J.K. LASSER'S

BUY, SELL, OR HOLD: MANAGE YOUR PORTFOLIO FOR MAXIMUM GAIN

J.K. LASSER'S™

BUY, SELL, OR HOLD: MANAGE YOUR PORTFOLIO FOR MAXIMUM GAIN

Michael C. Thomsett

John Wiley & Sons, Inc.

Published by John Wiley & Sons, Inc.
Published simultaneously in Canada.

This publication is designed to provide accurate and authoritative information in regard to the subject matter covered. It is sold with the understanding that the publisher is not engaged in rendering professional services. If professional advice or other expert assistance is required, the services of a competent professional person should be sought.

ISBN 0-471-21133-8

Printed in the United States of America.

10 9 8 7 6 5 4 3 2 1

For Lulu, with thanks for your understanding and support.

Contents

Preface

Creating Your Comprehensive Program

Why does anyone invest money? Why place yourself at risk and expose yourself to the volatility of the stock market? Why not just leave your capital in an insured savings account?

Of course, there are logical answers to these questions. As an astute investor, you already know that taking risk is an inherent part of investing your capital anywhere. For example, you could opt to place all of your capital in an insured account at your bank; in fact, many highly conservative investors do just that. This option also involves risk, however. The yield is so low that you risk losing the long-term purchasing power of your capital. The combination of taxes and inflation can cause the real value of savings to fall over time.

So even when you try to mitigate all risks, it's virtually impossible. The fact is, risk is the flip side of the coin we know as opportunity. So, in order to be "in the game" of the market or to be able to take the opportunities to earn profits, you also need to expose yourself to a corresponding degree of risk.

It's in the nature of investing that opportunity and risk are married in this way. The greater the opportunity, the greater the risk. So, every investor has to decide how much risk is appropriate, how much risk he or she can afford, and what portion of capital can be placed in higher-risk investments versus a base of lower-risk or moderate-risk ones. Within this body of decisions, many questions arise that demand self-education. These questions can be broken down into 10 major areas of study:

- Identifying how and why stock prices actually change
- Forms of analysis that can help you decide when to buy, sell, or hold
- Applying popular forms of analysis to your portfolio
- Market risk
- Diversification
- Liquidity
- Volatility
- Leverage
- Rate of return
- Professional advice

These 10 areas of study involve a study of facts and sorting through of various kinds of information. You need to become a competent investor in order to work through the maze of things you need to consider in making your own judgments. The alternative is to take advice from others, but sadly, good advice is difficult to find and experience shows that bad advice is far more abundant. So the bottom line is that investors really are on their own. In a market characterized by a large body of information, your biggest challenge is deciding which data are useful in the larger field.

We are not saying that it is impossible to manage your own portfolio. On the contrary, making your own decisions means that you are in control. Investors tend to operate analytically so that facts and figures are appealing and reassuring to the typical investor. Facts and figures by themselves are of little use, however, unless they are based on *true* underlying information. Among the information available to you are a lot of useless or baseless conclusions. The market is characterized by rumor, false assumptions, and decision-making based on poor information or even on no real information at all. As an investor, you want to be reassured with numerical information. You are looking for answers, and like all investors you would like to find that one solution that dependably tells you when you buy, when to sell, and when to hold.

That single answer does not exist, because no one can know what conditions will be like tomorrow. By gathering a body of knowledge and applying it in a sensible manner, however, you can make your decisions based on a logical and reasonable policy. You can manage your portfolio to maximize analysis, minimize risk, and earn profits. You can also take steps to overcome the most common flaw in the way people invest: depending upon unreliable information and making decisions without getting the facts beforehand.

This book is designed to explore each of the 10 areas of study that every investor needs to master. It is organized to present the popular fallacies that many people believe and then offer alternatives. These fallacies are widely believed, so the majority of investors continue to operate on a false premise in one way or another. As you will see in the 10 chapters that follow, however, the alternatives to these fallacies do point the way to market success. They demonstrate how you will be able to make intelligent decisions within your portfolio, based on sound information. The alternative—proceeding on the basis of widely held but false beliefs—will only prevent investors from realizing their goals in the market.

The first question faced by you and every other investor is, "When should I buy, sell, or hold a particular stock?" The old adage, "Buy low and sell high" should be followed by the equally important "instead of the other way around." It's true that many investors apply the adage in reverse. As values climb to record high levels, many investors want to get in on the profits—and, as a consequence, they buy at the top of the market. Then, when stock values fall, investors fear even larger losses and they sell their shares at the bottom of the market. So, the forces of greed and fear end up having more influence that the more rational forces of optimism and pessimism.

Once you are aware of this tendency, you will be able to move away from the "herd mentality" that characterizes the market. The tendency to move with the majority is natural, and it demands courage to keep a cool head when everyone is making decisions in the opposite direction; however, the key to market success is to make the important buy and sell and hold decisions based on solid information rather than on the basis of what everyone else is doing. This book's purpose is to organize and present the tools you need to achieve that end.

Acknowledgments

My thanks to Bruce Boyle for investment insights and for giving me a different point of view and to Virginia Gerhart for the years of encouragement. Special thanks also go to George C. Huff, who gave me the chance to learn so much in a marketing environment, in which the practical always buries the mere theory.

Also, thanks to Dave Pugh, editor at John Wiley & Sons, for the feedback and expertise and for supporting this project.

J.K. LASSER'S™

BUY, SELL, OR HOLD:
MANAGE YOUR PORTFOLIO FOR MAXIMUM GAIN

CHAPTER 1

The Pricing of Stocks

In the stock market, decisions often are made not on the basis of the facts, but on what ideas have captured investors' imaginations. This statement is true because investors seek answers to their questions, and one of the primary questions is "What makes stock prices go up or down?"

This basic and seemingly simple question actually is quite profound. The answer, too, might be complex and elusive. Investors seek certainty in an uncertain world. Their desire for certainty has produced a body of news, information, and analysis that contains the appearance of certainty, however. Each person has to decide how much of this news and information is reliable. If you plan to commit money to the decision to buy, sell, or hold a stock, then you also need to decide what information should form the basis for those decisions.

The most common deciding factors used in the market to attempt to anticipate future stock pricing are recent price history and patterns, current price relative to past price levels or other stocks, beliefs about future price movement (usually short-term), and a fourth area that can be described generally as "reckless optimism." While these three criteria form the basis of most market decisions by individual investors, none are reliable for making your most critical market decisions.

Recent Price History and Patterns

The desire for certainty—even in the uncertainty of the stock market—leads to a search for dependable information. So, a stockholder is likely to look to a stock's price history to judge how price movement will occur in the future. You can study the past in an attempt to understand what will occur in the future, but all you will arrive at will be an estimate, a reasonable understanding of likely outcomes. You will not be able to guess reliably at future price movements, however. There is, of course, an apparent rhythm to short-term price movements. For example, one stock might tend to move up and down within a confined range of price (the trading range). Another might be far more volatile, moving many points in either direction based on rumor or inconsistent earnings reports. In either case, does recent price movement give you the means for deciding which direction the price is likely to move in the future?

If you believe that recent price changes do predict the future, are you willing to commit investment capital to back up that belief? Price movement, studied visually, will create a pattern that can be studied. But what does that pattern reveal? Remember that the factors that influenced past price trends will not necessarily be repeated in the near future. If a stock's recent price trends show a narrow trading range, that does not set down a law that the pattern will be repeated. In fact, depending on such information can be quite misleading. It is easy to study pricing patterns and convince yourself that these are somehow dependable for the purpose of timing future buy, sell, or hold decisions. The truth is, however, that price movement is rarely so efficient that history can be used to time your decisions.

This statement brings us to the first big fallacy of market investing.

Fallacy: The pricing of stocks is efficient and fair.

The truth is that price changes tend to occur not in a reasonable manner but in overreaction to the underlying news. In other words, prices tend to swing too far above or below a logical value, based on good news or bad news. This situation is true for many popular stocks. To further complicate the matter, some stocks exhibit the opposite behavior: reacting *below* a reasonable level or swinging too little above or below a "fair" price level. While you can identify stocks falling into one classification or another, you also need to realize that a particular company's stock might overreact at times and underreact at others.

The pricing of stocks is neither efficient nor fair. If you study the price trends of a stock over the past year, you are likely to find many instances of price movement that make little sense in the short-term. In other words, while fundamentals such as earnings reports and dividend payments certainly have an immediate effect on a stock's pricing, many other factors also come into play. They include rumor and speculation and activity among institutional investors, such as mutual funds.

When a fund makes a decision to buy or sell a large block of a particular stock, it is inescapable that the decision will have an effect on pricing. When a large block is taken off the market (bought) or thrust upon the market (sold), the price reacts to the change in supply and demand. The decision by a mutual fund to invest in a company, however, or to divest itself of a company, could be made for reasons other than fundamental changes in the company's makeup. So, without understanding why large blocks of stock move in the market, we cannot really understand why a stock's price changes. This statement is most true for companies whose stock is held in large numbers by institutional investors. Whether individual investors like it or not, the institutional trades have far more to do with short-term price movement than any logical or reasonable analysis.

We are not saying that a mutual fund's decision to buy or sell a particular stock is ill-advised. It is important to remember, however, that a fund's management might make a particular decision for many reasons, including the desire to improve its own portfolio diversification, the need to meet a predetermined rate of return, or in reaction to economic changes beyond the company's fundamentals. So, tracking a stock's price and trying to identify what is going to happen in the future can be a frustrating exercise. The price movement in a company held by institutional investors could be artificially distorted by the decision of fund management (not just in one fund, but perhaps over many). It is important to remember that when you study price movement, you need to consider all of the possible reasons why it occurs; and chances are you will not even know all of those reasons. Some are not apparent. For example, when prices change due to economic reports, earnings, and other easily identified news about the company, everyone understands how the price changes in response. Beyond that, price change occurs for any number of reasons—many that never are easily identified by the investing public.

It is the uncertainty of price movement that makes the market so interesting. None of the certainties are particularly intriguing in comparison. In fact, most investors tend to remain interested in the stock market because of the uncertainty, which itself is appealing. Investors tend to think of market success as making a profit *against the odds*. In other words, success is defined in the market by beating the averages and not by finding certainty.

Given the nature of the market as uncertain, you are faced with two contradictory theories about the market and the pricing of stocks. These are the efficient market theory and the random walk hypothesis. Which of these is more accurate, if either, and which is helpful in trying to understand how and why stock prices change?

A theory, of course, is nothing more than the idea it expresses. In other words, the theory does not have to be pure in order to be useful. Either of these theories help to explain an aspect of market pricing that you will find helpful in the puzzle of price movement.

The efficient market theory states that the current price of all stocks reflects all of the information known currently to the general public. In other words, under this theory, the market is truly efficient because all of the changes in price movement are a reflection of the ever-changing supply and demand levels for that stock. The problem with the efficient market theory is that there might be many factors affecting price beyond what is known to the investing public, and these can also affect pricing of the stock; so while the efficient market theory might explain a lot of otherwise confusing changes in a stock's price, it is not a reliable theory for discovering dependable information. For example, the significant influence of institutional investors can distort price based on a decision made today, which essentially has nothing to do with the real value of the company. A mutual fund has to decide not only when to buy or sell shares of stock, but also how to move that stock within the market without causing a disruption. So to a degree, when a large block of stock changes hands, the very act of buying or selling can itself distort the market value. As the supply of stock changes, the price invariably is going to change as well—at least, momentarily. Such small changes are seen in the daily market reports, but they could have little or nothing to do with an efficient market.

The random walk hypothesis is a far more cynical point of view about the market. Under this theory, price changes are entirely random—at least, in the short term. Most investors who believe in long-term holdings for well-managed companies will acknowledge that interim price changes do not affect their portfolio decisions. In one respect, this policy reflects a belief in the random walk hypothesis. If applied to short-term price changes in particular, the random walk hypothesis makes some sense *and* is logical, as well. Even proponents of the Dow Theory (see Chapter 3) state that short-term price changes cannot be used as a reliable indicator of anything.

The random walk hypothesis certainly makes sense when applied to short-term price changes. The absolute belief that all price change is random is not supportable for long-term price studies, however. Obviously, well-managed companies that are profitable from year to year are going to rise in market value, and poorly managed companies that report net losses eventually will go broke and their stock prices will fall. In the long term, the fundamentals—sales and earnings—determine stock pricing. The market and its enthusiasts are far more interested in tracking short-term price change, however, even though virtually everyone agrees that such changes reveal nothing of lasting value. This scenario is a paradox of the market. Everyone knows that short-term price changes cannot be used reliably. Yet, most investors watch short-term price changes and make their decisions based upon those changes.

The random walk hypothesis is supported by statistical science, a reality that forms one of the basic tenets of the Dow Theory. In other words, no single change in price can be used as a signal to buy or sell. A change in price has to be confirmed by other signals, as well. Furthermore, any change has to be studied as part of a long-term trend. It is only the trends in the market that provide significant information; however, it is all too easy to fall into the trap of reacting to today's news and price change and to make the decision to buy, sell, or hold according to the point change in a company's stock (instead of in reaction to the fundamentals).

If you believe in the efficient market theory, you need to also understand that this theory applies to overall pricing and to daily changes in prices. Thus, the theory is interesting but does not really affect long-term value of stocks in your portfolio. Certainly, your basis for making decisions about stocks should not be based solely on the concept that today's price is efficient and therefore reflects a "fair" price in the market. That decision should rest with long-term strategies and analysis.

If you subscribe to the random walk hypothesis and believe that short-term price changes cannot be used to reliably predict a longer-term trend, then you have to also subscribe to the idea that your portfolio decisions should be made based on longer-term analysis. This analysis requires the study of trends based on the fundamentals rather than on market pricing. Most people will agree with this observation because it is reasonable; however, most people in the market—even those who describe themselves as proponents of the fundamentals—do in fact make decisions based on short-term price change.

From this point, it is logical to conclude that current (short-term) pricing in the market is neither efficient nor fair. It is unreliable and unstable in the sense that it does not show how longer-term trends are affected. The current price of stock, by itself, reveals nothing in relation to the fundamentals. Change in current pricing is simply the latest entry in a supply-and-demand marketplace that itself is subject to daily distortions. While those distortions are leveled out over time, they cloud the value of today's stock—especially with so much emphasis on price. Recent price history can only distract you from a meaningful analysis of the company and its stock as a long-term investment candidate.

So, the all-too-common question, "Is such-and-such a company a good investment at today's price level?" is itself unreliable. It's the wrong question. Replacing the fallacy that the pricing of stocks is efficient and fair, we need to arrive at a different conclusion: *The pricing of stocks is a short-term indicator and cannot be used to judge the long-term value of an investment.*

Current Prices per Share

In a tidy world that worked reliably and predictably, the current price per share of stock would move upward at a time and to a degree that you would know in advance—based on sales and earnings of the company. The fundamentals would dictate the fair price of the stock; in fact, the *price/earnings* (PE) ratio of a stock would be scientifically predictable because price and earnings would also be predictable.

In the real world, however, we cannot rely on current price to tell us very much about the company's value as a long-term investment. For many first-time investors, the beginning assumption is that current price (plus a recent movement in price) should be useful as an indicator of value. In other words, the novice tends to look at the stock's price for several reasons. First of all, it is the most readily available information. Second, consumers are used to using price as a starting point when shopping for anything, whether a sweater or a car. Third, price enables the shopper to make comparisons.

The error here is in confusing the pricing of stocks with the pricing of other goods. Whereas a sweater or a car will be priced according to understandable and sensible criteria, stocks are not. For example, a company prices its goods based on its costs and overhead and also based on what competitors charge. Ideally, a company wants to set its price lower than comparable goods offered by others but high enough to earn a respectable profit.

Forget all of that when it comes to stocks. Pricing of stocks is purely the result of what the seller and buyer determine by their actions. Thus, pricing can be far higher or lower than what it *should* be. In some cases, stock prices have risen so high that they make no sense whatsoever. The dot-com phenomenon of the late '90s makes this point. The stock of Amazon.com, for example, rose in its first two years of existence to more than $75 per share, and in the following two years it fell back to under $15 per share. Why the rise in price? Amazon.com never showed a profit during those years, so the price was not based on any current fundamental information.

In fact, stock pricing is based, for the most part, on a *perception* of future value. So, when the belief is widespread in the market that a company's future sales and profits are going to be higher than today's, the current stock price reflects that perception. While most goods are priced based on the cost to manufacture and market, plus competitive restraints, the pricing of stocks is far more complex and elusive. What this situation means for the investor trying to use price to comparison shop is that it is far too easy to be fooled by the current price. It really means very little in terms of future value, and as a comparative indicator, it is of no real value at all. Looking at the prices of two or more different stocks is not really a comparison at all, because those prices might well be the result of different supply and demand realities. One might be held by mutual funds while the other is not. One might be a well-established company and the other a relatively new one. A broad variety of reasons for pricing can affect a stock, so any form of price comparison is not only difficult but potentially misleading, as well.

The truth is that many investors select stocks based on what they can afford to invest. For example, if you have $5,000 to put into the market, you might look only at stocks prices below the level of $50 per share with the idea that you are going to buy only 100 shares. This search limits your review in terms of the price level, but is that a smart way to select stocks? In fact, it is not. So much emphasis is placed on stock prices, however—largely because of the way we are used to buying—that the valid means for stock selection are easily lost in the process. Comparison shopping on the basis of price works in the mall and the auto dealership, but the pricing of stocks is so vastly different that the usual shopping methods should not be employed.

If you want to comparison shop, the comparison itself should be based on criteria that are more important than the current price. You might study the PE ratio, sales and earnings trends, dividend yield, competitive strength of the company, capitalization, management, and a wide variety of other factors. Current price, however, does not provide you with meaningful information. Consider the real meaning of price. It is, in fact, the most easily accessible technical indicator. The current price of a stock has little to do with fundamental information. It represents the perception of future potential, that perception being held generally by investors in the market. When the perception is optimistic, prices are driven upward by demand. That perception often is right, and the stock's future performance will justify the belief. In the selection of stocks, however, one of the popular misconceptions held by investors is that they make decisions based on fundamentals, when in practice they operate exclusively on technical indicators. Current price is a technical indicator. This statement is true not only because pricing has little to do with a company's financial strength or operations, but also because the method by which prices are established and then change is almost exclusively driven by market perception. Thus, the technical side of the market has more to do with pricing than does the fundamental side.

The current price of a stock is best defined as the lowest price at which sellers are willing to sell and the highest price at which buyers are willing to buy shares. This basic observation characterizes the auction marketplace, which has to be distinguished from other markets. Imagine entering a car dealership with hundreds of other would-be buyers and bidding on a new model of a car. The person willing to pay the highest price wins the car. Of course, there would come a point where buyers would resist going above a specific amount because the buyers collectively know the approximate value of the commodity. When a new model comes out and a large segment of the market is excited about that car, however, it would be possible that it would be bid up to twice its actual value just because buyers were in a frenzy about having one of those cars.

This situation makes little sense to most people who have shopped for cars. We know how manufacturers price cars, and we also know that dealers mark up those cars so they will make a profit. It is not realistic to think that you can buy a new car for one-third of its sticker price, nor would it be realistic for a dealer to believe that buyers would be willing to pay twice the sticker price. From this illustration, we can conclude that most commodities that we buy—cars, for instance—are bought in one type of market, but stocks are bought in a completely different type of market. The expectations held by stockholders make sense, but they would be completely irrational in the automobile market. The entire structure of these markets is different. Even so, stock market investors often attempt to shop by using the same techniques they use elsewhere.

A novice might begin by looking for a "good $20 stock" in the same way that one might shop for a "good car under $25,000." Remember, though, that current price has absolutely nothing to do with the sensible definition of a stock as a "good" investment by any means. For that definition, we need to turn to the fundamentals. It is true that current price should be considered in the mix, because the price reflects a multiple of earnings. Thus, the PE ratio (see Chapter 2) is a pivotal indicator for the distinction between well-priced, under-priced, and over-priced stocks. While PE can be considered along with other indicators, looking at price alone can be quite deceptive. Imagine limiting your selection to only those stocks selling at $20 or below without also looking at the earnings per share. Obviously, this approach makes no sense whatsoever. It would be like telling a car salesman that you want to test drive all used cars priced at $10,000 or below. That would be an invitation to be over-charged. Every smart consumer knows that making a decision on that basis is a mistake; yet, stock investors do it every day.

Current price by itself tells you only the per-share market value of stock. It does not tell you whether that represents a PE multiple of five, 20, or 50. It does not tell you whether it is a bargain price or a premium. If you already own shares of the stock, current price is important to the extent that it tells you whether your stock is worth more or less than it was when you bought it; however, it does not tell you whether you should hold or sell. For that decision, you have to look, once again, at the fundamentals—the earnings, dividends, and other financial facts. Even so, many individual investors make their hold or sell decisions based almost solely on price. In practice, it is easier to take paper profits or cut short-term losses than it is to apply well-developed fundamental principles to the management of an individual portfolio. If you consider yourself a long-term investor, however, it makes sense to continue holding the stocks of companies whose fundamentals meet those tests and to sell the stock of companies who no longer provide you with the potential for continued long-term profits.

Being aware of the limitations of current price helps you to overcome the popular errors made in the market. Current price is the focal point of the financial press. Individual stocks are reported in terms of scorekeeping based on current price. Stocks make the news when they rise or fall enough points (in the view of the financial press) to be newsworthy. Even the method of reporting current price, however—as insignificant as a daily change might be—is misleading. For example, consider two stocks, each of which rise four points today. One stock is priced at $30 per share, and the other is priced at $60 per share. Under the system used by most financial news sources, the significance of these two reports is equal. Both rose four points. In reality, however, the day's change for the $30 stock represents a 13.3 percent increase, and the day's change for the $60 stock was only 6.7 percent. In other words, the reporting itself emphasizes points of change rather than percentage change in value per share.

The reporting of price is emphasized because it is easily understood and readily available. The change in price per share is important to current stockholders, so the perception is that the same level of importance applies to would-be buyers, as well. The reporting method is inaccurate and misleading. It also does not reveal the more significant information about a company; in other words, the comparative fundamental information. The financial press, of course, is like the rest of the press. It wants to convey information in a simple manner to report what is thought to be newsworthy. Every serious investor, however, has to be aware not only of the inaccuracies in reported information, but also of the fact that a daily change in a stock's price means absolutely nothing in terms of a company's value as an investment. It is only scorekeeping, and the game being reported—changes in stock prices—means nothing in the long term. The financial press identifies "winners" as those whose stock rose today and "losers" as those whose stock value fell. So that is the game. It has no relevance to the selection of stocks based on underlying, fundamental value, but it is misleading because so many investors make their decisions based not on a study of the company and its fundamentals, but on what they read and hear in the news.

Beliefs about Future Price Movement

Among the ideas that have caught on among investors is a primary belief that future price movement can be predicted. Certainly, the future *value* of a company as a sensible investment can be predicted with great reliability, using fundamental information to identify worthy buy and hold candidates. The very idea that price movement can be predicted is inherently flawed, however.

Considering the mechanism that creates changes in price—perceptions of future value tempered by institutional holdings—it is troubling that any belief in price level prediction can be as widespread, and yet it is. This belief demonstrates the illogic of the stock market. Short-term price movement in the market is recognized as unreliable by proponents of all major theories. The Dow Theory discounts short-term change entirely. According to the efficient market theory, prices reflect all of the knowledge about a stock at any given time, which means that the chances of a stock going up or down is 50-50—that is, if one accepts the efficient market theory in a pure form. Finally, under the random walk hypothesis, it makes no real difference whether a company's fortunes are positive or negative, because short-term price movement will be random in either event.

You will not find a theory about the market supporting the premise that short-term price movements can be predicted. Even so, a very popular belief is that price can be predicted by studying recent price patterns and trends. The *chartist* watches price charts of stocks to identify the direction that prices will move in the future. An entire industry has grown around the idea that patterns are established in price movements, almost as though prices had conscious will and would act according to statistical laws. The fact is that short-term price movement is entirely random. There is a degree of value in identifying certain characteristics of market prices for a stock, and those can be found in a study of charts. Beyond a few basic observations, however, it simply is untrue that price charts predict short-term price movements.

Fallacy: Future prices of stocks can be predicted by studying price charts.

You can gain value from the study of stock charts in a few limited ways. Virtually all online trading sites offer free quotes and charts for all listed companies, and this free service is invaluable in getting basic market information—either on stocks you own or on those you are thinking about buying. It is important to recognize that charts reveal very limited information about what is likely to take place in the future, however. The true believers in charting contend that trading patterns signal the next direction a stock's price will move, and they take great pains to prove their point. Like all belief systems requiring constant efforts to prove something, however, the thinking of these chartists is flawed. A chartist holds a more balanced view and recognizes the value of studying price trends. This individual knows that the information to be found on a chart is statistically valuable, however, but only insofar as it supports independently verified *likely* outcomes. In other words, if you believe that a stock's price is likely to rise over the next year based on what you see in a chart, that is useful information when it is also confirmed by other analysis performed using different means.

The basic premise of charting is that many stocks tend to trade within a predictable range, at least for a period of time (which, of course, is unknown). This trading range is further defined as having a top, the price above which a stock's price is not likely to move; this price is called the resistance level. It also has a bottom, the price below which a stock's price is not likely to move; this price is referred to as the support level. Resistance and support are valuable ideas because they help the analyst to identify when a stock's market price is likely to move above or below that range. Such an event is called a breakout.

Support and resistance levels are illustrated in Figure 1.1.

In this example, the trading range is progressing. That is to say, over time the resistance level and support level gradually move upward. This situation would indicate that the stock's price is likely to remain within the trading range,

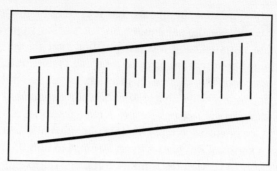

FIGURE 1.1 Support and resistance.

given its upward trend. Eventually, however, the price will move above or below the predetermined trading range pattern. Whether this event occurs due to random change or in response to rumor or financial news, the fact remains that when the pattern changes, the trading range is disrupted and has to be redefined. This breakout is illustrated in Figure 1.2.

In this example, the breakout takes place on the down side. Support level gives way as the price falls. The astute analyst would look for an underlying cause. For example, has the company released financial information recently? Was it disappointing? Is there a rumor or any news affecting the company? Any number of valid factors could affect a stock's price immediately, including economic factors like changes in interest rates, labor problems, lawsuits, new product introduction or problems with existing products, or changes in management to name a few.

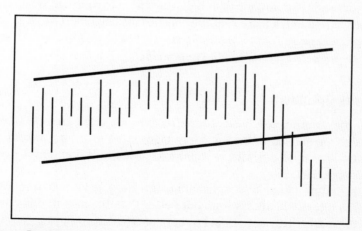

FIGURE 1.2 Breakout.

To some investors, a breakout signals that it is time to change positions. An owner of shares could see the sudden decline in market value as a sell signal, assuming that the news causing the fall justified that decision. A contrarian might look at the lowered market price as a buying opportunity, again based on the underlying cause of the change in price. It is not accurate to say that a change in direction or any other chart indication always signals a particular decision. You need to study the reasons for price changes while also understanding that some price movement is going to be unexplainable and truly random.

Chartists use a series of indicators in an attempt to identify when support or resistance are likely to be violated. Spikes and tests, for example, are analyzed in patterns. These have various names like "head and shoulders," and some chartists give great significance to the emerging patterns visible on charts. For chartists as with all investors, however, hindsight is always superior to foresight. Chartists can point to past price movement and explain what signals were clear; however, the record for predicting future price trends based on the same patterns is far more elusive.

You can gain insight by studying chart patterns. For example, it will become apparent that some stocks exhibit a relatively narrow trading range, whereas others demonstrate far more volatile trading patterns. This difference occurs for a reason, and a study of resistance and support levels for stocks is a useful comparative tool for the study of price volatility (see Chapter 7 for more information about the topic of volatility). As a short-term observation, trading patterns can be used to augment your personal program for stock analysis.

At the same time, however, it's important to recognize that stock prices do not behave in a natural manner, and statistically they are not going to move in adherence with any rules or predetermined patterns. The random nature of short-term price movement makes the attempt to predict the short-term future a troubling endeavor. Rather than believing that charting can be used to predict price movement, a more sensible conclusion should be: *Charting is useful for comparing price volatility among stocks, but short-term price movement cannot be predicted reliably using any method.*

Reckless Optimism

The chartist continuously looks to the recent past in an attempt to estimate what will happen next. In the same way, many other investors make their decisions based not upon any science, analysis, nor formula, but on the premise of reckless optimism.

It's the nature of risk-takers, including investors, to view matters with optimism. The future will always work out better than the past in this world view, and so the market has more than its share of reckless optimists. They view the future as "that period of time in which our affairs prosper, our friends are true and our happiness is assured."[1]

Optimism about investments is certainly no flaw as long as you also recognize that mistakes can be made and that situations change. Obviously, you would not purchase shares of stock unless you were optimistic about the company's future. A *reckless* optimism, on the other hand, enables you to delude yourself about the reality of the situation. Many decisions are made based on the idea that, in some way, a stock's market value will rise as long as the investor owns shares. In practice, everyone knows how difficult it is to judge the market in terms of timing. You might be right about the overall direction of a stock's price but wrong in the timing of your decisions.

This reckless optimism is encouraged in the financial press. For example, an overall rise in prices is referred to in glowing terms as "robust" or "a sign of renewed faith" in the economy, for example. When prices fall, however, the news is softened with descriptions of "profit taking" or "consolidation."

Why does the financial press encourage this approach, rather than reporting the news in a more forthright manner? The answer is found in a study of the advertisements seen in newspapers, in magazines, on radio and television, and on the Internet. Financial reporting is supported by financial institutions—brokerage firms, analysts, and information services related to the ownership of stocks. The majority of reporting, financial and otherwise, is supported by selling advertising space, so at least to some degree reporting is affected by the mix of advertisers. If the public becomes disenchanted with investing, subscriptions fall and ad sales follow. More to the point, if advertisers believe that news reports are contrary to the message that they want to send out, then their advertising dollars might go elsewhere.

Every investor faces the problem of bias in getting information. News as reported often presents a simplistic summary of the facts and often emphasizes the wrong points. A financial reporter might be able to write interesting copy, but this fact does not necessarily mean that the same person grasps the significance of the news itself. For example, when the market falls as measured by the popular index levels, it is possible to report that in more than one way. Consider the following two slants on the same story:

Example # 1
The Dow fell yesterday more than 450 points, the biggest drop in three months. This drop followed warnings by the Fed that interest rates could be increasing in the near future, which took the market by surprise. High sales volume in late trading yesterday shows that reaction is negative and widespread, and most experts expect further drops today.

Example # 2
The Dow corrected yesterday following a three-month price run-up. Index level retreated 450 points in late trading. While the Fed announced possible adjustments in interest rates, the change in the Dow level was the result of profit-taking and is not seen to signal a change in the market's direction. High trading volume in the late session shows continued interest among investors.

These treatments of the same news demonstrate that a vastly different tone can be put on the news. Investors should be aware of how easily this process can be done; it might even be unconscious on the part of the reporter. The tendency in financial reporting is to augment good news and to downplay bad news. This tendency permeates Wall Street, not only among reporters but among investors and analysts as well. Consider the case of brokerage firm recommendations. The majority of them are "buy" recommendations, and a downgrade usually suggests reverting to a "hold" or "accumulate" recommendation. In a story about the problem of investment bankers and a conflict of interest, CBS reported that at the time of their initial report, out of more than 8,000 analyst stock recommendations to the public, only 29 were to "sell."[2]

The problem arises when a brokerage firm also acts as investment banker, a role in which the firm markets an *Initial Public Offering* (IPO). The glaring conflict of interest in this situation is that the firm stands to make a big profit by selling shares of the newly issued stock while also in the position of advising clients which stocks to buy. This topic is explored in more detail later (see Chapter 10). The point to remember here, however, is that recommendations made by brokers of firms that also underwrite the IPO of a company are, by nature, problematical. This serious problem is widespread, but it continues for several reasons, including three primary ones:

1. *Reckless optimism as a characteristic of the entire culture.* It is not just the conflict of interest that has created the problem. That is only half of it; the other half is that investors practice reckless optimism daily. In other words, they would prefer hearing "buy" recommendations. That is good news. A "sell" recommendation is bad news, often a reversal of a previous suggestion from the same broker. So while the broker does not want to contradict previous recommendations, investors do not want to hear bad news. This culture of optimism clouds the facts and enables everyone—analysts, brokers, and investors—to proceed with the most optimistic point of view possible.

2. *Trust, perhaps too much, in the brokerage industry.* Investors like to believe in their advisors. Unfortunately, they probably give brokers too much trust, especially in the situation where a broker's firm is also the investment banker for the stock being recommended. The profit incentive for the brokerage firm and for the broker is on the side of making "buy" recommendations, so as a natural consequence investors are encouraged to buy and hold—even when the fundamentals contradict this advice.

A related problem comes from the idea that brokers have more information than the average investor. Brokers are licensed and have to possess information about the securities they market; however, this situation does not mean that they understand the fundamentals better than the typical experienced investor. In fact, because brokers in so-called full-service firms are compensated by way of commission, they are salespeople more than professional advisors. The idea that investors are paying for professional advice often is misplaced, and a study of outcomes as a result of broker recommendations makes this point over and over again. A four-year study conducted by Investars.com concluded that investors lost an average of more than 53 percent when they took the advice of their broker and that broker's firm led or co-managed the IPO. Even when the brokerage firm did not manage the related IPO, investors still lost money (4.24 percent on average).[3]

The big difference between these results makes the point that when brokerage firms underwrite an IPO, they do not give sound advice to their commission-paying customers. And even in cases where that relationship does not exist, customers still lose money. Chances are, those investors would have seen better results investing without the advice of a broker. The problem of trust is probably one factor in the growing trend toward the use of discounted trading services—notably, those online. In these cases, trades are made for a small fee, but no advice is given. More and more, investors are realizing that advice from brokers can be costly.

Perhaps the biggest problem in the obvious conflict of interest and poor track record of investment banking is the fact that there is no legal ramification for giving poor advice to customers. Although it might be difficult to identify an abuse in the many instances where poor advice is given, there certainly should be a distinction between underwriting and investment recommendations given by the same firm. The official position on the part of Wall Street firms is that their brokers give advice independent of the investment banking side of the business. The consistency of outcomes shows that a problem persists, however.

The *Securities and Exchange Commission* (SEC) regulates the industry, and the SEC would be the proper agency to enact changes in this area. In order to protect the investing public from abuses arising from conflict of interest, better-defined rules of conduct and due diligence on the part of the firm engaging in investment banking would go a long way toward solving this problem. Meanwhile, the unwary investor who continues to trust in a broker's recommendations takes his or her chances.[4]

To what extent does reckless optimism affect stock prices? In theory, optimism itself should not be a factor in the supply and demand for stocks. In practice, however, the degree of optimism has everything to do with price run-up, even when it is not justified. The late '90's dot.com industry and the run-up of stock price values makes this point, followed of course by the severe and rather fast turnaround in which values fell even more quickly than they rose.

The run-up of stocks like Amazon.com was typical of the reckless optimism and its effect on prices. Amazon had never shown a profit, meaning there was absolutely no fundamental information upon which to base an investment in the company—unless investors had some specific reason to believe that the high-moving price was justified on some basis. Such a justification is not known, given the lack of any net profits. Accompanying the run-up, however, was a prediction by an analyst named Henry Blodget that the price would rise. When Amazon's stock was at $243 per share, he predicted that it would go to $400, which it did. Blodget claimed that his prediction was based on sound analysis, but it is difficult to imagine how sound that process can be without any profits for the company. Unfortunately for the investors who believed in this prediction, the stock subsequently lost three-quarters of its value.

The point to this example is that reckless optimism can cause a stock's price to rise. If that rise is based only on prediction, however, that means that the frenzy of demand created as a result is itself the cause of the run-up. Ultimately, such situations will reverse themselves and many people will lose money. The case of Amazon.com is right on point, because there were no profits to support any optimistic prediction whatsoever.

The effect of reckless optimism has some historical references, as well. In the 1630s, Holland was caught up in a frenzy of investing in tulip bulbs. Unbelievably, bulbs sold for as much as 60,000 florins (about $44,000) until, in 1637, the whole market crashed. Until that point, speculators saw no reason to believe that the demand would fall and put their capital at risk in the belief that prices would only continue to rise. The reckless optimism of 17th-century Holland did not die with so-called tulipmania. It is only human nature to believe that a rising price trend will continue indefinitely. The frenzy of reckless optimism does affect price, but only for a while. Eventually, those with the most at risk lose their money, whether it is invested in tulip bulbs or the stock of companies that have never earned a profit.

Fundamentals and Stock Prices

The fundamentals—the financial and managerial information about a company—are the basis for selecting valuable and well-priced long-term stocks. Once stocks are held in your portfolio, the fundamentals also are most useful for monitoring the company to ensure that a 'hold' decision is justified. When the fundamentals change, the 'hold' might also change to the decision to sell.

This basic information is well known to most investors, whether acted upon or not. A popular fallacy, however, is the belief that price change of stocks is a direct reflection of the fundamentals. In fact, the fundamentals have very little effect on price movement. The market tends to batter stock prices around, usually overreacting to all news and rumor, so that price changes tend to make little sense in the immediate analysis. A rise or fall of many points often is not justified by the known news about a stock at the time. The *immediate* market is highly chaotic and makes no sense. In fact, sensibility does come into play, but it is seen not in day-to-day price changes, but rather in the long-term trends and price movements of stocks.

The fallacy, then, is the belief that short-term pricing of stocks is logical and can be followed; and more to the point, investors can gain some insight by watching a stock closely. In truth, watching daily changes in stock prices tends to confuse rather than enlighten. It makes more sense to study the fundamentals and largely ignore the small daily movements in a stock's price or to recognize that momentary change in market value has little or no meaning to you if you are holding an investment for the long term. Of course, while watching the fundamentals, remember that the purpose is to identify prospects for long-term holding, and once they are owned, to ensure that the hold decision remains valid. Don't expect the fundamentals to signal immediate changes in stock price. Even when prices do react to financial news, the reaction itself has little meaning. What counts is how the fundamentals support the contention that a stock's value will grow over many years; in the market, the tendency is to hope for price increases over many hours, and that is a mistake.

Fallacy: Prices of stocks change due to changes in the fundamentals.

It would be nice and orderly to invest in a market where this scenario was true. In the short term, it is not; however, the simple truth is that strong fundamentals do identify strong long-term investments, so those companies whose sales, earnings, and other fundamentals remain strong from one period to another also tend to work well as long-term investments. The market rewards patience, so truly following the fundamentals is a wise choice.

So how does the market work from day to day or hour to hour? Remembering that this environment is chaotic, it also makes sense that all momentary changes in price are the result of chaos. In that environment, we cannot expect order. The market is set up to provide some semblance of order even in the chaos, however. The way that buyers and sellers are brought together and their trades are executed is quite complex, but the market facilitates millions of trades daily with little error or misunderstanding. The pricing of stocks within this fast-moving, high-volume market is complex and as far removed from the fundamentals as possible. The complex forces of supply and demand react to *all* news, so any financial news just goes into the mix. An increase in declared dividend will likely cause a rise in price. The actual payment of a dividend will cause a corresponding fall in the price. If earnings are better than projected, the stock's price will rise in response. If lower than expected, the price is going to fall. Of course, far more information than the purely financial will also affect the pricing of stocks, often in ways that do not make sense to the analytical and financially oriented observer.

For example, a stock in an interest-sensitive industry like public utilities is likely to react to any news or speculation about interest rates. So, even an opinion expressed in a news piece can have an immediate effect on the stock's price. For example, the news might say, "The Fed meets this week to discuss interest rates, but no reduction in those rates is expected." This non-news could be seen as negative news in the utilities industry, so some utility stocks could lose some steam as a consequence. The statement might not be true, however. And if true, it might only confirm what was already know—that no reduction in rates is expected.

In other words, the market is going to react and overreact to every piece of news, opinion, rumor, and change. So, it is a mistake to pay too much attention to the hourly and daily changes in a stock's market price. There is simply too much going on to make momentary changes worth paying attention to, and in addition, those changes in price are the results of the chaotic environment. So, a small rise or fall in the price does not reveal anything of interest nor importance to you.

An alternative point of view about pricing of stocks and the fundamentals might be as follows: *The fundamentals point the way to worthwhile long-term investments, but short-term price changes do not reflect the fundamental condition of the company.*

The fundamentals are an historical body of information, so a quarterly or annual report tells you the status of the company over the past quarter or year and summarizes assets and liabilities as of the reported date. Price, on the other hand, is a projection of the market's perceptions of future value of that stock. Because the market overreacts as a whole, price is a poor indicator of what is really going to happen to a stock. As a relative measurement of the stock's value, performed through the PE ratio, for example, the price side is not reliable.

Many investors make the mistake of describing themselves as believers in the fundamentals, and in fact, the majority of investors describe themselves in this way. The majority also follows some very technical indicators, however. The market price of a stock is a technical indicator because it is based only partially on any fundamental information. Remember what the price of a stock reveals: It is the current level of perception about the future value of the company. The price, representing the highest price that buyers are willing to pay and the lowest price at which sellers will sell, is an illogical settling point in the chaotic market. It is a technical indicator. It provides the fundamentalist with nothing of value, but it can distract you if you pay too much attention to the alleged significance of price as reported in the financial press, where emphasis is on the point change during a trading day.

Many self-described fundamental investors also follow market indices like the *Dow Jones Industrial Average* (DJIA), which is based solely on prices of stocks. Because stocks that split hold greater weight in the DJIA than those that have not split, however, the index itself is a distortion. The level of the DJIA, considered by many as "the market," is a highly technical and inaccurate method for measuring the health of your stocks. It is scorekeeping in the most inaccurate form possible. In a country that loves baseball, however, the investing public wants to know the score. So, the DJIA, NASDAQ, and other index reporting provides the public with a sense of knowing whether our team is winning or losing. The inaccuracy of the index is not a concern in this sense, because the audience of investors just wants to be told whether the day was good or bad on some basis.

In this environment—where a simplistic report of changes in an inaccurate index is accepted as conclusive—you have both a problem and an opportunity. The problem, of course, is that the culture of stock market investing tends to be led by fallacy and inaccurate or meaningless reporting. So, to be truly well informed, it is also necessary that you learn to ignore the popular technical indicators. The DJIA and daily reports of winning and losing stocks tells you nothing of any fundamental value. You need to overcome the common and popular modes for understanding what is going on in the market.

The opportunity lies in recognizing the inaccuracy of the popularly reported market news so that you can look for information elsewhere. Because the majority is content with being told about the health of the market by way of point rise and fall in the index of a few stocks, you can find more important and valuable information, either about individual stocks or the market as a whole, by looking beyond price reporting and discovering longer-term price trends that reveal what is really going on.

For example, the "health" of the market is not really seen in index trends or in short-term changes in prices for individual stocks. The true health of the market has to be based on the fundamentals. Because you will buy, sell, or hold one stock at a time, it makes more sense to apply your analytical time to individual stock analysis than to market-wide study. The market as a whole might be experiencing a bull trend or a bear trend, but that broader trend might have little or no effect on the fundamental strength of a particular stock. In fact, larger trends and market-wide analysis are likely to distort the analysis rather than lend any insight to it.

An individual stock might be affected by economic factors like interest rates, international trade rules, federal regulations, labor news, and other outside influences. Of course, these outside influences have to be part of your fundamental study of a company as a prospect for long-term investment. In addition, the specific industry in which the stock belongs is going to be affected as a group, as well. The retail sector responds to different influences than does the public utility or transportation stocks. Pharmaceutical stocks will act and respond differently to changes in economic news than manufacturers. For example, consider the effect of changes in federal regulation of prescription drugs versus news of a pending strike by a large labor union. The various sectors are going to respond differently to these pending changes. The housing sector stocks are going to be affected by the price of raw materials, but not as much by the threat of a strike by auto industry workers.

These examples of news items can be expected to have a significant effect on stock prices in the industry affected by the news. They are forms of external fundamentals, and they have to be considered as part of your analysis. Even so, a well-capitalized company that has a decent market share and a history of growing sales and profits is likely to survive a bad year without any negative consequences in the long term. In fact, a momentary decline in market price of stocks resulting from negative economic news could represent a buying opportunity for companies you consider strong long-term investment prospects.

If investors were able to filter the news and analyze the significance of economic and internal fundamentals of a company, logical choices could be made. Many investors are confused, however, and don't really make a specific distinction between fundamental and technical forms of information. Price change is reported along with dividends, sales, and profits. The two forms of information are merged by the financial press, so it is easy to forget which is which. So, as a result, the investor who believes in the fundamentals ends up making decisions based on reports of purely technical indicators. Most popular are changes in the price of stocks and changes in the level of an index, such as the DJIA.

How does the news you hear today affect your decision to buy, sell, or hold a particular stock? In some respects, you need to insulate yourself from the news because there is so much of it out there. Financial journalists often feel compelled to tell you not only the news, but also what it means. So, you end up with a type of sound-bite analysis. For example, a company might report earnings this year of 8 percent. They earned 8 percent last year as well, and internally the rate of return on sales is considered strong and a positive outcome. In reporting this story, however, it would be quite easy for a journalist to put a particular slant on the story, such as:

Habicom Loses Momentum: The Habicom Corporation's annual report published this week shows 8% net profit on sales of $18 million. Although sales rose for the year over last year's $16.5 million, profits have stagnated. This loss of momentum could signal the end of Habicom's domination in the crowded field of tech stocks. Management reported that they were "very pleased" with the results, but analysts are alarmed at the failure of the company to surpass net profit levels with higher sales.

This example of interpretive reporting demonstrates the problem. One might expect the price of the stock to fall as the result of such a negative report, even though it is not necessarily a negative outcome for the company. It is not realistic to expect profit percentages to grow forever, and it often is not only acceptable but also superior for a company to hold its net profit levels from one year to the next. This idea, however, is not only difficult to convey in a short news report; it is also relatively uninteresting.

Remember, the financial journalist has the task of reporting information *and* making it interesting for the reader. That does not always mean that the report is accurate, nor does it mean that any decisions should be made only on the basis of a news story. Further investigation invariably reveals more information and could even contradict the tone of the report seen in the media.

The problem all investors face with trying to understand price is that the price itself is a very short-term indicator. When you look at a long-term price trend, you can relate market price to the fundamentals and select good long-term hold prospects. The temptation to concentrate too much on momentary price changes is made easier by the media, because seemingly dramatic price changes are easily reported. When you hear that your stock dropped three points today, it gets your attention. But that does not really tell you anything about *why* the price dropped. Financial reporting tends to assign sound-bite types of explanations. Prices drop "on news of softening earnings" or "due to pessimistic analysts' reports," and prices tend to rise for similar reasons like "anticipated robust sales in the coming quarter" or "growing strength in the company's international divisions." Deeper study is required before drawing any conclusions about daily price changes.

Perhaps one reason why investors believe prices change due to the fundamentals is because fundamental news is often cited as the reason for larger-than-usual price changes. In some cases, it is true—and in others, the fundamentals are only part of the larger story. You are likely to find that your analysis indicates no substantial change in a company's long-term fundamental strength, and yet daily prices still rise and fall at every small rumor or piece of news. On most days, prices fluctuate to some degree even with no news whatsoever. Remember the forces at work in the market. In stocks that are held by mutual funds, a major shift in buying or selling activity will certainly cause prices to change. Because investors tend to overreact to any news, a widely held stock might also tend to gyrate to a greater extent than is justified by the news. Stocks have specific characteristics, one of which is the "beta," a technical term describing a stock's tendency to change in price relative to the overall market. A stock with a high beta is believed to change in price to a degree higher than the market as a whole. A beta of zero indicates that the stock's tendency matches overall market tendencies. For example, if a stock's beta is 1.3, that means its price has moved 130 percent more than the overall market (up or down).

Because the beta is a technical term based on price, a technical indicator itself, any short-term information you gain from beta should be taken only as one of many types of analysis. Great importance is given in the market to such indicators; however, it remains a question of long-term strength in the fundamentals that really defines whether or not a stock should be bought or sold.

You cannot rely upon price or any of the indicators based upon price to decide whether or not a stock remains a strong long-term prospect today. The PE ratio, which compares price to earnings, enables you to judge how the market sees the potential of a stock; however, PE, like many indicators, has to be viewed in light of other fundamental data.

A reliance upon price information alone—the most popular way that investors judge the market—is the least dependable and least reliable method for determining whether or buy, sell, or hold a stock. The popular fallacies about price demonstrate that the popularity of price watching comes from the ease of access to that information, the emphasis of price by the financial media, and the broader tendency to judge the market using market index trends.

Notes

[1]Ambrose Bierce, *The Devil's Dictionary*, 1906.

[2]"Wall Street Prophets," CBS News, 60 Minutes II, reported June 26, 2001 (http://cbsnews.com).

[3]"Analysts' Links to IPOs Mean Losses for Investors, Study Finds," *The Wall Street Journal*, June 12, 2001.

[4]To see a summary of new or pending rule changes or to write to the SEC, check their Web site at www.sec.gov/.

CHAPTER 2

Fundamental and Technical Analysis

Do you follow the fundamentals? If you do, then you base your investment decisions on the financial reports of a company and related matters. These include dividend declarations and payments, management of the company, strength of the company compared to its competitors, position in the investment sector, and other tangible facts.

Most investors do indeed describe themselves as strong proponents of fundamental investing. Even so, they do not act or react to fundamental information as much as they do to purely technical indicators. Examples of popular technical indicators include the stock's current market price and changes in it, stock price charts, price predictions by analysts or brokers, and the ever-popular Dow Jones Industrial Averages. These are the most popular tools used by investors to judge the market's health and to decide whether to buy, sell, or hold. Yet, none of them are fundamental indicators. In fact, these technical indicators are probably the least-reliable decision-making tools you could use. In spite of their unreliability for investment purposes, they continue to serve as the primary and major selection methods among investors.

This statement is true because they are easily found and widely reported in the financial press. We have been told time and again that the DJIA and other indexes are *the market* in one important sense: when the market goes up (as measured by the DJIA), that is good news, and when it goes down, that is bad news. In spite of the fact that short-term changes are not relevant to long-term decision-making, most people accept this premise. Adding to the confusion, no index represents the characteristics of a specific company. So, even though the DJIA, S&P 500, or NASDAQ is rising or falling, the effect of this news on the stocks you are watching usually is insignificant. Chapter 3 includes much more detail on the Dow and its effect on the market as a whole.

Fundamentals—A Look Back

Overlooking the fact that so much concentration is spent on watching the Dow and other indexes, a quick review of the fundamentals might help to focus on what these indicators provide and how they can and should affect your long-term selection of investments to buy, sell, or hold.

The fundamentals include all financial information about a company. In that respect, fundamental analysis is the study of a company's financial history. A review of the balance sheet, income statement, and statement of cash flows (collectively called the financial statements) shows what the company did last quarter or last year in terms of sales and profits and what the company is worth as of the ending date.

The fundamentals are not only historical documents, however. The proper use of the fundamentals is to identify strongly capitalized companies. The study of fundamental analysis is intended to identify companies that present valid investment opportunities; to continue holding stocks in your portfolio whose financial performance meets standards or to sell when performance falls; and to make comparative judgments about companies based upon relative financial strength or weakness.

A company's financial position and performance should be judged on its own merit. In other words, how does the current report compare to the previous year? Did sales grow, and were profits maintained? Or did sales increase while the net profit percentage fell? A broad spectrum of fundamental tests should be applied beyond this situation, of course, but the point is that your decision to buy, sell, or hold a particular company's stock should be based on relative performance and financial strength plus position within an investing sector, strength of the company next to its competitors, and other fundamental comparisons. Unfortunately, this method is not always how Wall Street applies the fundamentals.

Instead, the fundamentals have become a method for judging how well a company's earnings come through compared to what analysts have predicted. If the analysts' expectations are met or exceeded, that is considered a positive sign, and if the performance falls below the analysts' expectations, then it is a negative sign. Buying, selling, or holding stock based on keeping track of how well analysts' predictions came out, however, is a dangerous method for stock picking. This scorekeeping approach to investing, as common and popular as it is, does not make the best use of fundamental information.

Perhaps the problem is that investors want to be told which stocks to buy, sell, or hold. This position would be entirely logical if the experts were usually right. But history shows again and again that analysts' recommendations—based on their own estimates—are wrong more often than they are right. So, giving any weight whatsoever to corporate earnings reports as they stack up against an analyst's predictions is entirely illogical. In fact, it places the priority in reverse order. The analysts' predictions are just that—guesses about the future. They might be based on in-depth analysis of corporate fundamentals and a sincere effort to forecast accurately what is going to take place within a company in terms of sales and profits. Even so, if you allow the analyst's predictions to set the standard, then it distracts you from what you should be monitoring instead.

It makes far more sense to view an analyst's predictions as one of many sources for information. Your final decision to buy, sell, or hold a particular stock should be based on the fundamental outcome—performance of the company—rather than the accuracy of mere predictions. Any accountant will tell you that forecasting and budgeting is a means for setting internal standards but that these devices were never intended to mark the final word in what *should* take place in terms of results.

Comparisons from period to period are where informed decisions can be made. Seek companies as long-term investments whose fundamentals show a consistent pattern of growth. That means, among other things:

- *Sales growth each year.* Growth does not have to be dramatic, just steady. A company whose sales growth demonstrates it can hold a market share or increase it is on track from the investor's point of view; sales growth anticipates long-term profit growth, as well.

- *Profit consistency.* Profits should be judged on the basis of their relation to sales. The acceptable level of profits varies by industry. It is not realistic to expect profit percentages to increase each and every year, however. Achieving and maintaining a competitive return on sales is the real test. A promising sign is a company's capability to yield the same return on sales even when the sales dollar amount changes from year to year. A danger signal is the combination of increasing sales but a falling return on sales.

- *Dividend trend.* Is the company maintaining its dividend yield? Shareholders expect to be given a dividend each quarter, and this situation is one test of a company's profits and operating capital. If a company misses a dividend or cancels payments, that is a negative indicator; if dividends are paid consistently and increased as profits grow, that is a positive indicator.

- *Capitalization tests.* Study the relative degree of long-term debt to total capitalization. Corporations issue bonds or borrow from banks to finance part of their growth; however, if you see that debt capitalization is growing over time, that is a troubling sign. The more debt a company carries, the less net profit remains to pay dividends or to fund future growth. So, a healthy situation involves maintaining debt capital at a steady or diminishing level.

These are some of the major tests that can be performed to identify prospects for possible buy decisions. And once in your portfolio, a company's stock can be evaluated further using such tests to ensure that the trends continue in a positive manner. When a company's return on sales begins to deteriorate or when debt capitalization grows too quickly, you might decide it is time to sell.

This information is by no means a comprehensive overview of fundamental analysis. It is meant to convey the approach that makes sense, however—using financial information to make your own decisions. If you buy, sell, or hold based only on how accurate the analysts guessed at sales and profit levels or how they rate stocks, that is a misguided approach to the selection of stocks and to the decision about whether to continue holding stocks in your portfolio. Professional advice is worth seeking and following only if you believe that someone else has the insight to know more than you do about these basic decisions. Unfortunately, the insiders and so-called experts are not always the most qualified to advise you on where to invest your money.

Problems of Financial Reporting

The preoccupation among investment analysts is with accuracy of predictions, even though business analysts know that prediction, specifically forecasting, is a good monitoring tool but by no means a precise science. The game has become one in which the price will rise if analysts underestimate earnings and vice-versa.

Price ultimately defines profit and loss. If you sell at a price higher than the price at which you bought, then you profit. Even so, price itself as a short-term factor in evaluation of a stock is quite meaningless. Because we know that a stock's price is affected by so many non-fundamental matters, it is a troubling indicator to use for making important decisions in your portfolio. Some investors choose stocks on the basis of price because they want to buy 100 shares, but they have a finite amount of capital to invest; even so, this situation does not mean that a stock at one price is a good buy and a stock at another price is not.

The problem of price reaction to predictions versus outcome is chronic in the market. The astute investor should identify long-term investment prospects based on fundamental tests and then largely ignore interim price movements unless price changes significantly and in an unexpected manner. The *fundamental* reasons for price changes invariably are going to be tied to the basic facts about a company's capitalization, sales, profits, and dividends, however (as well as related dollars and cents issues).

So, investors with a long-term perspective on the matter would naturally emphasize the study of quarterly and annual reports and would apply fundamental tests. These include analysis using a moving average of debt capitalization, sales, profits, and dividends. A long-term correlation between a stock's market price and consistency in the fundamentals could be expected as a result. Ignoring short-term price fluctuations and analysts' predictions, the long-term investor should pay more attention to monitoring the business aspects of the company—performance within its competitive market and its standing in the investment sector. Beyond that, the opinion of analysts is nonsense. After all, those opinions are aimed exclusively at the speculator, one who wants to trade in stock to maximize immediate gain and who is not at all interested in long-term holding of a stock.

With the distinction made between speculation—short-term profit seeking— and long-term investing, the fundamentals clearly are the keys to selection and monitoring of stocks. There are some potential problems associated with the fundamentals, however. Even though the comparison of financial strength between companies and periods identifies likely candidates for long-term investing, how do you know that the fundamentals are accurate?

The *Securities and Exchange Commission* (SEC) monitors publicly listed companies and their reports to stockholders to ensure that no deception takes place. Before the 1930s, companies were not regulated carefully and many wild claims were made, investors swindled, and stocks traded in highly leveraged situations. This "house of cards" characterized the market to such a degree that the big crash of October 1929 should not have come as a surprise. Following that crash, a series of important federal laws were enacted, creating the SEC and defining the rules under which publicly listed companies had to report their financial condition and results of operations. These rules have led further to a rather large volume of rules for accountants and auditors called *Generally Accepted Accounting Principles* (GAAP). The same acronym is used for Auditing Principles. The *Financial Accounting Standards Board* (FASB) is a private-sector organization that sets standards for accounting practices in the United States. FASB develops the rules and guidelines for reporting by accountants and auditors in an attempt to standardize the methods used for evaluating companies during audits and ensuring fair and accurate reporting.

> **TIP**
>
> The FASB Web site provides information about current issues and new rules. It can be viewed at http://accounting.rutgers.edu/raw/fasb/.

The work of the FASB is important because it attempts to apply standards that all auditors should follow. Accounting systems are complex, and the questions that arise concerning valuation of assets and liabilities, timing of accrued or deferred transactions, recognition of costs and expenses, and inventory systems all affect the reports that go to stockholders. Because of the complexity of these matters, it is possible to see a variety of different interpretations within similar circumstances, without those interpretations being fraudulent or misleading. The interpretation of financial transactions can be conservative or liberal. It is a mistake to believe that an audited financial statement is 100 percent accurate. As long as it is substantially fair and accurate, it is considered acceptable under the broad accounting standards.

The purpose of independent audits is to ensure that no outright fraud is taking place. Thus, companies listed on public exchanges are required to undergo audits by independent accountants at least once per year. In addition to annual full-blown audits, the same companies also have periodic reviews for the quarterly reports they are required to file for stockholders. In addition, the SEC also audits publicly listed companies on a selective basis and occasionally finds a case of fraud. In those relatively rare instances, the SEC can assess civil and criminal penalties, suspend trading, and in extreme cases close down the whole operation. Given the extensive nature of the regulatory environment, though, the cases of serious fraud are rare.

Within the rules and guidelines, companies can report their sales and profits in a number of ways. Some devices are used to defer earnings to a future year, for example. By "deferring" income, a corporation can create a pattern of consistency. The alternative might be a rather volatile report in which year-to-year comparisons are difficult because sales and profits change a lot. The truth is, stockholders and analysts like to see steady growth; they want dependability and predictability, and corporate decision-makers like to deliver what their stockholders want.

As long as the reported sales and profits and valuation of assets and liabilities are not deceptive, the practice of managing transactions within the guidelines is not frowned upon, either by the SEC or in the auditing industry. Even stockholders should ask themselves what they consider to be the primary responsibility of a CEO of a publicly listed company. Is it to manage the operations of the organization? Or is it to maintain and improve the market price of shares of stock?

A CEO would break the rules if decisions include "cooking the books." That refers to making changes in the reported results of operations in such a way that the public would be deceived. The pressure on the CEO might come from the board of directors as well as the stockholders, who watch analysts' predictions and expect the CEO to come through with ever-higher sales and profits. Within this environment, interpretations of financial results can be stretched within the rules so that the "right" answer could involve various outcomes. The "right" or "true" result is not easily identified because so many interpretations are possible. In a complex corporate environment with many diversified subsidiaries and divisions, an audit is likely to turn up a number of transactions that could or should be altered to more accurately reflect outcome. In fact, at the conclusion of an audit it is not uncommon for an auditing team to meet with the financial executives of a company to review proposed changes. Some changes are negotiated. In other words, the financial officer might agree to an outside auditor reclassifying some transactions as long as they leave others alone.

Some corporations, including banking, securities, and insurance, for example, are required to set up reserves. These can be extremely large funds that exist in reality or only as journal entries. The reserve requirements are complex and subject to many different interpretations. And the financial strength of a company, as well as its reported profits, can be significantly affected by interpreting reserve requirements in different ways. The timing of matters like reserves, bad debts, or write-offs of obsolete inventory, for example, can affect profits as well.

In these industries, it is especially easy to "bank" earnings. In an exceptionally good year, some earnings are deferred to a later period. This action achieves a report consistent with the previous year and in line with analysts' predictions. It also provides a cushion for future years that might be disappointing in comparison to prior periods. You might review the results of a large, publicly listed company and see that in fact, sales and profits are remarkably consistent from one period to another. It could be that some banking of earnings is taking place. As long as the auditor is comfortable with the methods used to achieve this goal, and as long as the SEC is satisfied that no fraud is taking place, this practice is allowed.

One way to look at the practice is to be troubled by it, with the attitude that the same standards should be applied every year without fail. From a stockholder's point of view, however, the practice of banking earnings could be not only appreciated but expected. A stockholder is reassured when the company's sales rise steadily over many years and when profits are correspondingly consistent. This situation also translates to consistent dividend payments and periodic increases. Stockholders in this scenario also see the market price of the stock rise steadily over the years. The analysts' reports are right on the money, because such situations are fairly easy to predict. Any long-term stockholder could probably predict the outcome with equal accuracy.

So, as an investor, you have to ask yourself whether you want absolute accuracy—even if that means the possibility of wild gyrations in sales and profits—or a well-managed and consistent growth pattern in which dividends are paid regularly and the market value of stock rises in a nearly predictable manner. One test of a company's safety is the volatility in its stock price. A company whose stock has a broad trading range often reflects an inconsistent financial record, as well. So, banking earnings tend to smooth out the volatility and make the whole matter more reliable and predictable, which investors like. In fact, the volatility of the financial outcome often is reflected in the volatility of market price as well. (See Chapter 7 for more discussion of volatility as a test of a listed company.)

Relation between Fundamentals and Pricing

Volatility in price is one measurement of the relationship between the fundamentals and pricing of stocks. Remember, price is affected more by non-fundamentals information than by the fundamentals. There are strong ties between the fundamentals and price, however. In the example in the previous section, the point was made that widely divergent changes from one year to the next in financial information can also lead to a volatile trading range for the stock. An unsettled record of financial results is also unsettling to investors, so a lot of trading in and out of such stocks has to be expected.

Prices of stocks rise and fall when dividends are reported and paid, when earnings reports are published (in comparison with analysts' predictions), and when other fundamental events take place. These can include news affecting the corporation, such as changes in federal interest rates, pending labor strikes, lawsuits, and product information (such as approval of a new drug for a pharmaceutical company, for example). The competitive position in a market sector also affects a company's stock value. If a company is not a leader of the sector, it also is prone to the effects of the leader. So, when the leading retailer has a disappointing year, the stock value of many other retail concerns might fall as well, even when their financial reports were better

The relationship between the fundamentals and market pricing is not direct, but it is real. If it were direct, you could track market price to reports of sales and earnings and see the cause and effect. This function is not possible because financial reports usually trail by at least one month, often by more time. So, while market price is extremely current, financial reports are historical—and, in market terms, outdated.

Fallacy: The fundamentals and market price of stocks are directly related.

The fact is, these two are not directly related at all. Remember, corporate earnings are reported as a return on sales, but investors tend to think in terms of return on investment. So even when you try to relate a series of financial numbers to the market price, you are really looking at two different sets of rules—and the results derive from different forces. Because investors approach their portfolio from an investment orientation, they often misunderstand how corporate profits come about. It's not a matter of ignorance; it is, however, a mistake to think that corporate management takes the same approach as investors.

From the corporate point of view, management does involve keeping the stock price up and hopefully making it rise over time. To the extent that managing the books and planning out sales and profits helps achieve this goal, top management can take credit when it succeeds in its efforts at controlling market price; and certainly, all stockholders appreciate the results as well. The emphasis of managing a corporation is far removed from the investment questions that stockholders possess, however. While the stockholder tends to think in terms of supply and demand for shares of stock, corporate executives are more oriented toward the three immediate questions of market share, economic conditions, and customer/client service. The management functions performed in the corporation are far different than the public relations functions that executives and the board have to perform in order to maintain the stock's price.

1. *Market share* is constantly on the minds of corporate executives. In each industry, a finite amount of demand for goods or services means that each member of the sector has to fight to gain and maintain a market share. Everyone wants to be the leader in his or her sector, but only one can succeed. Market share limits growth because there is nothing a corporation can do to make it grow. They can only attract a larger portion of market share by becoming more competitive or improving customer service and long-term product loyalty. Thus, the key to growth is not only holding onto the limited market share but diversifying into other market sectors to improve overall profits. In evaluating the fundamentals of a company, a study diversification in terms of markets often helps in the comparison. As long as all divisions of a company are profitable, diversification in terms of markets is the most practical way to augment the primary market share. In other words, over the long term, corporate profits can be helped to grow. In the immediate market, however, the relationship between diversification and market price is virtually nil. In fact, it could be fair to say that the market often is oblivious to corporate markets other than the primary market sector.

2. *Economic conditions* affect corporate profits, some to a greater degree than others. Most analysts like to watch interest rate changes, not only because many industries are particularly sensitive to the effects of rate change, but also because this change is considered a barometer of market confidence. The traditional point of view is that investment capital

goes either to the stock market or to the bond market. Thus, when rates go up, bonds are more appealing; and when they go down, capital returns to stocks. While this point of view is somewhat logical, it is not as clear as it might seem. In recent years, the stock market has seemed to not react to changes in interest rates in the same manner as in the past. This situation is due in part to a tremendous growth in capital within the market and in part to the significant influence of mutual funds and other institutional investors. So much capitalization of listed companies takes place through mutual funds that it is difficult to judge the real effect of changes in interest rates. The economy certainly can be measured by interest rates to a degree, and corporate management pays attention to interest rates. The market prices of stocks are not likely to react on a case-by-case basis. Short-term price changes do rise and fall, however, even on rumors that interest rates are going to change. This short-term cause and effect has little to do with real long-term investment value based on a study of the fundamentals.

3. *Customer/client service* has always been a primary concern of management. Recognizing that market share is affected not only by price comparison but also by the degree of service provided, well-managed corporations constantly strive to improve their customer service program. Some succeed more than others. As a fundamental aspect of a corporation's capability to maintain customers through loyalty to product, however, it is also necessary to offer and deliver the best service possible. This mission is a cornerstone of management, so it is an important fundamental test. In other words, when you are comparing two companies in the same industry, prices and quality of products are likely to be very similar. What might distinguish one from another, though, is the commitment to customer service. As an important method for comparing companies, the customer service test—which is not always a test noted by analysts—helps make a fundamental comparison for the purpose of long-term investing. This test is far removed from the minds of most investors, however, and the analysts' preoccupation with short-term pricing means that important tests like comparisons of customer service are ignored altogether.

It is not accurate to believe that fundamentals and a stock's market price are directly related. The cause and effect are associated in the long term, of course, because the fundamentals define corporate strength; however, today's concern is oriented almost exclusively toward the market price of a share of stock, how much it rises and falls, and most of all whether it will rise or fall tomorrow or next week. The fundamentals are given a lot of lip service in the market, but in practice, emphasis and attention go right to the price.

Replacing the widely believed notion that fundamentals and market price are related directly is a more realistic idea: You cannot rely on the fundamentals to judge the price of stocks. Of equal importance, today's stock price tells you very little about the relative health of a company and its fundamental position. The two areas are almost entirely unrelated. You might think of market price as a short-term measurement and a technical indicator while the fundamentals are detached and completely separate.

Technical Analysis: A Look Forward

While fundamentals are a look back, technical indicators are the opposite—a look forward. The fundamentals are a study of yesterday's numbers and management issues. They serve the purpose of identifying companies with the best prospects for growth based not only on sales, profits, dividends, and capitalization, but also on a study of market share, response to economic conditions, and customer service. Technical indicators, on the other hand, are a study of price and related matters.

Investors often confuse the concepts of price competition and financial strength. When a stock is selling at $25 and another is selling at $50, however, that really tells you nothing whatsoever about the financial strength of a company. Having seen in recent years that some stock prices rise to incredible heights even when the corporation has never earned a profit, it becomes clear that price (in fact, the whole arena of demand for stocks) can be far removed from the realities of the fundamentals.

This statement brings us to another popular fallacy about how the market works.

Fallacy: Technical analysis helps you to identify companies that are strong today.

This notion finds many ardent supporters. Technicians like to point to sustained price strength in a stock as proof that the market believes in the strength of a company. Price by itself reflects only the current market demand for shares of stock, however. It does not tell you how well a company is managed, what kind of long-term vision it has for growth, whether it offers a diversified product or service base, or even whether or not the company has earned a profit. The fact is, market price sometimes has a life of its own, and a stock might rise to price levels that are unsupported by any fundamentals. At times, the fundamentals are completely lacking. For example, a company that has never shown a profit might still experience a tremendous run-up in price, which makes no sense on any fundamental basis. By the same argument, a company whose fundamentals are superior could see its stock remaining flat or even falling. This situation occurs at times when there is no fundamental explanation; demand is low for shares of that stock often because analysts are not enthusiastic for the company or because mutual funds are not buying shares in the company. Whatever the reason, a stock's price is set not by fundamental standards but by market supply and demand.

Remember, price is *not* a fundamental indicator. It is a reflection of the perception among investors of the future potential of a company. This potential might have little or nothing to do with reality and might not even be based on fundamentals. How do you apply fundamental tests to a company that does not earn a profit? The fact is, you can look at some fundamental-type indicators and ratios, but the important test has to do with profits. A company should be able to demonstrate that it can produce a profit. When sales rise at impressive multiples but no profits are seen as a result, that is a problem (fundamentally), but the market might not care. To a great extent, the market is blind to fundamentals when it likes a company. The whole structure of a price run-up often is based entirely on perception.

When it comes to the price of stocks, investors might not care about the fundamentals at all. Even when a corporation is in trouble, meaning that its net losses are growing as sales increase and it is losing market share, laying off employees, and cutting back in every way possible, investors might continue buying shares and running the price to ever-higher levels. In other words, as one observer said it, "When the foundation of a pyramid erodes, the top can still be supported on nothing but money."[1]

The belief persists, however, in spite of logic or proof, that technical analysis is the best tool for identifying good investments. Because it is forward-looking rather than historical, the technical indicators enjoy popularity among many investors who see the potential for price growth as the key to market success. It is critical to make a distinction, however. *Price* reflects only the current supply and demand for shares of stock, whereas the fundamentals are an entirely separate range of facts. The two are not related, and investors often overlook this fact. Price does not tell you about a company's current financial position, but it is easy to confuse the two and to come to believe, wrongly, that in fact price does serve as a thermometer of a corporation's profits and losses. As a consequence, many investors who describe themselves as faithful followers of the financial side of things are, in practice, technicians. If you are more concerned with price of a share of stock than with sales, earnings, dividends, capitalization, and other important fundamentals, then you are not a true believer in fundamental analysis.

Getting away from the fallacy that price and other technical indicators are the key to finding good investments, we need to rethink the whole idea with another point of view: Technical analysis is concerned primarily with supply and demand for shares of stock and not with the nuts and bolts of financial strength of the company.

Problems of Technical Analysis

Technical indicators, primarily associated with market price of stock, cannot be accurately associated with financial facts and figures. Even so, there is a tendency to merge the two dissimilar forms of analysis into a single entity. This problem is important for every investor. If you find yourself having trouble distinguishing between what constitutes a technical or fundamental indicator, then you are not alone.

Making the distinction deserves the effort, however, because confusing these two vastly different forms of analysis can lead to trouble. Investors who understand the importance of fundamentals may respond to technical information inadvertently, believing that they are continuing to operate on a fundamental course. This problem is common and widespread.

We are not saying that technical indicators are negative in any way; in fact, using technical indicators or a combination of technical and fundamental information can serve you well. A well-rounded problem of analysis can and should include any indicator that provides you with insight about whether to buy, sell, or hold a particular company's stock.

The problem arises when the analysis itself is not understood. The majority of technical indicators deal with price, so the selection of a company as a long-term investment based on a technical indicator probably is misguided. Technical indicators can be most useful in identifying stock price volatility, notably a change in volatility. Such a change can, in turn, signal that some fundamental changes are also taking place within the company, and that deserves further research. In other words, the study of price (such as through the use of charts and monitoring a stock's trading range) can be used as one method for producing warning or danger signals, from which you might research the fundamentals to identify important changes. These changes might be in the fundamentals but might also be too subtle to show up in earnings reports. For example, a company might experience a change in management, emerging problems with litigation related to product liability, labor union problems, or changes in its competitive stance within its market sector. Any of these fundamental indicators could work as a sign of future trouble for the company, also meaning a change in status from hold to sell; but the first signs of this situation could be seen in price volatility. So, in this situation a technical indicator can serve as an early warning system in monitoring your portfolio. It can also help you in the process of selecting companies as long-term investments before you decide to buy. A pure analysis of the fundamentals can be augmented by technical indicators such as relative price volatility.

Problems arise in the use of technical indicators when investors are distracted from their intended course. So, when you identify a good long-term hold based primarily on fundamental strength and associated indicators, you can be distracted by the game played among analysts—guessing at earnings levels and then evaluating stocks according to how well the outcome matches the analysts' guess. This method is the usual way that the matter is handled, with forecasts actually leading the market in a comparative mode. This technique is a misuse of both fundamental and technical information, however. The purpose of earnings reports, of course, is to keep investors updated on the most basic information needed to evaluate the company. When a company sees increased sales and profits for a quarter or a year, the outcome is positive. Just because an analyst predicted that earnings would be higher, does not mean that the company is failing. In fact, the resulting effect that a company's stock falls is puzzling in itself. If management meets its fiscal goals by producing higher sales and profits, maintaining its earnings margin, and rewarding stockholders with dividends, the stock's price should continue to rise.

In fact, when you ignore the short-term effects of analysts' forecasts on stock price, you discover that when corporations increase the strength of their fundamentals, their stock prices do rise. The longer-term perspective overrules the short-term price changes seen on the market and in reaction to the overrated comparison between forecasts and outcomes. It is far more important to compare outcome to what the corporation predicted than it is to give so much weight to the opinion of an outside analyst.

Where do the technical indicators serve you well? This topic can and should be the important question and distinction that you apply in the development of your program. As you manage your portfolio, how can you apply technical indicators? Comparative analysis is always the way to go, and comparisons should be made within one company from year to year and between stocks that you consider to be similar in characteristics.

The first routine involves trend analysis over a period of time. The process of watching the fundamentals can be helped with some technical trend analysis, as well. For example, a review of the trading range helps you to identify a changing trend in price volatility. Because volatility is so important in identifying market risk, change over time can and should lead you to a review of the fundamentals, as mentioned before. More to the point, a study of emerging changes in volatility can help round out your overall program for analysis of your stocks, whether you are thinking of buying shares or you currently own shares and you need to know whether to buy more or to sell what you have. While a change in volatility should not be the sole determinant in this decision, it can and should be a primary starting point in your analysis. Chapter 7 involves a more detailed study of the importance of volatility.

The second form of technical analysis should involve comparisons between stocks. Assuming that you begin your analysis with a study of several stocks that you consider similar in terms of capital structure, growth potential, and market risk, comparisons of changes in technical indicators are most useful. Whether you are monitoring several companies whose stock you might buy in the future or just monitoring stocks in your portfolio, we have to assume that the starting point involved some form of similarity. If you have identified your personal "risk tolerance" level, you are most likely to diversify your holdings among several companies similar in features. If you seek long-term growth, you are most likely to own shares of companies you consider to be similar in many fundamental characteristics.

As you monitor these companies, the fundamentals are of primary concern, of course. Much of the fundamental information comes after the fact, however. Earnings reports are several weeks behind the event, and in fact, technical indicators can lead an emerging change in the fundamentals and deserve watching. The change is especially apparent when you are reviewing several companies and their technical indicators begin to vary. Why would one company see a change in volatility, its PE ratio, or even stock price when others with the same characteristics remain unchanged (as measured by those technical indicators)? The answer can be complex and elusive at times. When you approach any analysis on a comparative basis, however, it is the divergence of one member of the pack that gets your attention. When one stock becomes more volatile, when its price changes for no known reason, or when trading volume increases dramatically, something is going on. It is worthy of further investigation.

You might find out that in fact, no fundamental changes are taking place whatsoever. Technical change (in other words, price) takes place at times for reasons beyond any analysis and cannot be explained analytically. At other times, however, you might uncover information that is, indeed, very significant. It might be fundamental in nature (changes related to management, product liability, or economic factors, for example), but the consequences might not show up in the financial results for several quarters. At such times, it is important to note that the technical indicators that change in one of the companies being monitored could help you to make fundamental distinctions in your portfolio.

The PE Ratio

Of all the indicators at your disposal, perhaps the most interesting is the PE ratio. To compute it, divide the current market price (a technical indicator) by the earnings per share of stock (a fundamental indicator). The importance of the PE ratio is that it combines both technical and fundamental information and can be viewed as a bridge between the two. It further enables you to compare companies on the basis of their PE ratio.

Essentially, the PE identifies what effect price has in the perception about future value. The price is expressed as a *multiple* of earnings. In other words, a PE of 10 means that the price is 10 times greater than the value of earnings per share. If a stock's current price is $50 per share and the earnings per share is $5, then the current price is at a multiple of 10 times earnings.

Is the PE an accurate indicator? To answer that, it is also necessary to understand how most investors view the PE ratio; in other words, how do most investors react to stocks with a high PE and to stocks with medium or low PE ratios? Remember, because price is a *multiple* of earnings and the ratio is expressed in that way, the PE expresses the market's degree of faith in a stock to rise in the future. So, the higher the PE ratio, the more enthusiasm there is on the part of the market as a whole for that company. In other words, when a PE is high, that means that the market has a stronger-than-average belief that the stock is a worthwhile investment; and when a PE is relatively low, that means the market estimate is that the stock is not as worthy an investment as is a high-PE stock.

Of course, within these general conclusions, some investors also recognize the potential for stocks to become overpriced—and one easily recognized symptom is an exceptionally high PE ratio. It is intriguing that a stock's price is run up to a point that the PE ratio is exceptionally high, however, given the recognition that high-PE stocks might present greater risk. The answer, of course, is that the majority of investors continue to believe that high-PE stocks represent greater future potential for profits. That is why the PE is higher than average; investor demand drives up the price, and that demand comes from a belief that the stock's market value will go higher still in the future. From this information, you might draw one of several possible conclusions, including the following:

1. Many investors do not pay attention to PE when deciding which stocks they believe will be more valuable in the future.

2. Many investors believe that as a PE goes higher, it acts as a signal to buy more shares.

3. Some investors do not understand the significance of PE as a risk element in the selection of stock investments.

4. Some investors think low-PE stocks have less potential to return a profit and high-PE stocks have more potential—in other words, these investors accept the majority view and act accordingly.

To some degree, any or all of these conclusions might be accurate. The truth is that perceptions about stocks as represented by the PE ratio are wrong, however. It is a fallacy to believe that a higher-PE stock is going to perform better than average, just as it is a fallacy to believe that a lower-PE stock will perform poorly in the future.

Fallacy: The PE ratio is a dependable way to judge a stock.

This statement is a fallacy in the sense that investors generally have greater faith in higher-PE stocks. Because the price has been driven up to a higher multiple than the average, many investors believe that means the stock's future profit potential is higher. In fact, the opposite is true. A 14-year study of stocks between 1957 and 1971, testing the efficient market hypothesis, revealed that with consistency, lower-PE stocks out-performed higher-PE stocks. The study included all stocks listed on the *New York Stock Exchange* (NYSE). Results showed an average annual rate of return in six groupings:

6—lowest PE	16.3%
5	13.6%
4	11.7%
3	9.3%
2	9.5%
1—highest PE	9.3%

These results are further summarized on the bar chart in Figure 2.1.

Putting these results another way, if an investor had placed $1 million in the lowest PE stock group at the beginning of the period, it would have grown to $8,282,000. The same amount invested in the highest-PE group would have grown to only $3,473,000, however.[2]

While this study is outdated, it was confirmed by a later, similar study conducted between 1966 and 1983. This study also ranked all NYSE-listed stocks by PE ratio at the end of each year. This study showed the same trend of disparity between PE ranges, divided into 10 groups:

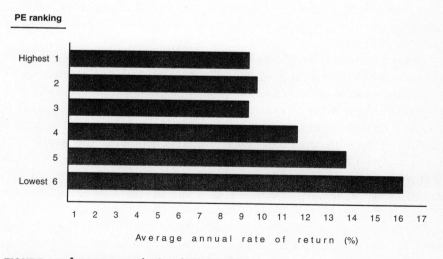

FIGURE 2.1 Average annual return based on PE.

10—lowest PE	14.08%
9	13.81%
8	10.95%
7	10.29%
6	9.20%
5	6.43%
4	7.00%
3	5.57%
2	5.50%
1—highest PE	5.58%

This study confirms that the structure of PE ratios on the NYSE did not change from one test period to another. In fact, it showed that with remarkable consistency, lower-PE stocks have outperformed higher-PE stocks.[3]

The PE studies reveal that over long periods of time, lower PE stocks perform better for investors than the higher-PE stocks. Even so, the PE, by its very nature, continues to act as a reflection of investor sentiment. The higher-PE stocks represent greater optimism about future profit potential, which of course is demonstrably wrong. So, the PE could be considered as a contrarian indicator.

In practice, of course, you should realize that these long-term studies involved the entire market and would not apply to any individual stock. There are many examples of high-PE stocks that have returned higher-than-average profits to investors as well as low-PE stocks that were lackluster over many years. These studies dealt only in averages, and in that respect they make the point: the general perception about PE as a method for judging investment potential is wrong.

We need to replace the widely held fallacy with a different conclusion: The PE ratio serves as a contrarian indicator when applied to the market as a whole; higher-PE stocks produce lower than average annual returns, and lower-PE stocks achieve better than average annual returns.

This conclusion will be startling to many people who view the PE with great confidence. As with many indicators, the facts contradict the widely held belief. In fact, PE can be used as a good method for isolating a range of stocks that you would consider including in your portfolio. Instead of seeking a higher-than-average PE, however, it makes more sense to seek a lower-than-average PE and to monitor PE to determine when stocks should be sold.

The problem with using the PE extends beyond the truth as shown in studies. Whenever you compare the fundamental and technical indicators, you need to also question the reliability of the outcome.

The Reliability Problem of the PE Ratio

The PE ratio as a test of value, present or future, presents problems to every investor due to the timing of information. The price is current, of course, because it is today's market price for stock. The earnings report, however, is a value at a moment in time, usually the end of the last fiscal quarter. The farther away in time from that report, the less reliable the PE ratio.

A completely accurate PE would involve a comparison of the closing price as of the date the earnings were reported. PE tends to be a daily market statistic, however, and few people seem to acknowledge the inaccuracy of the ratio itself. If you are planning to use PE to judge stocks as potential buy candidates or for the purpose of deciding to hold or to sell, an alternative method of calculating PE is recommended.

Under this method, use the price and earnings on the same date. Recognizing that short-term price movement is undependable as an indicator under any market theory, the day-to-day changes in PE are meaningless— especially as the earnings information becomes increasingly dated. So, view the PE ratio on a quarterly basis, using end-of-quarter market prices compared to end-of-quarter earnings per share. Using this method, you have dependable and consistent information and the PE ratio can be studied as it works in a long-term trend. From this point, you can also see how the PE is changing over time, not on a day-to-day basis but on the basis of how price on a closing date compares to earnings for the *same* day. In other words, use PE as a part of trend analysis over time, but not to monitor the status of a company's stock from one day to the next.

The problem of accuracy in the PE extends beyond the timing of information. Given the change in the mix of listed companies over many years, some investors have come to rely less on PE. Some industries, notably in the technology sector, might have low profits or even losses for many years before becoming profitable; so how do you measure growth in such companies? An alternative to the PE is the price-to-revenues ratio. Especially with Internet-related companies becoming more widespread, the analysis of stocks based on profits will not always produce accurate results. If the purpose to the analysis is to identify future potential, then in some instances a comparison between price and revenues makes sense. This statement assumes, of course, that the fundamentals of the company make sense as well. In other words, as sales increase, the profit margin should at least hold pace—even if it is lower than it could be in the future. The reasoning in support of price-to-earnings analysis is based on accuracy. It might be more accurate to consider a company gaining higher market share as its sales increase—even when that increase is not reflected in earnings.

Some analysts have jimmied the numbers to produce higher earnings reports, especially for semiconductor companies. Arguing that these companies made large long-term investments, a modification of PE was devised to increase the earnings side of the PE ratio. This revised value was named EBITDA, or earnings before interest, tax, depreciation, and amortization.[4]

Of course, this adjustment will increase the earnings number being used as part of the PE ratio. To be fair to *all* listed companies, however, the same formula should be applied to make comparisons truly comparative. Otherwise, the EBITDA is nothing more than an analyst's device to alter the outcome and invalidate any comparison between the stocks of dissimilar industries.

Solutions for the PE Puzzle

The key to using PE and making it an accurate indicator is to ignore current information and depend exclusively on recent historical facts. Proponents of both the Dow Theory and the Efficient Market Hypothesis—the two primary theories about the pricing of stocks—agree that short-term price changes cannot be used reliably to draw conclusions about investment value. Even so, PE is widely recognized as a daily test and comparison for companies.

The problem of unreliable current price is compounded by the previously mentioned problem of outdated earnings reports. Depending on when the latest quarterly report was issued, earnings could be three or four months out of date, which makes the current PE unreliable and inaccurate. Furthermore, because different industries have vastly different characteristics, it could be very inaccurate to compare an airline to a technology company or a 150-year-old Wall Street brokerage firm to an Internet sales company that started up last year.

Recognizing these disparities, we have to also conclude that market-wide surveys are revealing but that they tend to average out the problems every investor faces when trying to make valid comparisons. We can see that high-PE and low-PE stock ranges perform quite differently, but how does that help in the decision-making you have to execute in deciding which stocks to buy, sell, or hold? Of course, when making comparisons between companies in different sectors, it is important to recognize the differences in the fundamentals and also to acknowledge that those differences could invalidate your analysis using PE and many other indicators.

As one possible solution, consider restricting comparative analysis to two levels. First, study PE for the specific company on a historical basis, comparing end-of-quarter market price to end-of-quarter earnings per share. Look for trends in these stationery statistics as a means for making decisions about how well that stock continues to meet your investment criteria. Second, if you are going to make comparisons between companies, limit the comparison to the same market sector. Compare transportation companies to other transportation companies, and compare technology stocks to other technology stocks. If you believe that a study of earnings is inaccurate given the need to build market share over time, consider price-to-revenues analysis, but again, limit the comparison to stocks within the same industry before drawing any conclusions. And, for companies that have especially large capitalization requirements, consider using the EBITDA method for calculating earnings. Make such comparisons within the same market sector, however, to avoid further distorting the comparison. Remember that it is not reliable to compare companies that are dissimilar in terms of industry. It is also less than reliable to attempt to make comparisons between large, well-established, and well-capitalized companies and smaller companies going through their early years of development. So, all comparisons should be made in acknowledgment of the intrinsic problems involved with company-to-company comparative analysis. A comparison should be made whenever possible between companies that share as many characteristics as possible—market sector, approximate age, and capitalization level.

The reliability problem in company-to-company comparisons is supported by a series of market studies concluding that smaller companies tend to perform better than the market averages and that larger companies tend to perform poorer than market averages. A long-term study of stocks between 1931 and 1974 involved dividing all NYSE-listed companies into groups based on market capitalization. The largest group underperformed the market by 1.3 percent per year on average while the smallest companies (in terms of market capitalization) outperformed the market by 5.5 percent on average.[5]

This "small company effect" contradicts a widely held belief that larger-capitalization companies perform better as investments. On the contrary, it would seem that smaller companies do better on average, and that conclusion seems to be consistent over many years. In 1982, another study was conducted involving 3,000 stocks on the NYSE, AMEX, and over the counter. The study involved the decade from 1968 to 1978. In this study, capitalization groupings were made in 10 groups. The largest-capital stocks underperformed by 4.2 percent per year. The smallest-capitalization stocks outperformed the market by 5.4 percent per year.[6]

A third study involved the longest period of all, 43 years from 1951 to 1994. In this study, the 10 percent representing the largest-capitalization stocks and mid-cap stocks underperformed the market by 2.7 percent per year. In the same period, so-called micro-cap stocks (those with capitalization below $25 million, representing the smallest 30 percent of listed companies) outperformed the market on average by 10.4 percent per year.[7]

When looking at PE and company valuation, it is clear that the entire matter resides under a cloud of contradiction. The belief that higher-PE stocks have greater-than-average profit potential is proven wrong. The belief that stronger-capitalized companies perform better also is proven wrong by long-term studies. You will need to exercise great care when analyzing companies in terms of their PE ratio. Stronger-than-average growth potential might not show up in the PE but is more likely to be found in the fundamentals—strong sales and profit growth over time. This statement naturally leads many to look for strong capitalization, however—in other words, the ability to fund growth over many years. Studies also show that smaller-cap companies outperform larger-capitalization concerns, however, so that can also be misleading. Much of the impressive performance among the micro-cap companies occurred in the boom between 1975 and 1983, according to one source;[8] however, the point remains that many of the traditionally held beliefs about what makes one company a better long-term investment than another have to be re-evaluated in light of what the studies reveal.

1. In fact, effective analysis of stocks you consider as prospective buy candidates, as well as stocks held in your portfolio, have to be monitored with a view to what the studies have shown. It makes the most sense to apply these rules to the analysis of stocks by using the PE ratio: Calculate the PE at fixed end-of-quarter dates and follow the PE trend over time.

2. Make company-to-company comparisons within the same industry or market sector.

3. Attempt to compare stocks to one another with similar capital structure.

4. Consider price-to-revenue comparisons in place of PE for market sectors with relatively young companies whose growth curve might take many years.

5. Consider adjusting earnings to exclude non-operational costs and expenses, but apply the same adjustments to all companies in your analysis.

6. Question the widely held beliefs about PE ratio based on long-term studies and their outcomes.

Notes

[1] Laurence J. Peter, "Why Things Go Wrong," 1985.

[2] "Investment Performance of Common Stocks in Relation to Their Price/Earnings Ratios: A Test of the Efficient Market Hypothesis," *Journal of Finance*, June 1977; study conducted by Sanjoy Basu.

[3] "Decile Portfolios of the New York Stock Exchange, 1967-1984," working paper, Yale School of Management, 1986; study conducted by Roger Ibbotson.

[4] "How the PE ratio developed," Matt Marshall, *Mercury News*, March 11, 2000.

[5] Study conducted by Rolf Banz, reported in 1978.

[6] Study conducted by Thomas Cook and Michael Rozeff, reported in 1982.

[7] James O'Shaughnessy, *What Works on Wall Street*, McGraw-Hill, 1998.

[8] Jeremy Siegel and Peter L. Bernstein, *Stocks for the Long Run, 2nd Ed.*, McGraw-Hill, 1998.

CHAPTER 3

The "Practical" Dow Theory

The stock market often is defined in terms of one measurement: the *Dow Jones Industrial Average* (DJIA). This index consists of 30 of the largest stocks traded on the major exchanges, representing approximately one-fifth of the capital value of all publicly listed stocks in the United States.[1]

Is it fair or accurate to consider the DJIA as "the market" in making judgments about the timing of investment decisions? Is it enough that about one-fifth of the value of the market can be tracked in terms of market price by watching the DJIA? And do the stocks in your portfolio follow that one-fifth of stocks closely enough to make the DJIA a worthwhile measurement? In fact, the most important question every investor needs to ask about the averages is, "Does movement in the DJIA help me to decide whether to buy, sell, or hold a specific stock?"

Because the DJIA is a composite of 30 different companies, the index movement is a mix of the ups and downs of its components and not just a representative conclusion about the entire market. This feature is the flaw in any index or average; they cannot be used to accurately judge your own portfolio. While significant change in the DJIA and the current trend can be helpful in measuring the mood of the market, that is its limitation. So, you can identify an optimistic mood (a bull market) characterized by rising market values or a pessimistic mood (a bear market) characterized by falling market values.

In this chapter, we take a close look at the DJIA to determine its value as an indicator of market mood or as a means of deciding what actions to take, if any, in your portfolio. To begin, it is necessary to first understand the background of the DJIA—how it was first developed and how it evolved into the influential market statistic that it has become today.

Origins of the Dow Theory

In 1880, Charles Dow arrived in New York, having spent his career until that time as a reporter. He found a job reporting on mining stocks and quickly gained the reputation as a capable analyst of financial information. While working for the Kiernan News Agency, Dow met Edward Jones. In 1882, the two men formed Dow Jones & Company, located in the back room of a soda fountain at 15 Wall Street, next door to the NYSE building.

The company began publishing a news sheet in 1883 under the name *Customer's Afternoon Letter*. This sheet eventually became *The Wall Street Journal*. The paper was first published on July 8, 1889. Dow began writing a series of essays about his observations. In them, he noted the recurrence of cycles in trading; he believed that a dependable method of trend analysis could be developed by tracking market leaders. His idea was that these leaders would set a pace and the market would follow. He identified 12 stocks as the first index of market leaders.[2]

Dow's essays led to the development by others of what we know today as the Dow Theory. An associate of Dow, Samuel Nelson, wrote a book, *The ABCs of Stock Speculation*, in which Dow's observations were organized into a more formal methodology. Dow's successor as editor of *The Wall Street Journal*, William Peter Hamilton, took the ideas further, publishing a series of predictions that became a popular feature in the paper.

By 1916, Dow's original list of 12 stocks grew to 20, and by 1928 it grew to its current level of 30 stocks. Dow's original observations, which were aimed at business management rather than investors, could be defined as market-wide trend analysis. Business cycles and trading cycles often correspond, and Dow's observations grew after his death into a major theory about how and why prices change in the market. Today, the 30 so-called "industrials" represent the major index serving as the core of what is now called the Dow Theory. In addition, the Transportation and Utility averages (plus a Composite of all three averages) are used by many analysts to study market-wide trends and cycles. The 30 stocks in the DJIA, while representing only one-fifth of total capital value in listed stocks, have taken on an identity far beyond Charles Dow's original essays—they have become "the market" in the minds of many analysts and investors.

The 30 stocks in the industrials as of mid-2001 are as follows:

Ticker	Name
AA	Alcoa, Inc.
AXP	American Express
T	AT&T
BA	Boeing
CAT	Caterpillar
C	Citigroup
KO	Coca Cola
DD	E. I. DuPont de Nemours
EK	Eastman Kodak
XOM	Exxon Mobil
GE	General Electric
GM	General Motors
HWP	Hewlett Packard
HD	Home Depot
HON	Honeywell
INTC*	Intel
IBM	International Business Machines (IBM)
IP	International Paper
JPM	J. P. Morgan Chase
JNJ	Johnson & Johnson
MCD	McDonald's
MRK	Merck
MSFT*	Microsoft
MMM	Minnesota Mining & Manufacturing (MMM)
MO	Philip Morris
PG	Proctor & Gamble
SBC	SBC Communications
UTX	United Technologies
WMT	Wal-Mart Stores
DIS	Walt Disney Company

*These stocks trade on NASDAQ; all others are listed on the NYSE.

Basics of the Dow Theory

As it has grown over the years, the Dow Theory has been firmed up and its points have become established in the minds of market observers. These points can be divided into several theories or tenets:

1. *The market goes through three distinct trends, or movements.* The Dow
   Theory defines three trends in the market. First is the primary trend,
   lasting several months or years. A primary bull trend is optimistic and is
   associated with rising prices, and a primary bear trend is the opposite. A
   secondary trend lasts between several weeks and several months and normally runs in a direction opposite the primary trend. The third trend is
   seen in day-to-day price changes and is given no importance in the identification of major market movements.

   As the stock market becomes increasingly accessible to investors through
   the Internet and speculators influence market prices through online day
   trading, the traditional analysis of price trends might be more difficult to
   establish. At the time that Dow first observed market trends, most Wall
   Street concerns did not even have a telephone (including Dow Jones &
   Company). Today, trading online is becoming widespread, and the sheer
   volume of activity could make trends as they developed in the past more
   difficult to identify in the near future.

2. *A trend is confirmed by the same movements in Industrial and
   Transportation Averages.* According to the Dow Theory, you need to analyze both Industrial and Transportation trends together; both have to
   demonstrate the same direction in order to establish a trend. A bull
   trend is established only when both averages exceed previous high levels,
   and a bear trend is taking place only when both averages fall below previous low levels. As a second part of this tenet, a trend remains in effect
   until both averages reverse their direction by exceeding previous highs
   or lows.

   Why do these averages need to conform, according to the Dow Theory?
   The relationship between production and transportation of goods is
   directly linked. This statement might have been true 100 years ago when
   the Transportation Averages (then made up of railroads and called the
   Railroad Average) were more directly linked to manufacturing products
   for the consumer. The Dow Theory assumes that the fundamentals *and*
   price trends of industrial and transportation stocks will react to the relationship between manufacturing and delivery. As the U.S. economy
   becomes more and more service-oriented, the significance of manufacturing and transportation of products might be becoming less important as
   indicators of market direction.

3. *Only closing prices should be used in analysis.* This idea is based in part
   on the idea of what makes a price settle—that is, buyer and seller agree
   on the price and it reflects all that is known about the company at that
   time (the efficient market hypothesis). Originally, though, closing prices
   were used on the basis that these were the prices that informed investors
   were willing to settle for overnight.

The original reasons for using closing prices are obsolete today. The idea that a buyer would be willing or unwilling to hold stock at a specific price overnight is based on traditional limitations to trading activity. Today, trades can be made online or via telephone within mere seconds, and execution of trades is done and confirmed with lightning speed. While closing prices do mark an obvious point for any form of analysis, the original justification for this rule under the Dow Theory should not be given a lot of weight.

4. *Trends are firmly established when three events take place.* The Dow Theory goes on to specify that in order to establish that a trend is occurring, three events are required. In a bull market, those events are as follows:

- A well-informed investor buys stock when prices are low and when the mood of the market is fearful and negative.
- Earnings in companies are growing.
- Technical indicators as seen in increasing prices follow the fundamentals, as seen in higher earnings.

In a bear market trend, the three events are:

- Well-informed investors sell high-priced stock even though the mood of the market is enthusiastic.
- Softening demand for shares leads to the beginning of decline in stocks' prices.
- The market in general moves toward the selling of shares, leading to an acceleration in falling prices.

This tenet of the Dow Theory is a study of the forces of supply and demand, observed within the market as a forum. The context of this tenet also observes the tendency among most investors to become most enthusiastic as the market approaches a high (whereas informed investors act in a contrary manner), and most become most pessimistic as the market approaches its low (and again, the minority of informed investors recognize the low as the time to begin buying shares).

In respect of its observation of supply and demand and the typical behavior among investors, this segment of the Dow Theory is the most useful. It is a recognition of the tendencies leading to missed opportunities and to losses among most investors. By failing to observe the basic rules of trading cycles, many investors fail to see that it is all a matter of timing. It also is human nature to react with elation when caution makes more sense, however, or to hold back out of fear when the logical behavior is to step in and buy.

5. *Stock prices determine trends.* This tenet states that trends are established by stock prices alone. Thus, watching the DJIA and applying the

other Dow Theory tenets limit the nature of information required to determine when long-term trends turn around. As rallies set high levels twice in a row, the pattern is called a bullish indication; and when prices establish lows twice in a row, the pattern is called a bearish indication.

While the importance of price trends as overall indicators cannot be ignored, the emphasis on prices alone is troubling. As most investors own a handful of stocks, overall trends might indicate a market mood but they do not address the fundamentals of the companies whose stock resides in that portfolio. This tenet forms the basis for the same rules followed by chartists, observing that support and resistance define the perimeters of a trading range; and when those levels are broken through, a new trend begins. As applied to individual stocks, there might be a degree of logic to the concept. Applied to the market as a whole, the limitation of analysis to prices in an average of 30 stocks is purely technical and does not reveal anything useful about the individual companies in your portfolio.

Problems with the Dow Averages

The DJIA is so widely used for establishing the tone of the market that for many observers it is the final word. A "good" day on Wall Street means the DJIA rose, and an especially good day is one in which the DJIA *and* the NASDAQ Composite Index both rose. The most significant belief or assumption in the market is that the DJIA represents the broader market in every important respect (health or mood, up or down tendency, and so on).

Two related fallacies are at play in the minds of most investors, whether they consciously believe them or just operate under the false assumptions.

Fallacy: The DJIA is "the market."

Fallacy: The DJIA is an accurate index.

The Dow Jones Company does not publicize its methods for selecting stocks for its averages. Periodic adjustments are made, however, consisting of replacing one stock with another. Is the replacement stock more representative of the economy? Or is there some other reason to make the replacement? Without specific knowledge about how these decisions are made, these questions cannot be answered; however, considering that many investors and analysts treat the DJIA as representing the market as a whole, it is unsettling that a single company can replace one component with another. For example, the DJIA was adjusted a few years ago by removing Woolworth's, Westinghouse Electric, Texaco, and Bethlehem Steel. These were replaced by Hewlett-Packard,

Johnson & Johnson, Traveler's Group, and Wal-Mart. Are the four replacement corporations more representative of the economy today than the companies they replaced? To some extent, they are; but we still do not know the reasoning behind the removal of corporations, not to mention the timing of the decision to do so. It is certain that replacing one set of components with another is going to alter the nature of the DJIA, so a long-term trend will be far from accurate. In fact, as a basic requirement for accurate long-term analysis, it makes no sense whatsoever to change the components of the average without also adjusting the trend line itself.

Even given these points, the DJIA trend is not disrupted nor adjusted even when some components are replaced with others. Because the DJIA itself is only a sample of large corporations in the U.S. economy, it is but one way to measure the market. To what extent have replacements changed the direction, degree, and strength of the DJIA, however?

The fact that the level of the DJIA might be artificially sustained through replacement of components is enough to invalidate its value, at least to a serious statistician. Imagine a market study in which consumers were asked to select a preferred flavor, and over a period of time the preferences were recorded. During the study, however, some company brands were not being picked, so the study group replaced them with alternative flavors. In this case, the market study would be considered completely unreliable because the components were changed during the study. As a basic requirement for analysis of anything—whether stocks or consumer goods—the study should be based upon consistent and reliable information. Thus, replacing components of the 30 industrials from time to time makes the DJIA a problematical indicator. At the very least, the numerical value set for the DJIA should be altered to reflect what it would have been if the replacement stocks had been included for some period of time.

Equally troubling is the fact that the DJIA is price-weighted, meaning that each stock is given equal value regardless of the amount of outstanding stock. A company's total capitalization, which of course has much to do with its capability to operate and compete, is not taken into consideration; only price affects movement of the DJIA. Many other indexes are weighted by market capitalization and that makes a certain amount of sense. The Dow Theory states that price alone determines trends, however. Under that tenet, price is considered as the only ingredient of the DJIA regardless of capitalization levels—even if those levels vary widely among the 30 companies.

The effect of stock splits over more than 100 years has been to create a weighting effect among the 30 stocks in the DJIA. Some stocks have greater weight than others, and this weight changes each time a stock splits. As of July 3, 2001, the weighting of the DJIA was as follows:[3]

Name	Weighting
Alcoa, Inc.	2.5642
American Express	2.535
AT&T	1.423
Boeing	3.5752
Caterpillar	3.2998
Citigroup	3.367
Coca Cola	2.9158
E. I. DuPont de Nemours	2.9957
Eastman Kodak	2.9437
Exxon Mobil	5.5434
General Electric	3.1354
General Motors	4.1077
Hewlett Packard	1.8025
Home Depot	3.0395
Honeywell	2.2278
Intel	1.9333
IBM	7.1707
International Paper	2.2963
J. P. Morgan Chase	2.8942
Johnson & Johnson	3.2395
McDonald's	1.7289
Merck	4.1065
Microsoft	4.4727
MMM	7.4151
Philip Morris	3.0338
Proctor & Gamble	4.102
SBC Communications	2.5781
United Technologies	4.6301
Wal-Mart Stores	3.1239
Walt Disney Company	1.7993
Total	100.0000%

If this weighting reflected relative capital strength of the Dow components, it would look much different.

The large disparity in weight between MMM (7.4151%) and AT&T (1.423%) is derived from the stock splits over time, and not on any capital-based test. Thus, the weight of a particular stock does not reflect sales, profits, capitalization, or even price history.

Overcoming the Problem

Is there a better way to make use of the Dow Theory? Obviously, the DJIA contains a number of problems. The fact that it is accepted throughout the market as a valid criterion for making judgments does not mean that it is unflawed. In fact, just because the majority believes that the DJIA is an accurate index does not mean that anyone should accept that as conclusive. On the contrary, the majority is more often wrong about such things. In this case, it is more likely that most people have never given it much thought. They do not question the DJIA or its accuracy or relevance because the topic simply has not come up.

As an astute investor, you might want to question all information and most especially all forms of information that are long-standing and traditional. The DJIA is a convenient tool for identifying one aspect of market-watching, specifically the test of "up" versus "down" for a fictitious index of big companies. People who watch the news like to get information in a simple and straightforward manner, and financial journalists like the DJIA and other index reporting because it is easy to explain and easily understood. If you challenge the assumption that price alone determines a trend, then the DJIA is inaccurate in your view. The fact that it might be inaccurate does not matter to a large segment of the investing public, because the audience gets what it wants—a simple answer to their question: Did the market go up or down today?

When investors hear that the market has moved in one direction or another, their next step usually is to check the stocks they are watching or already own. Experienced investors already know that except for large-scale price changes, however, the direction of the DJIA usually does not reflect what happens to individual stocks. Sometimes these stocks follow the market, and sometimes they move in the opposite direction or do not move at all. Experienced investors also understand that short-term price changes cannot be taken into account when viewing long-term viability of a company as a whole; the short-term fluctuations have to be disregarded under either the Dow Theory or the random walk hypothesis.

When the DJIA takes a big jump in either direction, it usually is caused by some news to which the market is overreacting. Thus, the market—as measured by the DJIA—probably will correct itself in subsequent sessions. Any change in your stocks that is caused as a reaction to market-wide change will probably be corrected as well.

In summary, no changes in the DJIA—large or small—are likely to affect the viability of your stocks as investments. The current price will change, but only temporarily. The big surprise to many faithful DJIA watchers is that in spite of a widespread belief to the contrary, the index itself is not the market. More to the point, the index does *not* lead the market. We need to arrive at a new point of view replacing the commonly-held belief about the DJIA as "the market" in a broader context: Changes in an index of stocks does not affect the investment value of any individual company; the DJIA has no effect whatsoever on the important fundamental tests that define whether to buy, hold, or sell a particular stock. On the contrary, an index is an *average*, so using index movements to judge individual stocks can be most misleading. The important test of a company's investment value should rest with the fundamentals, and any price-related trends established by average change should not be considered.

Beliefs about the accuracy of the DJIA need to be replaced, as well. No statistician or scientist would tolerate a change in the components of a sample population; that would invalidate the entire matter as a violation of the scientific method. This practice is tolerated and left unquestioned, however. The knowledge, though, that the DJIA is adjusted from time to time gives you the insight to discount its value as an indicator. The mistaken belief that the DJIA provides accurate information about the market should be replaced with another point of view: the DJIA is not a reliable indicator, and it provides no guidance for the individual decisions about individual stocks or about the market overall.

Recognizing the intrinsic flaws of the DJIA, it becomes apparent that the reporting of change in value is a simplistic tool for conveying information. Financial journalists use the DJIA to tell readers or listeners whether the market had a good day or a bad day. The DJIA cannot be used to make serious decisions about your portfolio, however, not only because it does not represent the stocks you own, but also because its calculations are distorted as well. As an investor, you are not an owner of shares in "the market." You own shares of one or more companies, even if you invest through mutual funds. So, the DJIA is representative of only 30 large companies; it might lead price trends to some degree in the rest of the market, but even that point itself does not mean that the DJIA validates index watching as an analytical method. You still need to return to the company's fundamentals to make accurate judgments about its investment value.

Timing Your Market Decisions

The main complication of deciding when to buy, sell, or hold is a matter of timing. Some investors study one or two indicators, looking for a relatively dependable but simple method for making decisions by formula; but in fact, this approach is not practical.

One of the worst ways to make decisions is to base them on the DJIA; even so, many people believe that the up or down trends in the DJIA are, in fact, reliable indicators for timing market decisions. Most of the people who believe this idea also are mystified when their timing turns out to be wrong and when individual stocks do not act according to the indicators gleaned from the DJIA— and for good reason. The DJIA is not a worthwhile indicator for timing buy and sell decisions.

Fallacy: The DJIA helps you to time buy and sell decisions.

Why should the DJIA be considered a valuable analytical tool when it is flawed? Not only do the 30 stocks not act as representatives of the entire market, but the occasional replacement of components makes the entire procedure suspect. Given these problems, it should be clear that the DJIA is not reliable for any serious analysis of the market, either as a whole or as it applies to individual stocks.

What can you use to determine when to buy, sell, or hold? If, in fact, the DJIA cannot serve as a reliable indicator, what index can be used? The S&P 500 is a broader index of stocks, and it seems to track market-wide activity in a far more accurate manner. NASDAQ is a composite, so it is an accurate measurement of NASDAQ-based securities. Even with accurate index systems, however, the decisions to buy, sell, or hold individual stocks remain a difficult issue for most investors.

The desire to find an accurate index might be part of the problem. Why pay attention to market-wide indicators at all? It is not realistic to expect a particular stock to act in a way indicated by an index, and yet many investors follow this principle. Remember that indexes do *not* lead the market, however. In fact, "the market," essentially, is not led by any one factor or series of factors. It is the composite of thousands of economic, fundamental, and illogical pieces of information all added together. The classic examples of optimism and pessimism within the market generally have been overreactions unjustified by any fundamental facts. Invariably, taking part in the frenzy that occurs from time to time in the market is a mistake, and many people lose money by following illogical trends. Those trends often are defined in terms of the index watching itself. For example, the best-known "trend" is a large rise or drop in the point value of the DJIA.

As a market trends upward, the tendency in the short term is for prices to be run up by growing demand. This demand comes from many investors trying to jump onto the trend, however, even though it has no logic to it. Thus, the run-up is artificial. It might continue for quite a while, but ultimately it will end and those investors will lose money. The same thing happens on the down side. A panic causes more investors to dump stocks, so prices are driven downward. The farther the point drop, the greater the panic and the higher the number of people selling stock at low prices.

In these short-term timing overreactions, the cool-headed investor knows to resist the frenzy. When prices are rising for no logical reason, that is the worst time to buy; and when everyone else is in a panic and selling shares, that itself is the best buying opportunity. When the general mood goes one way, however, it takes some courage and clear-headed thinking to recognize the flaw in the herd mentality and to make decisions contrary to the general trend.

The belief that the DJIA is useful in identifying trends is perhaps the most illogical belief about the science of stock pricing. That fallacy needs to be replaced with a different point of view: The market operates on the basis of supply and demand for *individual* stocks, and short-term changes often are an overreaction to the information at hand. Serious investors need to select stocks to buy based on strong fundamentals, to hold those stocks as long as the fundamentals continue to meet standards, and to sell stocks when the previously strong fundamentals weaken.

From the long-term investor's perspective, the market price of a stock is insignificant to the degree that it changes from day to day. Such an investor is far more interested in how the stock's value changes over the long term. The market rewards patience, and that makes it imperative to ignore short-term price changes. These changes are inaccurate, misleading, and even upsetting to the otherwise structured approach to long-term investment based on a study of fundamentals. More to the point, intelligent investors can take comfort by discounting the value of the DJIA as a tool for measuring the value of their stocks. It might be fun to watch the DJIA in the same way that it is fun to watch other people gamble in Las Vegas. If you are going to put money down on a gamble but your strategy is based on a belief that is entirely false, however, then you will most likely lose your money.

The same principle that applies in the casino applies on Wall Street. If you are going to develop a system, it should be a system that is sound, that is proven to be valid, and that produces long-term profits. Some investors (like some gamblers) believe in ideas based on luck, superstition, or false science. That is why it is far easier to lose money in the market than it is to make a profit. This situation does not mean that the odds are against you; they are only against you if you use illogical or false indicators to make important decisions. Those investors who concentrate on the fundamentals have a solid chance at profiting over time and of realizing long-term success in their portfolios.

Applying the Dow Theory

As you overcome the flaws associated with watching the DJIA, you can arrive at a valuable application of the Dow Theory in your portfolio. The principles that Charles Dow first established are themselves not illogical, and some aspects of his ideas can be used to manage individual stocks.

The Dow Theory is almost always applied to the market as a whole, which is inaccurate and illogical. Aspects of the Dow Theory can be used, however, to aid in making decisions about individual stocks—an idea that makes sense but is rarely put into practice.

Remember that Dow recognized the importance of long-term trends as a business principle, and his original idea was to develop methods for business analysis. These principles are used widely in the corporate environment, where accountants and analysts study markets and their reaction to products or services in an ongoing effort to gain more market share. As they succeed in the science of analysis, sales and profits grow. Analysis also is applied to improving internal efficiency so that expenses are minimized, again improving net profits. In the corporate environment, the primary administrative activity is aimed at improving profits. It is ironic that the same emphasis does not take place in the market.

Business managers are fundamental-based from necessity. The fundamentals of business management are devoted to dollars and cents, the production of profits. So, business people do not try to predict what customers will buy based only on averages; they study fundamental trends and test their markets. This method is the equivalent of investors studying a company's overall fundamental success. When investors are distracted by the DJIA and other technical indicators, however, they can easily lose sight of the important tests that help them determine the value of the stocks in their portfolio.

Most investors would dispute this statement by claiming that they want to buy stocks at a low price and sell them at a higher price. That might be the intention, but it does not always work out that way. Investors do tend to watch the DJIA (and, in fact, short-term price changes for their stocks), but they sometimes forget to apply sound business principles that can and do define profitability in business, as well as in portfolio management.

The tenets of the Dow Theory can be applied to individual stocks, and that idea makes perfect sense. These tenets and their applicability to stocks are as follows:

1. *The market goes through three distinct trends, or movements.* Just as the market as a whole tends to work cyclically, so do individual companies. It is important to make a distinction between stock price behavior and the cycles experienced by specific companies, however. Stock price cycles might be a reflection of a company's cycle, but that is confused by the overall market trends that are reflected in stock prices. So, when prices generally are on the move, the prices of all stocks tend to go in the same direction.

   A company's cycle, on the other hand, is caused by more pragmatic matters. Some industries are seasonal, so an annual cycle can be seen readily in changes in sales volume and profits. A company might also be said to go through a predictable growth curve. When it is small, growth tends to occur at a more rapid pace than its larger competitors. Well-established, strongly capitalized companies can afford to produce significant profit margins with steady growth at lower rates; conversely, a very large corporation might be unable to sustain growth due to size and breadth (diversification) of its many subsidiaries and divisions.

Admittedly, these observations oversimplify the cyclical patterns of a large corporation, which are quite complex and can contain numerous variables. The point remains that cycles, however—whether annual, related to a company's capital strength, or industry-specific—are among the realities of corporate management. Part of running a big company includes management of the cycles and how those cycles affect cash flow, profits, and even the stock price. No corporate manager wants the stock price to fall, but pricing cycles often are outside the control of management. And that is the key.

If you want to apply the Dow Theory to corporate fundamentals, it is also necessary to identify the specific cyclical trends. In the financial analysis of business, those trends take place in three distinct ways, just as stock prices do. The same rules apply as well.

A short-term movement has to be discounted as unreliable. A corporate analyst knows that the daily levels of sales, costs, and expenses cannot be used to identify any sort of trend of value to the analytical process. For example, in the preparation of a corporate forecast and budget, the daily levels of transactions cannot be taken into account.

An intermediate movement is where most analysis takes place within the corporation. A study of monthly numbers over a period of several months reveals what is taking place in terms of forecasts and budgets (versus actual transaction levels), production of sales and profits, and marketing changes. Are customers buying the product? Are they buying more or less than the marketing forecast thought? Is a particular division producing the return it is expected to yield? If not, why? These are the on-going forms of analysis that take place in corporate trend analysis. The intermediate trend spells profits or losses, and as those trends emerge, corporate management can take steps to reverse negative changes or to encourage positive ones.

Long-term trends are seen in quarterly and annual financial statements and multi-year expansion plans. At the highest levels of corporate management, the "big picture" is constantly on the minds of executives. The vision of future market share, new product development, and ever-higher sales and profits are driving forces in the corporate world. Because all of these ideas have to be based on financial outcome, they all represent long-term fundamental analysis.

Once you recognize that the three movements apply to business management, you will be able to make more informed comparisons between companies to arrive at portfolio-based decisions. By selecting companies whose long-term vision is aimed at well-planned and controlled forms of growth, you are most likely to end up with a portfolio of long-term growth stocks. The identification of these companies is based on how well organized the company is and upon how well its management is able to control its long-term marketing trend.

2. *A trend is confirmed by the same movements in Industrial and Transportation Averages.* The idea of "confirmation" is a key to all trend analysis. Any singular movement cannot be considered a trend; it has to be confirmed by changes in related areas. In the case of the DJIA, a trend is believed to be confirmed when the same direction reversal takes place in both Industrial and Transportation Averages. This belief is based on the traditional relationship between the production and transportation of goods. With today's makeup of the Transportation Averages including so many non-goods related companies (such as passenger airlines), the validity of this original idea should be questioned. The original point applies to business trend analysis and to analysis of corporate fundamentals, however.

For example, if you are monitoring a specific company and you notice that sales and profits begin to rise, you might ask why that takes place. The trend will be related to some fundamental change that can be identified. For example, a company might have acquired another company so that the increase in sales reflects the elimination of competition, thus a larger market share. In this case, there is not a legitimate "increase" in sales but an adjustment in the trend. When you study corporate fundamentals, you need to ensure that your comparisons remain valid. When sales grow due to a merger, for example, the previous sales history has to be adjusted to include the sales of both sides in the merger so that you can identify the real trend.

Another example of confirmation occurs whenever an unexpected change takes place in sales or profits. Have specific divisions or subsidiaries introduced new products, lost market share, or undergone other fundamental changes? The important function in the fundamental analysis process is in the identification of *causes* for change. Without knowing the cause, you cannot understand what the change means. In the previous example, a merger caused an increase in sales and profits. When you study the two companies together and include both histories, you might discover that the combined sales and profits are on track with the previous activity or that there was actually a drop-off in activity.

While the Dow Theory requires independent confirmation by way of analysis between two separate indexes, corporate analysis requires confirmation of a change in the trend through identification of the cause. Because corporate analysis is complex, the cause is not always apparent. It might be necessary to investigate in depth and even to contact the company's

Stockholder Relations Department to make inquiries. Corporate management knows why sales and profits rise or fall; entire departments of
accountants and internal auditors spend their efforts each and every day
identifying these causes. While the budgetary and forecasting routines
within corporations can be highly political, the underlying cause of
change is the most interesting subject for corporate study. It is known
and understood in the executive levels of the company. It is the main
ingredient in determining what to do next. Defining the cause of change
helps the corporate decision-maker decide how to hold onto market
share, sustain profits, and ultimately keep stockholders happy through
also sustaining stock prices.

3. *Only closing prices should be used in analysis.* In the analysis of stock
prices, it makes perfect sense to study a closing price only. Interim price
changes can be misleading, and they change rapidly. This tenet of the
Dow Theory is based on the belief that the closing price had significance
between buyers who were willing to hold securities at that price
overnight. In today's 24-hour market, a closing price is a mere stopping
point, and new analysts give as much weight to it as was given in the
early 20th century.

The concept, however, has a fundamental equivalent in corporate analysis. The "closing" price in terms of sales and profits is represented by a
month-end, quarter-end, or year-end total. In an operating period, a cut-
off point identifies the end of the period for reporting purposes. When a
fundamental rule is applied that only closing prices should be considered, that means that only the final, audited financial statements can
really be counted for the purpose of making any long-term fundamental
comparisons.

For example, if you follow a company's PE ratio, what numbers serve as
the basis? Each day's closing price is used for the first component; however, how dependable is the earnings-per-share value you also use? It is
necessary to use quarterly earnings numbers for interim analysis,
because that is all you have available. It is also practical to recognize the
unreliability of the PE as you move farther in time from the latest
reported numbers. Because price changes daily and earnings-per-share is
reported quarterly (and even then is out of date), a current PE should
not be treated as conclusive by any means.

Given the fact that quarterly reports are not audited in the same detail as
annual reports, the earnings-per-share should be in line with previous
patterns in order to be considered reliable. If there is a significant depar-
ture from past trends—if, for example, earnings suddenly jump to unexpected high levels—then the PE should be considered questionable.

Using validated closing numbers for analysis is part of a long-term monitoring process. Using historical fundamentals to track your portfolio is a dependable manner for identifying the fundamental strength of a company, and for ensuring that the attributes do not change over time. In that respect, the "closing" numbers you should use in your fundamental analysis can be identified without trouble. They are the quarterly and annual results taken as they are unless unusual changes have occurred. Just as an analyst of stock prices would want to investigate an unexpected price spike, the fundamental analyst would want to know why a fundamental indicator (for example, earnings per share) would change drastically from a past pattern.

4. *Trends are firmly established when three events take place.* The Dow Theory identifies a series of three events that are considered reliable indicators that establish trends. For a bull market, these are buy-low actions by well-informed investors, growth in corporate earnings, and technical indicators such as price following the fundamentals.

The observation of a series of events as a prerequisite for the firm establishment of a trend is among the tenets of all trend analysis, and it is practiced widely in corporate applications. The price-related occurrences make perfect sense in the study of price trends. When it comes to the identification of fundamental trends, the same sort of distinctions can be made and are helpful in monitoring companies over time.

One of the most important observations of the Dow Theory analysis is that the technical indicators follow the fundamentals. Thus, price increases would be expected to occur as profits were reported at higher levels. This situation is both logical and predictable when studying intermediate and long-term trends; this event is also easily observed. By digging deeper, however, you might also find other confirming information of a fundamental (and thus, leading) nature. These include insider buy decisions. When corporate insiders begin buying their own stock, that is a strong sign of improving fundamental strength—especially if the trend is established over many periods. By the same argument, recurring sell decisions by insiders should be studied carefully, too. If a number of executives are retiring at the same time, that could explain cashing out of stock options, for example; but if current management is selling its shares, it could be a sign of trouble in future growth patterns.

When companies buy shares of their own stock on the market, it is retired as treasury stock. Why would a company perform this action? It normally occurs when a corporation considers its stock to be at bargain prices. So, buying and retiring the stock increases the capital strength of the company.

These are only examples of how trends can be confirmed by related information. On the highly detailed analysis of a company's fundamentals, it is easy to manage moving averages to identify trends. Sales might tend to rise for a period of years and then plateau. When this situation occurs, what does it mean? Is the slowdown of a growth pattern a negative? Or, does it mean that the company has consolidated its market share and now is concentrating on solidifying it through strengthening customer service and controlling its costs and expenses? Analysis reveals the causes and the reasoning behind such subtle changes in long-term trends. Each piece of related information either verifies, explains, or confirms what a trend already shows. Or, in some cases, information might contradict what appears to be taking place, which requires further investigation. The purpose, remember, in applying the tenets of the Dow Theory to fundamental analysis of individual companies is to ensure that the conclusions you reach are reliable, based on good research, and truly predictive.

5. *Stock prices determine trends.* This idea is at the center of the Dow Theory—not as envisioned by Charles Dow originally but as developed by his successors many years after his death. Because the Dow Theory contends that price is the sole factor in determining market trends, it would follow that other factors can be discounted or that they are important only to the extent that they cause prices to react.

A serious study of long-term trends shows that many factors affect and even cause pricing trends in the market. To apply the concept to corporate analysis, however, you might ask what factors cause trends. That is the key to understanding how and why sales and profits rise and fall, why corporations gain or lose market share, and why certain stocks and sectors go in or out of favor among investors. Experts such as marketing analysts and accountants study trends to identify areas needing greater controls, opportunities for larger sales and market share, and for mere raw data for use in reporting. Convincing arguments are those that prove a point, support a point of view, or leave one obvious alternative. At the top level of the corporation, executives depend upon information supplied to them by their analysts. The same is true for investors in the market; but just as a corporate executive would fire an analyst who is consistently wrong, investors should determine first of all whether the advice they receive is reliable or misleading.

Once you identify the factors within the corporation that affect *fundamental* trends, you will understand the value of the principle in the Dow Theory. That, of course, is based on the belief that market price is everything; within the corporation, a more enlightened and realistic view is that many things affect outcome. You cannot simply start up a corporation and wait for the market to come to you. Every corporation has to fight for market share, create sales, and manage costs and expenses. Profits are not created easily. There are no easy or magical ways to create profits, either in the business world or on Wall Street. Following the advice of analysts who are wrong more often than right is not a wise method for creating long-term profits. It makes more sense to put in the effort studying the causes of fundamental trends and then determining how those trends are likely to affect long-term growth.

The Intrinsic Flaw of Indexing

The whole matter of creating and monitoring an index of stocks is both popular and widespread. Despite the fact that a broad index tells you nothing about when to buy, sell, or hold a particular security, the entire realm of market indexes and averages has its true believers.

Why is indexing a popular idea? There are three reasons:

1. *Models are consistent, and humans are not.* People know instinctively that a model is going to report consistently, whereas a human being has to struggle against ego, error, and the occasional bad day. A model, such as the DJIA, calculates the rise or fall and reports it each and every day with remarkable consistency. If you are able to ignore the fact that components are replaced from time to time, the indexing of stocks can provide comfort. It does reveal in a broad sense the mood of the market, again assuming that you accept a particular index as being representative of the broader range of listed stocks.

   The problem, of course, is that the model itself does not provide you with what you need. It only describes its own movements in terms of "good" (up) and "bad" (down). That tells you nothing whatsoever about how *your* stocks are performing. For that, you need to go to the fundamentals. One observation has been made that buying the 10 highest-yielding stocks in the DJIA each year is a strategy that works consistently.[4] Of course, that is true. But it is *not* true because the DJIA exists. It's true because the issues included in the DJIA are high-performing stocks as a matter of their selection. You can use the model of the DJIA to identify likely investment candidates, but you can perform the task without the DJIA, as well. The error is in believing that the DJIA somehow creates the investment opportunity. It does not; it is only a model that includes 30 stocks that, in the opinion of one organization, represent the overall direction of the market.

2. *Statistics are accepted without question.* Most people accept what they hear statistically. So, when the DJIA is on an upward trend, that means

the market is healthy. It's time to invest. The market is healthy. People readily believe what they hear when it is reported on a population (statistically, a population is sample data) without question. For example, if you read a statistic in the newspaper stating that 80 percent of all people surveyed are of the same opinion, that is pretty convincing. This conclusion occurs in spite of the possibility that the question itself might have had a built-in bias that distorts the outcome. This situation is the problem with reporting statistically; it is most difficult to arrive at an objective test that creates dependable results.

The same problem applies to market analysis. No single method of calculating returns on a sample population is going to definitively and conclusively describe what is going on in the market. More to the point, the statistics themselves are inapplicable. Statistical methods are used to judge the market on the basis of 30 stocks, 500 stocks, or a composite—but none of the indexing methods tell you whether you should buy, sell, or hold a particular stock. The fact remains that no stock is going to be accurately described by any index. The indexes are the wrong data to study. You can only calculate the value of a particular stock as an investment by going back to the corporate numbers and making comparative studies, tracking internal and market trends, and identifying solid growth patterns.

3. *People want to believe the stories they hear and are more likely to react to their intuition than to relatively boring statistics.* Human nature requires that our imaginations are caught by legends, rumors, and stories. On Wall Street, this situation is not only an aspect but also a defining quality of the culture itself. The rare occurrence captures everyone's imagination. How often have you heard these stories yourself? Typical are statements such as the following:

"There's a stock that everyone says is going to jump 500 percent next week."

"I know a guy who made half a million day trading in his first month out."

"This kid used his dad's credit card to trade options and made $2 million. He bought his dad a new car and a house in Florida."

These claims, wild as they are, might even be based on true stories. But even if true, they are *rare* exceptions to the way that things really work. They are not typical, and investing in an effort to duplicate an experience is like using someone else's winning lottery numbers. They are unlikely to come up again in the following week.

It also is human nature to trust one's intuition more than reliable research. It's easy to believe that your hunches will be right, because if you have a healthy ego, you need to believe in yourself. This problem tends to overshadow logic and common sense. It is further supported by the related problem that financial reports are dry and boring, and research—even when it proves a point—is not very interesting. So, when you hear that lower-PE stocks out-perform the average and larger-PE stocks underperform, that reality defies the more popular intuition about the market. You see PEs driven up in popular companies as more and more people buy stock, and so you want to get shares as well; you don't want to miss the opportunity. In the moment, higher-PE stocks have far more intuitive appeal than the long-term studies showing that lower-PE stocks are better long-term investments.

Indexes are flawed methods for making individual decisions, even if you believe that they serve as a method for judging overall market mood. It is true that without some form of index reporting, it would be impossible to get a sense of the market's overall mood. When most indexes are reporting a trend in one direction or another, you get an idea of sentiment, confidence, and mood in the market. Historically, we identify major bull and bear markets by price trends overall. We peg stock market activity to emerging recessions just as we use Federal Reserve interest rate policy to determine likely reaction in the stock and bond markets—not to mention real estate and other sectors of the economy.

There is a value in indexing, without any doubt. It is a useful tool for making judgments about economy-wide matters. The mistake is to make individual decisions about stocks in your portfolio based on movements in the index, however. Even when your stock reacts by moving in the same general direction, it makes no sense. Stock prices that do react to large index movements usually are corrected in a very short time. For example, if the market as measured by the DJIA falls 600 points, it is likely that many large companies within the DJIA contributed to that fall. (After all, the fall itself is defined by activity in those 30 stocks.) If you are holding shares of a corporation that is not included in the DJIA, it is likely that it, too, will lose several points. This result occurs because many people panic as prices fall and sell off their shares. This panic creates the point loss; it is a self-defining phenomenon. Rather than following suit and also selling, it makes sense to wait out the drop in prices, realizing that as disturbing as it is, the problem will reverse itself within a few days as the causes of the price drop are sorted out. If any action makes sense at all, it would be to *buy* more shares during the price dip. It is accurate to say that the contrary strategy works at such times and makes far more sense. Taking no action is normally the wisest course of all, because as long as the company continues to be a viable long-term investment candidate, price changes are temporary—even when the market drops hundreds of points.

The same argument applies on the up side. When prices rise dramatically, it probably is the worst time to invest money in the market. Just as the panic factor affects judgment on the down side, the greed factor is at work as prices peak. And just as down-side corrections occur, so do up-side corrections. An over-priced market is expensive, and it is the worst time to buy more shares than good judgment dictates. Depend instead on analysis of fundamentals aimed at identifying long-term hold candidates and resist the temptation to follow the more popular market activity.

Notes

[1] Source: Dow Jones & Company; of the 30 stocks in the DJIA as of mid-2000, 28 were listed on the New York Stock Exchange and two (Intel and Microsoft) were listed on the NASDAQ.

[2] These were: American Cotton Oil, American Sugar, American Tobacco, Chicago Gas, Distilling & Cattle Feeding, General Electric, Leclede Gas, National Lead, North American, Tennessee Coal & Iron, U.S. Leather Preferred, and U.S. Rubber.

[3] Source: Dow Jones & Company, July 2001.

[4] James P. O'Shaughnessy, *What Works on Wall Street*, p. 6.

CHAPTER 4

Identifying Investment Risk

The majority of investors know all about market risk; that is, the risk that capital value will be lost. In the stock market, this scenario takes place because prices fall after shares of stock are purchased. As important as market risk is in the scheme of things, however, you also need to be aware of several other kinds of risk and how those risks can affect your investment success.

Risk is often talked about in the market but not described specifically enough to be helpful. Your task as an investor is to first identify the level and type of risk that you are willing and able to assume and then to match that risk profile to appropriate investments. This simple-sounding task can be daunting, however, when you realize that the very topic of risk is not explained or understood by most advisors. The usual position is to emphasize *opportunity* and to ignore the risks that are invariably associated with those opportunities.

You need to study risk from a larger perspective than the all-too-common cursory glance. Wise investors know that a portfolio filled with risk-appropriate stocks is a good portfolio—one that is likely to perform according to your long-term goals.

Risk and Opportunity

With so much emphasis on the *opportunity* presented by a particular investment decision, it is likely that the question of risk will be discussed only minimally, if at all. Unfortunately, one truth about the nature of investing is that risk
cannot be avoided. All investors face some form of risk. The relationship
between risk and opportunity is specific and undeniable. The greater the
opportunity for profit, the greater the associated risks. Likewise, the lower the
risk, the lower the profit potential.

These associated properties of investments cannot be ignored by the wise
investor. You need to be aware of the direct relationship between risk and
opportunity. To hear the proponents of day trading or futures and option purchasing, however, the potential for fast money is where all of the emphasis is
placed. Yes, it is *possible* to make a very large amount of money in a short
period of time. It is also *likely* that in such a situation, you will lose a large
amount of money in just as short a time period. In addition, the fact that some
people profit the first time out in ventures like day trading can blind them to
the reality. Ultimately, high-risk speculation is going to create more losses than
profits.

Understanding the nature of high-risk speculation, you need to remember
that even a one-time profit is not necessarily going to repeat itself. Losses tend
to be just as immediate and severe as profits in such speculative approaches.
Ultimately, it is extremely difficult to build a long-term portfolio for many years
by taking high risks. Some promoters make the argument that younger people
can afford greater risk because they have more time until retirement. This
statement is another way of saying that you can afford to lose money now
because you have time to learn from your mistakes. It makes more sense,
though, to take a four-step approach to the question of risk and opportunity:

1. Begin by defining your "risk profile." What can you afford to risk, and
    what kinds of risks are you willing to take?

2. Seek investment opportunities that are a good match for your risk profile.
    Avoid investments that are not appropriate under your definition.

3. Review your risk profile periodically. As your income level, net worth,
    investing experience, and age change, your risk profile is likely to change
    as well.

4. Act on information in accordance with your current risk profile.
    Remember, setting standards works only when you also follow those stan-
    dards regularly.

So, the process of definition, identification, review, and action is the key to
investing within a defined risk profile. The profile should define your "risk tolerance," the amount of risks of various kinds that you are willing and able to
undertake. Some investors would reply, "Of course, I would prefer to take no

risk whatsoever." It would be nice to have opportunities without risk; however, every investment has some risk features that define them in terms of risk profile and opportunity levels. Avoiding risk altogether is not a practical idea.

You define the risks that are appropriate for yourself by examining your financial status. That includes current income and money available to invest—not only the amount you can afford to set aside each month, but also the division between liquid funds and long-term investments. Also include an evaluation of your net worth, including value in pension plans, your home, and other investments. Finally, review your family status. The risk profile for single people will differ from one for a married couple with children. It should also change with your age. Younger investors probably need to begin their program by building equity over the coming decade; older investors begin to think about retirement and how to preserve spending power. Thus, as you grow, you are likely to become more conservative in your investment approach—which in turn translates into a more restrictive risk profile for yourself.

Another factor affecting the definition of risk is your understanding of particular investments. You might stay away from certain areas because you are not familiar with the characteristics of those products, which is wise. You should never place money at risk unless you know what to expect. For example, most investors believe that investments like options and futures are too risky for them. To a large extent, this statement is true. Those who have studied this area gain knowledge about how the rules work, however, and might even find some ways to invest without taking significant risks.[1]

The process of defining your own risk profile can be complex, especially if you have many investments and obligations. It is a necessary phase, however. Married couples are likely to discover during the definition phase that they do not share the same risk profile levels, which requires a degree of compromise in order to find investments that will work for both sides. The process of defining what kinds of risks and how much risk you can and will take is essential in order to take the next step: identifying the *elements* of risk and then choosing investments that are a good match.

An element of risk refers to the kind of exposure that you have with a particular investment. Just to limit this discussion to stocks, consider the different attributes of stocks when you begin to make comparisons: from one sector to another, at different capitalization levels, between different PE ratio levels, among high- and low-volatility stocks, between young companies and very well-established ones, and so forth. The comparisons are endless. Some sectors are highly sensitive to interest rates, such as public utility companies that depend heavily on debt capitalization. Other sectors tend to work on short cycles, such as technology stocks, and others are especially sensitive to consumer retail sentiment. So, each investment sector and each type of stock—not to mention specific companies—can be defined in terms of risk elements. Some stocks will be very similar in this regard, but does that mean you should select only stocks that share the same characteristics? That would mean you would lack diversification in your portfolio. The importance of identifying risk elements is not to select stocks with identical attributes but to identify a range of risk that would be considered acceptable and to then select stocks that fit within that range.

Once you define your risk profile and identify stocks that are a good match, the difficult part is completed. It is also necessary to review your risk profile from time to time, however. People change over time, and their risk profiles have to be expected to change as well. When you are first starting your career, you might be single, renting an apartment, and earning a low rate of pay. Eventually, you might be married with children, own a home, and be earning a much higher salary. This change in circumstances on all levels necessitates a periodic review of your risk profile, as well. It should be obvious to everyone that the life changes we experience will also affect the kinds of investments that are appropriate. Risk profile is not a permanent condition; it evolves over time. Just as you need to review your various insurance needs as your circumstances change, you also need to review and modify your risk profile.

It's a mistake to identify yourself as being a particular type of investor and then make one of two mistakes: either invest contrary to your self-definition or fail to make changes as you yourself change. Many people make one or both mistakes. It is a common error to define oneself as a fundamental investor but to invest primarily in response to technical indicators—the DJIA, stock prices, or charts for example. It is also an error to decide that you have a particular set of attributes and to continue to act upon that definition even when your economic and personal situation changes. Flexibility is essential, because change in one area requires a change in strategies and approaches to the market. This review phase is all-important. It is more than just a monitoring function; it is a continual renewal and maintenance of your portfolio to ensure that you are investing in accordance with your own goals.

Finally, even when you periodically review and change your self-definition of risk profile, you still need to set a rule for yourself: that you will act within your own guidelines. Many people have observed that self-discipline is a crucial attribute for successful investing. That means that once you have defined an appropriate risk profile, you also need to ensure that you pick only those investments that meet your needs. You probably know someone who defines himself or herself in one way but acts in another. As an investor, you want to be sure that you do not fall into the same trap. If you consider yourself moderately conservative, it is a mistake to put money at risk in a highly speculative way just because someone else claims that they are making big money. The temptation to look only at the opportunity side, and to ignore the very real risks, is a constant threat to your long-term goals. Virtually every investor wants, as one goal, to preserve purchasing power while growing their net worth—so taking chances you consider unacceptable is gambling rather than investing. If you define yourself as a speculator and you are willing to take bigger-than-average risks to gain the opportunity for bigger-than-average gains, then you also accept the fact that you will lose at times. The problem comes when someone is a conservative investor and he or she takes a risk that is not acceptable and then loses. That is a painful lesson. It happens because the individual did not go through the four steps listed earlier.

Perhaps one of the most serious risks you face should be called "self-discipline risk." The temptation is there constantly, and you are exposed time and again to rumors and wild claims of easy money—but there is very little talk of the associated risks. We all know the risks are there, so being a self-disciplined investor means you know yourself, you have defined what works for you, and you follow your own rules. To begin defining what works, it is first necessary to consider and quantify for each investment decision all of the applicable forms of risk.

Market Risk

Most investors know about market risk. It is, in fact, the lifeblood of Wall Street. The opportunity that your shares will increase in value, offset by the risk that they will decrease in value, fairly well describes what most investors think about on a daily basis.

The fact that market risk is well known and well understood does not necessarily also mean that investors know what to do to manage that risk. One widely-held belief is based on a rather short-term idea: that timing decisions to buy stocks when prices dip temporarily and then sell them when prices rise temporarily is a popular notion about how to manage, or at least how to overcome, market risk. This idea presents a whole range of other problems, however. For example, if you do take short-term profits, what will you do with the money next? Because most speculators tend to follow a similar range of stocks, they tend to be up or down in value at the same time—so timing subsequent decisions is difficult to say the least. Such short-term activity as profit-taking is not a characteristic of the long-term investor, which most people consider themselves; yet, it is a popular practice.

Fallacy: A trading strategy is not management of risk.

The belief that finding the right formula for successful timing of buy and sell decisions is somehow the key to successful investing misses the point. Market risk is, by definition, a short-term problem. If you carefully select stocks in companies whose fundamentals are appropriate given your risk profile and long-term goals, then day-to-day changes in market price have little significance to you, other than just as a point of interest. Trading strategies are also short-term in nature. Your strategy as a long-term investor should be to determine the appropriate timing of stock selection given evolving changes in your risk profile, not day-to-day timing to earn a few points in a stock because of some temporary news.

The tendency among investors who take profits is to seize opportunities because they do not really have faith in the long-term prospects of the company. They have not studied the fundamentals carefully enough to hold that stock, or they have studied the fundamentals but they are too impatient to hold shares as long-term investments. The widespread tendency to "play the market" rather than to invest results in a common outcome: Rather than just taking short-term opportunities, it's likely that a temporary drop in price causes undue fear and shares are sold prematurely. So, rather than buying low and selling high, playing the market often results in doing just the opposite.

Trading strategies are appropriate for speculators, but for others looking for ways to preserve capital buying power and build equity over time, it is not a necessity. The *market risk* you actually face is the risk of selecting the wrong stocks. As long as you understand how the fundamentals affect long-term investment value, however, and as long as those fundamentals do not change, the investment will continue to represent a worthwhile market risk. Prices do follow the fundamentals, but long-term growth takes time. By "long-term," it means that you need to be patient—and, in that respect, to ignore the day-to-day changes in market price.

We need to replace the mistaken belief that a trading strategy is a form of management over risk with a more accurate idea: that market risk as it is commonly described is a short-term issue and not of immediate interest for the long-term investor. Thus, a trading strategy belongs in the realm of the short-term investor or speculator. We are not saying that market risk, should be ignored in your selection of stocks based on the fundamentals. Highly volatile stocks are that way for a reason, so the higher the market risk, the more you need to review fundamental causes for price volatility. The cause and effect might define and distinguish the degree of risk based on otherwise similar fundamentals.

The difference between the forces affecting market price and the fundamentals is significant. For this reason, it makes sense to distinguish between market risk and *price risk*. Market risk should refer to the range of dangers (and opportunities) associated with the selection of companies based upon their fundamental strength. You probably realize that even when you apply the best strategies and analyze a company thoroughly, it might not end up being profitable as a long-term hold. The key is to be right more often than wrong. By developing sensible methods for the analysis of corporations and their fundamentals, you will be able to select likely and viable candidates for long-term profits. In other words, over many years the company's value will grow, and that growth will be reflected in dividend growth and in market price growth. That rate and degree of growth can be further accelerated if dividends are reinvested in additional partial share purchases of the stock.[2]

The market risk that you face even when you invest strictly on the basis of fundamental attributes of a company is that the long-term values will not be there. Signs might show up along the way, of course. A company's anticipated growth rate simply doesn't occur, or sales and profits don't get booked at the rate or consistency you expect. In those cases, a "hold" should be changed to a "sell" and your capital should be invested elsewhere. So, even the most conservative investors face market risk based solely on selection problems arising from poor financial performance.

The other form of market risk should be clarified as price risk because it is short-term in nature and limited solely to the market price of the stock. It is a technical risk because it is price-related *and* because, for the most part, it is unaffected by fundamental attributes. You might observe that price movement occurs for two broad reasons. The first is in response to fundamental news, and the second is due to short-term perceptions, rumors, news, and unidentified causes.

In short-term prices due to fundamentals, the response of the market is often a result of comparisons between analysts' predictions and actual outcome. If an analyst's prediction is that profits will grow by 5 percent but they only come in at 4 percent, the market sees this result as a negative—and the short-term effect is a drop in the stock's market price (and vice versa). The game on Wall Street is to give much influence to the analyst's prediction as a standard and to then measure corporate performance against the prediction. This situation is backwards from the way that it *should* work, of course. The real test of a company's success is how well it meets its own forecasts and how well it creates and then controls market share over the long term.

The second form of influence that the fundamentals have over market price is more subtle because it is a long-term feature of a company. As the fundamentals remain strong over time, a company's market value grows. Stockholders recognize the success and reward it by being willing to pay more for shares. So the fundamentals affect stock market prices in the long-term sense, regardless of short-term price fluctuations.

The second cause of price change is the purely technical, which also tends to be short-term in nature. Those who study charts believe that they can predict movement in a stock's price based on patterns of the recent past. For the most part, this method is not scientific and has never been proven effective. The study of price ranges and analysis of support and resistance, however, is a valid topic for identifying price volatility and trends or changes in price trends as they emerge. The astute technical investor also recognizes that short-term changes are not reliable as indicators, however—even for price movement. The study of price risk (and opportunity) is properly a long-term effort, based not so much on the immediate cause and effect of technical indicators but on the attempt to identify the rate of change that is likely to occur in a stock's market price.

When you make the distinction between market risk and price risk, you will be able to also understand the different forces at work in the market and how those forces affect the value of your investments. Following the fundamentals requires not only ensuring that a company remains on the course you expect, but also taking action when the fundamentals change. When a company does not continue to hold its market share, for example, that usually foretells a decline in sector influence and in future market growth rates as well. Every company wants to hold onto its market share and gain more. That cannot happen for every company in a sector, of course; so some of today's leaders will lose market share in the future. As long as you monitor your holdings carefully, you will recognize emerging signs and take action to sell shares before most investors recognize the emerging problem.

The consequence of not taking action is that you might end up with capital invested in underperforming issues. This situation not only impedes your profitability but also comes to represent a "lost opportunity" risk. If you had that capital invested elsewhere, it could be growing at a better rate and producing more acceptable profits in your portfolio. So, the function of monitoring the stocks you hold is not limited to checking financial statements periodically. It also requires an action plan for selling shares when a company loses its momentum.

Recognizing that not every company can continue to grow and dominate a single sector, many companies go through periods of diversification. They attempt to acquire subsidiaries or merge with other corporations so that they can participate in more than one sector. A diversified company can produce profits on many fronts and might not need to dominate any one sector to achieve growth. This strategy is wise, and enlightened corporate management recognizes the need to diversify its product or service lines. Not only does a single-sector corporation have to worry about competitors, but it also might be vulnerable to cyclical changes that can be overcome through sector diversification. Companies might also be vulnerable to other forces. For example, a corporation such as Philip Morris might have been content to remain one of the stronger tobacco-producing corporations several decades ago. Given today's trend against smoking, however, it makes less sense to continue to expect long-term growth in that sector alone. Thus, Philip Morris has diversified into food and beverage sectors—a smart move for the long term because it is not necessarily true that tobacco sales alone will continue to dominate the future. Just as livery stables and horseshoe companies were strong in 1900 but virtually out of business a few years later, new technology, medical advances, and social forces can make today's leaders much weaker or even obsolete in the future.

Economic Factors and Risk

One feature about price in the market is that a lot of weight is given to outside influences. Many investors believe that even small changes in the economy have an immediate and lasting effect on the health of the stock market in general. This belief is only partly true.

Most economic change does indeed have an immediate effect on market values of stocks; however, it is not necessarily a lasting effect. For example, the market is especially sensitive to interest rate news and even to rumors about decisions that *might* be made in the near future. If the Chairman of the Federal Reserve gives a speech and makes the vague statement, "Interest rates might go up in the future," that could have a significant and immediate impact on stock prices. That does not mean the price drop would last, however. The market reacts in the moment, and price changes tend to be overreactions in either direction to the cause of the change. So when the word is put out that interest rates *might* change, as meaningless as the statement might be, the market takes that as a sign that rates are going up. This anticipation causes a drop in stock prices, often a broad drop that is not really justified. Even if prices did go up in the future, the immediate reaction often is too severe to be justified by the rumor, true or not.

Whether real or only perception, the influence of economic factors does affect market values in the short term. Cyclical stocks such as those in the retail area are especially sensitive to economic news concerning consumer buying trends, credit buying, and other so-called confidence indicators. If the general belief is that buying levels are going to be down, notably toward the end of the calendar year when most retailers depend on high-volume retail activity, then the market value of retail stocks can be expected to react negatively. This statement makes sense; obviously, the corporate profits are going to be lower when sales do not meet expected volume levels. Stock prices should reflect lower profit performance. The point, though, is that the reaction to news and rumor tends to be overly severe—and for the observant investor, that can present a timing opportunity.

The same argument applies to good news. Chances are, stock prices will rise too much in expectation of good outcome. For example, if a corporation announces that current quarter earnings will exceed expectations, chances are that the company's stock price will rise in response. Like most overreactions in price movements, however, it will be corrected in the opposite direction in the near future. A highly volatile stock should be expected to react with a more than average price change than a less-volatile stock. Thus, if you invest in stocks whose trading range is broader than average and whose price tends to move up or down to a greater degree than the average stock, you should also expect more severe overreactions to both good and bad news and rumor.

Some sectors—such as retail, for example—are more sensitive than others to cycles. A cycle might be tied to calendars, as in the case of retail stocks whose sales are seasonal. Or, it might be cyclical in following interest rate trends or the construction market. In cyclical stocks, the ranges of price change are actually predictable even though you cannot know with any certainty the timing of every cycle or its duration. It's a certainty that the cycle will occur, but timing is the hard part. If you invest based on fundamentals, however, a smart way to accumulate shares of a long-term prospect is to wait out cycles and buy additional shares at cyclical low points. This technique maximizes profit potential by keeping your basis low. This advice might be difficult to follow, however, for several reasons:

1. *Identifying the low point in the cycle is not always easy.* You can plan to buy shares at a cyclical low point, but such points are more easily identified in hindsight. Knowing you are there at the moment is far more difficult. So, this situation is partly a guessing game. One guideline is to buy shares when you believe the current price is a bargain compared to past price levels and in consideration of the potential for long-term growth (the fundamentals).

2. *The apprehension among investors is highest at cyclical low points.* It is difficult to make a decision that goes against broader thinking. At a low point in a cycle, the mood of the market often is highly pessimistic, and predictions are for continuing falling prices—perhaps even a long-term bear market. These predictions accelerate as the low point is reached. The cool-headed investor recognizes the contrary nature of the market and picks up shares when most investors are deep in despair. It requires independent thinking and fortitude to make such a decision, however.

3. *You might not be financially able to buy additional shares at low points.* Some low cycles tend to be widespread, and investors do not always have capital available to buy more shares at these times. Shares of many stocks in your portfolio could be depressed at the same time so that you would not have capital available to buy at cyclical low points.

The cyclical nature of investing, broadly speaking, can be identified by looking back to the past. Cycles can be tracked and anticipated with study, however. This process is a largely technical pursuit, because cycles—like prices—tend to be passing features of stocks and sectors, and cycles affect current price without really having much to do with long-term prospects for growth.

A related risk is investing in too many stocks that are subject to the same economic changes or market cycles. You might prefer to diversify among stocks whose cycles are dissimilar. If all of your stocks are depressed at the same time or up at the same time, then you are vulnerable to those cycles. A solution is to buy shares of companies whose products and services reach entirely different markets, and that will not react in the same way to the common changes in the market—interest rates, consumer buying trends, or overseas competition, for example.

Inflation and Tax Risks

A lot of market-watching is dedicated to watching economic factors, perhaps because they are widely published and easily accessible. In the long run, however, economic factors do not affect a company's investment value nearly as much as the more subtle risk of lost spending power.

This risk is subtle because it is gradual and invisible. It contains two elements: inflation and taxes. Together, these factors can erode spending power so that although it looks like your investments are growing well, they are gradually losing ground. Corporate analysts know that the production of profits is a fight against inflation and taxes. Growth in profits that does not overcome the double effect of these forces is actually going to represent a net loss when analyzed in terms of return on invested capital. If a company is overly committed to debt capitalization and interest rates are high, then its profits are eroded by payment of interest. The more interest paid to bondholders, the less profit is left over to pay dividends to stockholders (translating to a lower return on invested capital). In addition, lower profits also mean the company has less capital available to fund future growth. The expansion of a corporation's market share requires capital, and if the spending power of capital is being eroded by inflation and taxes, then that expansion is not going to occur.

To demonstrate the effect that inflation and taxes have together, consider what you need to earn on your investments just to break even. Figure 4.1 provides a formula for a break-even calculation.

To apply this formula, begin with the assumed rate of inflation in the future. Then divide that by the inverse of your effective tax rate.[3]

For example, if your effective rate, including both federal and state tax liabilities, is 28 percent and you assume that inflation next year will be 3 percent,

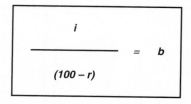

$$\frac{i}{(100 - r)} = b$$

i = Assumed inflation rate
r = Effective tax rate
b = Break-even interest rate

FIGURE 4.1 Break-even interest.

then your break-even rate—the return on investment you require just to break even—is as follows:

$$\frac{3}{(100 - 28)} = 4.17\%$$

You require a return on investment equal to 4.17 percent just to break even. If your net return is less than this number, then you have lost the buyer after inflation and taxes. This result is the *real* effect of inflation and taxes. In this example, you need to consider 4.17 percent as the floor for all evaluations of your portfolio. If you earn an overall rate above this level, you are profiting; if your overall rate is lower, then you are losing spending power.[4]

This evaluation does not take into consideration the usually tax-free appreciation of your primary residence, nor does it allow for the deferral of taxes achieved when you hold shares of stock over many years. The value of break-even analysis is that it provides a model and can be used as a standard for comparison. If you are paying taxes in a high bracket today but you won't sell your stock until retirement, then using current effective tax rates is misleading. So, as a standard for comparing performance, break-even analysis is useful but not completely accurate in every situation.

A useful table showing break-even for a range of inflation and tax rates is provided in Table 4.1.

As you can see, when considered together, the consequence of a rise in effective tax rate and the rate of inflation is to accelerate the required break-even level. Does this situation mean that as you move into a higher tax bracket, you

TABLE 4.1 Break-Even Interest Chart

Tax Rate	Assumed Rate of Inflation			
	2	3	4	5
22	2.6%	3.8%	5.1%	6.4%
25	2.7	4.0	5.3	6.7
28	2.8	4.2	5.6	6.9
31	2.9	4.3	5.8	7.2
34	3.0	4.5	6.1	7.6
37	3.2	4.8	6.3	7.9
40	3.3	5.0	6.7	8.3
43	3.5	5.3	7.0	8.8
46	3.7	5.6	7.4	9.3
49	3.9	5.9	7.8	9.8

need to be willing to assume more risk just to break even? No, it means that it becomes increasingly important to take steps to invest to avoid or defer taxes and to offset inflation. You can take a number of steps to achieve these goals, including the following:

1. *Invest in a tax-deferred environment.* You can defer taxes in several ways. First, you can invest through a self-directed *Individual Retirement Account* (IRA) in which taxes are deferred until withdrawn. This benefit is doubled if you are also able to deduct your IRA contribution as an adjustment to gross income. You also control the timing of profits by deciding when or if to take your profits. With a long-term perspective, your plan might call for holding shares of stock until you retire, when your tax bracket would be lower. This plan is based on the assumption that tax rates as they apply today would still apply later. It also assumes that your monitoring of your portfolio continues to indicate a hold rather than a sell decision. It makes no sense to keep nonviable stocks in your portfolio just to defer taxes.

2. *Build equity in your home.* One of the best offsets against inflation is home ownership. Traditionally, home values beat inflation over time. If you select a property in a good location and in an area where values are growing, you will be able to beat inflation. Home sales are also free from tax up to $500,000 in net gain as long as you live in the house as your primary residence for at least two years. So, homeowners also benefit by escaping the tax consequences of making a profit. Meanwhile, during the years you own your home, you can also claim itemized deductions for interest and property tax expenses—further reducing your effective tax rate.

3. *Seek long-term growth, but be aware of market risk.* Being aware of the double problem associated with inflation and taxes, it makes more sense than ever to look for strong fundamentals in companies and to buy for long-term growth. In the interest of growing equity *beyond* your break-even point, however, you still need to be aware of market risk. Remember, the break-even point is only one standard for comparison purposes. When you consider the fact that you choose when to sell and be taxed on your profit and when you offset your portfolio with growing home equity, you might not suffer from inflation and taxes to the degree the calculation indicates. Avoid the mistake of trying to earn a better return (and, as a consequence, increasing your exposure to market risk).

The problem of inflation and taxes makes the point that as an investor, you need to take some action to protect your buying power. One aspect of this risk is that having no investments whatsoever does not free you from risk exposure; it only means that your spending power is eroded over time. If you take no action to create future growth, then the inflation and tax risk is automatically attached to your net worth; spending power is eroded over time. Even selecting highly conservative but low-yielding investments does not overcome this risk. For example, if you put your capital only in an insured savings account, the yield might not be adequate to offset the double effect of inflation and taxes (even when estimated conservatively). You need to take action and offset the required rate of return against known risks.

Short-Term Risk versus Long-Term Risk

When you review the overall risk elements of your portfolio, you probably can identify some stocks that represent long-term holds and others that require closer watching. The latter group probably represents a degree of higher market risk, and a mix among stocks with dissimilar fundamental features is one form of diversification. "Risk" usually is described in terms of "high" or "low," however, when in fact it would be more accurate to separate speculative or short-term risk from long-term risk.

This distinction is not the same as between market risk and price risk. The differences between short- and long-term risks bring up new aspects to the question of risk evaluation. A long-term risk is normally based upon a thorough review of the fundamentals. You are willing to hold such issues in your portfolio because the fundamentals as you read them today support your contention that the value of that investment will grow over a long period of time, usually several years. It is also possible to undertake short-term risks that also are based on fundamentals, however, but that are not limited to market price.

Some situations arise in which you recognize a short-term opportunity. For purposes of this discussion, that could mean a period of one year or less. Such an opportunity might arise when you recognize a cyclical adjustment in the stock, when new products are introduced, or when other similar events take place. You might buy shares of stock in a company with strong sales and earnings when the stock's market price is depressed (because analysts have predicted too high an outcome). An out-of-favor stock could be far below its reasonable value in many circumstances. If you buy shares of stock in those cases, you recognize that it could be a relatively brief hold and you will be selling those shares in the near future.

Is this method a form of speculation? It is not if you base your decision on more than just the price. A speculator usually takes high risks in the pursuit of short-term profits so that activity is strictly related to price and price risk. A short-term market risk should be based on the fundamentals, however, but in situations where you might not want to hold shares for the longer, more permanent term. You might have capital available to invest for the coming year, but you want to keep it available for other buying opportunities. Rather than just parking those funds in a money market account earning minimum interest, it could make more sense to look for viable short-term market risks.

The attributes of companies meeting your requirements—again, a study of the fundamentals—would be based on the same tests you apply to long-term market risks. The difference, however, is that you believe the opportunity is short-term, too. As always, the opportunity and the risk are going to be married to one another. You cannot always limit your portfolio to only long-term stocks because you might not be able to find enough securities meeting your long-term standards. It also makes sense to move in and out of short-term opportunities as long as you have developed a reasonable analytical means for identifying such stocks.

One example of viable short-term market risk stocks could be those with relatively volatile price history *and* volatile sales and earnings history. While some companies report consistent sales and profit growth from one year to the next, others are all over the map. This year could be profitable, followed by low sales and a net loss next year. In this situation, the fundamentals are impossible to pin down because the inconsistency means that you have no long-term history to follow and no trend to analyze. Companies that have price and fundamentals swings can represent short-term investment opportunities, however. For example, if a company is the leader in its industry and you have heard that a merger is in the works with the company's closest rival, that could be a positive fundamental event that would have a positive impact on the stock price within the next year. This situation is only an example, because such information could also be based on an unfounded rumor; the stock price might not react as you expect; and just because two corporations merge does not mean that the new company's stock will perform well in the market. Given all of these risk elements, you might continue to view the situation as a worthwhile investment opportunity.

In this example, the short-term market risk was based on fundamentals to a degree, and the level of risk (and opportunity) was high. It often is true that short-term risk is higher than a fundamentally based, long-term risk. A subtle problem can develop in long-term investments that can spell higher risks in your portfolio, however. This situation can be called erosion risk.

The purpose of taking a long-term risk should be to establish a *dependable* rate of return and growth in your portfolio, at least for part of your capital. You need to ensure that you are beating the combined effect of inflation and taxes or at least meeting a standard you have set for yourself. Beating the market as a whole is a worthwhile standard and one that most analysts and even mutual fund managers do not meet. So, as long as your stocks perform at the level you require, a long-term investment should be considered a success.

If earnings begin to lag, however, problems usually follow close behind in market value, and that long-term investment begins to erode. As a stock's growth slows down and dividends flatten out, your long-term rate of return will lag and you will begin to lose ground. As a stock's growth curve flattens, the hold indicator should become a sell action. Too often, investors commit themselves to a particular company because it has always been a good performer and past experience has been profitable. As a realistic outlook on a publicly listed company, however, every concern has its day—and eventually that day ends. The age of railroads, for example, was a powerful period dominated by a big industry. Today, though, the railroads do not have the economic influence and power they did 100 years ago. That has been replaced by airplanes, the automobile, and the trucking industry. In fact, the economy as a whole has been moving away from big manufacturing activity over the past decade. The combination of international business and service industry emergence has caused many changes. These types of changes should be expected to continue into the future, where change definitely will occur—perhaps at an accelerated rate in comparison to the past.

A long-term prospect that has great fundamental strength belongs in your portfolio as long as the growth continues. That pattern will slow down if other companies move into the leading position and begin taking market share from your company, however—if economic and technological change makes your company's products or services obsolete or even if your company grows so rapidly and becomes so diversified that its growth prospects peak early and begin to flatten out. All of these events indicate that the company is no longer a long-term growth candidate. You need to seek replacements when these events take place in order to avoid erosion risk.

A related form of risk in your long-term portfolio is called "lost opportunity risk." If you are strongly loyal to a company or a set of companies and you own their stock, you need to ensure that their performance remains at or above your required level. Otherwise, your capital is tied up in underperforming stocks and you are losing other opportunities. You probably have already experienced the situation in which you see an opportunity to buy shares of stock but you do not have capital available. It is tied up elsewhere. In that case, you lose potential profits because your plan doesn't have adequate flexibility. To avoid this situation, you need to be willing to sell shares as soon as they begin to underperform.

Many inexperienced investors make the mistake of taking profits as soon as they can. When stocks go up in value, they sell shares and end up with several short-term gains, but their portfolio becomes filled with underperforming stocks. As these investors replace profitable shares with shares that do not perform well, they tie up their capital with stocks that do not meet their long-term requirements. To avoid lost opportunity risk, it usually is necessary to sell not only profitable stocks but those that are losing ground, as well. If a company's fundamentals are not meeting your standards, it makes no sense to continue holding shares even though the tendency is to want to hold to get back the

OPPORTUNITY MANAGEMENT ASPECTS OF RISK

paper losses that have found their way into the portfolio. This situation is ill-advised.

If you wait out your paper losses, you will end up with a portfolio that has lost overall capital value and is likely to continue to underperform. You are better off taking a relatively small loss today and placing your capital elsewhere than you are waiting out investments that are not producing the profits you expect.

Opportunity Management Aspects of Risk

In many respects, monitoring your portfolio is a form of "opportunity management." In other words, you need to identify the good and bad performers and make adjustments as information develops. Reacting to trends makes sense as a basic routine in portfolio management, because decisive action is the primary method for cutting losses and maximizing profits.

As your own portfolio manager, you look for signals that foretell change. Your purpose should be to react quickly as those signals emerge to avoid losing ground. A good rule of thumb for fundamental analysis is that change shows up in earnings first, then in dividends. Using the example set by Charles Dow, an unexpected drop in earnings works as a primary indicator, and a reduction in dividends (or even more severe, a missed dividend) serves as a confirming indicator.

When a company anticipates earnings at a given level and actual earnings fall short, you need to determine why that happened and what it means to you as an investor. This situation is not the same as the more common market approach based on an analyst's predictions. As that game goes, the analyst forecasts an earnings level. If actual results come in below that level, it is bad news; and if they come in above, it is good news. This test is not fundamental but a guessing game, in which the analyst is given far too much influence over market price.

It is different when corporate earnings fall below the prior period's level, especially if the company's management has not anticipated it or when they cannot explain it. In spite of the inevitably optimistic tone of the message you read in a corporate annual report, management is responsible for *managing*—and that means the development and control of growth. If sales and profits swing wildly from year to year, it often means that no one is at the helm, and a company that is poorly managed is not a viable long-term hold. In addition, the market as a whole does not appear to understand some important aspects of growth from the corporate point of view. Five important insights about growth are as follows:

1. *Growth does not necessarily mean endless expansion without control.* Growth has to be planned over the long term. In other words, management is responsible for identifying current and future markets and then

developing methods for marketing its products or services—not only to get a *larger* share of the market but to out-compete just to maintain what it has today. If unbridled expansion were a practical matter, then every big company would grow by leaps and bounds and pick up every smaller company. For numerous reasons, this method is not practical or possible. Not the least of those reasons is the natural limitation of corporate resources, including management's ability to oversee its staff, facilities, and assets in a reasonable manner. Control goes hand in hand with growth, and from your point of view, a well-controlled program for corporate expansion is an important sign of a strong, fundamentally based sign that management knows what it is doing. The long-term vision of professional management includes the ability to understand the limitations of growth and to plan for expansion accordingly.

2. *Management's job is to plan growth so that it does not outpace capitalization.* In addition to coordinating growth plans with necessary controls, management also needs to pace its growth plans so that its capitalization structure remains adequate. Too many rapidly growing companies end up going out of business because they grow so quickly that they cannot hold onto their market share. When customer service levels fall off, when corporations become unresponsive to their markets, or when product and service quality fail, the inevitable consequence is rapid loss of market share. When growth happens so quickly that corporations lack the basic needs to service that growth, trouble always follows. It requires time and capital to hire the right staff at all levels, locate and develop facilities, purchase capital assets, and put an internal system in place to make sure that marketing and administrative support remain able to handle the very pace of growth. Lacking these basic requirements, the apparently promising rapid growth of a company can fall like a house of cards. Capitalization at adequate levels as a prerequisite for permanent growth cannot be emphasized too greatly. As you evaluate the fundamentals of a corporation, avoid making the mistake that most market analysts make: applauding growth without also evaluating the quality of that growth and without judging whether management and capital are going to be adequate to manage the pace of growth.

3. *Sales growth tends to plateau in predictable ways.* Observing long-term growth trends, you will observe that sales tend to grow in stops and starts representing a series of long-term trends. They look like cycles, and to a degree they might be cyclical; but in fact, sales growth tends to plateau based on the corporation's capabilities in terms of capital and facilities. A well-managed corporation will go through a series of growth plateaus predictably. Pausing in the growth curve often is a wise move because management needs time to consolidate, to review its often large staffing

and organizational structure, and to make needed revisions before heading for the next plateau. A common but inaccurate criticism in the market is that corporate sales fall off or level off. A more in-depth analysis of corporate growth patterns might reveal that slowing growth temporarily to make plateau adjustments is not only inevitable but a wise move on the part of management. Actually creating the environment in which growth is held off is often the only way to ensure continuing a high standard of customer/client service and the long-term ability to hold hard-won market share. So, when analysts observe that sales are leveling off following a multi-year growth period, that does not mean the upward growth trend is over; it could mean that management knows what it is doing, and the pause is only a preparation for the next growth phase.

4. *Profits cannot be expected to grow in the same way as sales.* Another area in which many Wall Street analysts fail to grasp the business realities of corporate management is in the widely studied area of net earnings. The earnings per share is the critical number reviewed by everyone in a comparative manner, even when it might be unreliable—especially if the number of shares outstanding has changed during the year. Net returns, though, do not continue growing over time as sales do. You would expect a growing company to see ever-higher sales, and the dollar amount of profits should follow suit. The *rate of return* in sales is not going to grow indefinitely, however. There is going to be a natural limitation to that growth. It is often the case that well-managed companies are defined by management's ability to maintain a rate of return. That means the return on sales is going to be consistent over time, while increasing sales mean a corresponding increase in the dollar amount of profits.

One danger signal in fundamental analysis is when you see growing sales and profit dollar amounts but a declining rate of return on sales. That rate of return should remain constant as a minimal standard. When the rate of return of profits to sales falls, that usually means that management is failing to control its costs and expenses. As sales go higher, the tendency is to relax controls that were critical when a young corporation was young. Thus, with a shrinking return on sales, the corporation is experiencing growth but profits are eroding at the same time. Real growth in terms of return, either computed on sales or invested capital, means that profits should be maintained. It's unrealistic to expect the rate of return on sales to continue rising indefinitely, but that rate should be kept at a reasonable level (which also varies by industry). You can identify what constitutes an "acceptable" return on sales by comparing several companies in the same sector over time. As you discover what industry leaders achieve in terms of long-term profits, you will discover a consistency in rates of return, both in flat sales markets and in markets characterized by sales growth.

5. *Growth is naturally limited.* The expectations on Wall Street often follow the idea that as long as a company is expanding, it is succeeding; and that once growth stops, the company is on the way out. This concept is based on the premise that growth is always good and non-growth is always bad, and that concept is misguided. Growth is not only a mistake when uncontrolled; it also cannot continue forever. Within each industry, there is going to be a limited market for each product or service, and those markets can only be expanded to a finite degree. Once market share is established, the only way to expand in the future is by developing additional products and services or by diversifying into different industries. These steps are also finite. Even a widely diversified corporation can only expand so far given capital, facility, staffing, and quality control limitations. Expansion beyond reasonable limits or into markets that are not suitable mixes of different lines of business often fails. When a large retailer attempts to enter the financial services market, for example, as Sears did many years ago, it should not have come as a surprise that the venture did not succeed. Sears, a well-established retail giant, was not able to compete in a new industry with other well-established and expert corporations whose specialization was financial services. Capital alone and the ability to buy up new subsidiaries do not ensure success; it often presents a new problem, that of having to learn the rules of unfamiliar sectors for which the corporation is poorly structured. Even big, professionally managed companies will be limited in terms of expansion if only because their management can only specialize so far, and beyond that, expansion is not going to succeed.

The Need for Risk Management

As you study the fundamental trends of corporations and track their sales and profit expansion over time, you are executing one form of risk management. This term has several meanings in the financial industry. To some, risk management is a fancy term for various types of insurance; to others, it is a generalized phrase used to convince people that they should pay for investment advice. A more down-to-earth definition relates to how you select and review parts of your portfolio and how you assess your holdings over time.

Some investors believe that once they invest money in a stock, they should forget about it and let it grow. This method is a dangerous practice, however. Even in the company with the best fundamental strength, situations change. As expansion is taking place in the corporation, it is also taking place in competing companies—and market share might shift over time. So, as you see the fundamentals change, you also need to adjust your portfolio so that your capital is continually committed to companies whose long-term prospects remain high. Just because you intend to hold a stock in your portfolio for many years does not mean you should do so; as the fundamentals change, you need to change a hold to a sell. Adjusting your holdings in response to changing fundamentals is a form of risk management—the elimination of stock whose corporate fundamentals have declined and replacing it with another whose fundamentals are stronger.

This situation does not necessarily mean that you have to keep capital "at work" in the market at all times. It would be nice to believe that there is an endless supply of companies whose fundamentals are excellent and you only need to pick ones that you like. Depending on the kind of standards you set and upon how much risk you are willing and able to assume, however, it might not always be easy to find viable investment candidates. You might need to remain out of the market for a while and wait. In addition to the decisions to buy, sell, or hold, a fourth decision is justified at times: staying away altogether.

Fallacy: Risk is easily managed by keeping money at work in the market.

Managing risk is not a simple matter at all; it requires work and is ongoing. The decision to buy and hold particular issues should not be made just to keep capital invested; in fact, staying in the market when the timing is wrong is itself a form of taking on more risk than you can afford. The timing of market decisions needs to be based on long-term fundamentals and not on the current market price trends, but still, the timing for fundamentals is cyclical, just like the more popular price in the market.

For example, when the economy is going through a recession, several characteristics affect the fundamentals. Because sales are likely to be down or falling in many sectors, corporate profits are also lower than expectations. Higher interest rates will also affect the profitability and financial strength in some sectors. So, major economic trends will have a direct affect on large segments of the market. Sectors like retail, technology, or public utilities are going to be especially sensitive to the major economic news dominating the day.

If you believe that the timing is not right to invest in a particular sector or in the market as a whole, based on weakness in the fundamentals, then you might consider picking stocks in sectors that do not react as strongly to economic news. Alternatively, you can select stocks that remain viable long-term growth candidates even though the economy is going through a recession. You also could purchase shares of a mutual fund, perhaps one seeking short-term income rather than long-term growth. Or finally, you can decide to stay out of the market with available capital.

The point is that the mistake can be made all too easily to buy shares of stock because capital is available and because you believe that you have to keep your money at work. The belief that keeping money at work is a form of managing risk derives from the idea that just buying shares of stock in several different corporations is adequate because it diversifies your portfolio. This statement is not true. Risk management requires far more thought than just purchasing stock and keeping all of your capital invested. At times, it means making no decision (at least, not yet).

The fallacy that your money should be kept at work needs to be replaced with a somewhat different point of view: If you are going to keep your money at work, take all the steps you can to ensure that the money is at work profitably. If you are not convinced that the fundamentals support this plan, invest the capital elsewhere (at least, for the short term). Remember, the market rewards patience—and, by the same philosophy, it punishes rashness.

Risk and Diversification

The topic of diversification is among the most popular in the market. As the best-known form of risk management, diversification usually is understood only in its most basic form: the buying of shares in several different companies. Diversification itself contains some risk, however, and the many forms of diversification should be considered overall as part of your risk management program.

The basic idea of diversification (or, as some financial experts call it, "asset allocation") is that you need to spread your money around among many investments whose characteristics are dissimilar. In this way, you are not likely to lose money in your entire portfolio when a single negative cause arises. For example, if you buy nothing but retail stocks, your entire portfolio is vulnerable when the retail sector goes out of favor or has generally lower sales volume and profits than expected.

Although diversification among different stocks makes sense, there is a form of risk in over-diversifying. If you want broad diversification but have limited capital, the obvious solution is to buy shares of a no-load mutual fund and reinvest all dividends. That solves the problem, and for millions of investors it is a simple solution that produces profits at a relatively small cost. If you diversify too broadly, however, the return on your portfolio is likely to approach the market average. For many investors, the goal is to *beat* the market average and not to match it.

Diversification is misunderstood by a large segment of the market. Assumed to always be a necessary element in your portfolio, diversification can be taken too far. It makes as much sense to identify a single corporation with exceptional fundamental strength and long-term growth potential and invest a lot of capital in that company. In fact, you might perform well above market averages if you pick an exceptional growth stock. That, of course, is the problem: How do you locate the exceptional growth stock?

Because you cannot pick long-term stocks with consistency, some form of diversification is necessary. The risk you assume has to be in balance with diversification, however. Risk is found in many forms, and the simple act of spreading capital around among many different stocks does not eliminate all forms of risk. In some respects, it exposes your portfolio to a wider range of risk than you would experience with a more focused investment plan.

Fallacy: Risk is an isolated factor that is best managed through proper diversification.

Those technical investors who are preoccupied with price movement and spend their time and energy on short-term changes tend to understand risk only as it relates to the market price of stocks or to the movement of longer-term averages and indices. Because technical investors are interested primarily in price movement, they might be unaware of the longer-term and more subtle forms of risk at work in the market.

In fact, short-term price fluctuation is nothing more than a mundane form of short-term risk. It does not affect long-term investment value, and in fact, as long as your investments contain long-term value, short-term price changes are not important. They can serve as momentary indicators of market perception, and unexpected price dips might represent opportunities to accumulate additional shares. Price itself should be discounted as a risk element in the selection of investments, however, except to the degree that it reflects something changing in the fundamentals.

Diversification is of equal importance in a broader sense. For example, rather than simply owning shares of several companies, it makes more sense to select long-term investment prospects in sectors whose characteristics are dissimilar. In that way, stocks will not react to the same economic cycles in the same way—and different sectors experience dissimilar cycles as well—so that a truly diversified portfolio performs on balance rather than in the same manner at the same time.

On an even broader scale, diversification risk is mitigated by investing in several different markets. For example, you might keep capital at work in the stock market divided among directly owned stocks and shares of a mutual fund. At the same time, you might build a savings account in the money market and own your own home. These three major markets—stocks, money market, and real estate—make up a form of broad diversification. Because these markets, in a broad sense, are going to respond to economic change in vastly different ways, you offset diversification risk by participating in all three.

The tendency among market experts and investors is to be aware of these very basic risk strategies and to talk them up quite seriously but to not really act on the observation. Many investors unfortunately prefer to ignore risk or to believe that their judgment and intuition are sufficient to offset any market risks. Many investors believe that, in fact, they are not going to be exposed to risk because they are better than average at timing and picking stocks. The "ego approach" to investing is understandable but dangerous. The high self-esteem is an attribute of successful people, and it goes hand in hand with success in the overall sense. It also can act as a blind spot, however. We are not saying that motivated, successful people should be more conservative than their nature; it does mean that risk is very real and can be avoided or offset with a few easy steps. Diversification in a broad sense is just as simple as diversification among individual stocks, and the outcome makes a portfolio far more secure. Picking stocks with similar characteristics exposes you to specific risks for the entire portfolio. It is simply more logical to spread capital among many different risks that are not going to occur at the same time or in the same way.

Remember, those different risks all have the flip side of opportunity. So, a positive way to view this argument is that exposure to dissimilar risk is one way of placing capital in the position to benefit from a diverse range of market opportunities, as well. That is the essence of diversification.

The fallacy that risk is an isolated factor should be replaced with another observation: Diversification should apply in a broad sense between sectors and even markets. It works as a positive force to expose capital to many different opportunities, and spreading capital around among dissimilar risks simply makes sense.

Risk Tolerance Levels

In any discussion of risk, the term "risk tolerance" invariably comes up. This term describes the amount of risk you are willing and able to take in the market. As a general rule, your circumstances dictate your risk tolerance level (or they should). Young, single people are likely to have a higher tolerance for risk with their capital than a young married couple. And, lower-income families need to be more cautious with their investments while wealthy individuals and families can afford to take more risk in some respects.

Identifying and defining your risk tolerance is the first step, of course. Even if you believe you already know how much risk and what types of risk you are able to take, have you reviewed this question lately? Have you checked the holdings in your portfolio to see whether your stocks are a good match for your risk profile? If you are married, have you compared notes with your spouse to see whether you both have the same risk tolerance levels?

The whole question of risk tolerance can go wrong if it is not applied. Many investors go through the definition stage and actually develop a fairly clear idea of what types of risk they should be taking and what they can afford based on assets, income, and other circumstances. When it comes to where they invest their money, however, the risk profile and portfolio is no match at all.

A periodic review—in fact, an ongoing review—is essential to ensure that you have picked stocks that match your risk tolerance level. Remember, this level changes over time. Whenever your life circumstances change—meaning change in income or job, marriage or divorce, the birth of a child, college education, starting your own business, or a death in the family, to name a few—you also need to completely review your risk profile. Some changes that lead to alterations in your risk profile can be mitigated through buying insurance. Protecting your income, health, or home equity can all be achieved through the purchase of insurance policies. To protect against the taxes associated with a growing income or the ever-present threat of inflation, you need to find ways to invest that will preserve the purchasing power of your capital. This approach requires finding investments that beat inflation, such as real estate, and the selection of investments that are tax-free (like your residence) or tax-deferred (like investments in an IRA and other qualified plans).

Without a doubt, major changes in life circumstances have to be taken into consideration when defining your risk tolerance level. Your risk profile does not have to be restricted to the way you understand it today, however. To a large degree, risk is defined not just by attributes of particular investments, but by how well (or how poorly) those investments are understood. As you learn about the risk characteristics of particular investments, you are more likely to discover that in many respects, a particular investment is appropriate for you when you thought that it was not.

For example, most people are fearful about owning real estate before they actually can afford to buy a home. The unknown problems, such as the cost of utilities and maintenance, for example, are small details that worry the unfamiliar. When those individuals do buy their first home, they usually discover that the normal costs and maintenance problems are taken in stride and are not as big a problem as they feared. The same is true about a first-time investor in the stock market (or for that matter, in any market). Before you owned your first share of stock, you probably were worried about price changes, the mechanics of making a trade, and the vague question about selection of the best stock. You probably worried that your stock would fall right after you bought it and you would lose all of your money, that you would accidentally buy 1,000 shares instead of 100, or that you would pick the worst possible stock at the worst time.

These apprehensions are normal, and everyone experiences them. As you became familiar with the terminology and the mechanics of trading, however, and as you actually executed a few trades and made or lost money, those initial fears disappeared. They might have been replaced with a sense of accomplishment, tempered with a healthy degree of confusion or frustration. The point, however, is that you overcome initial fear by taking action.

This statement is true of many other markets, as well. Highly specialized markets, no matter how much or how little risk might be involved, are better defined in terms of risk when you understand their attributes in context. This method works on the high side as well as on the low side. You might not have the risk profile to risk everything selling short in commodity futures, but consider the risks you accept when you try to avoid all risk. Investing in a low-interest, insured savings account usually means yielding *less* than you need just to break even after taxes and inflation.

You cannot avoid risk; it is a characteristic of all investments. If you want to be exposed to the opportunity, you also have to accept the corresponding risk. By becoming educated about the actual risk elements of a particular investment, you improve your chances of succeeding—if only because you need to know your risk exposure before you put your money at risk. With so much emphasis on profit opportunity, the risk is the dark underside of the decision that often is ignored altogether. By knowing the full picture, you are better equipped to make informed decisions and to avoid unexpected surprises in your portfolio.

Notes

[1] For example, while it is a very high-risk venture to buy options, selling "covered" calls is a very conservative strategy. That involves placing 100 shares of stock under an option, which gives someone else the right to call away those shares. Because time works to the seller's advantage, selling covered calls is an example of how a risky investing area can also be used in a conservative manner. Chapter 8 includes more information about using options for leverage in your portfolio.

[2] Many listed companies participate in *Dividend Reinvestment Plans* (DRIPs), allowing stockholders to take dividends in additional partial shares. For more information, check the Web site www2.netstockdirect.com/index.asp?redir=0.

[3] The "effective" tax rate is the rate paid on your taxable income. To compute, check last year's return. Divide your total tax liability by the taxable income; the percentage is your effective rate. To accurately compute the effective rate, add together the tax liability on both federal and state tax returns and divide that by your taxable income.

[4] This evaluation should not be limited to the capital you have invested in the market. You also should consider the equity in your home. If your investments earn only 3 percent but your house's market value rises by 10 percent, then obviously you are beating the effect of inflation and taxes. To further complicate matters, the equity in your home is probably exempt from future income taxes—so as long as its market value matches or beats inflation, your spending power is preserved.

CHAPTER 5

The Egg and Basket Idea

As one of the basic tenets of wise investing, diversification—the spreading of capital among different investment products and risks—is perhaps the best known. Although it is taken for granted that diversification is important and necessary, many people do not fully understand the methods of diversification. In some cases, capital is spread out in such a way that the same risks apply over an entire portfolio. As a result, little or no real diversification is achieved.

It is not adequate to simply invest in the shares of several different corporations. While that does diversify your portfolio in some respects, it does not always ensure that risks have been diversified as well. To truly achieve a diversified portfolio, you also need to identify and mitigate risks. Some investors, of course, are content to remain exposed to particular forms of market risk in exchange for exposure to the opportunities that come with them; however, it remains important to avoid building a portfolio with issues so similar in risk profile that you become vulnerable to singular risk elements. For example, if all of your stocks are sensitive to interest rates, a small increase in interest rates could affect your entire portfolio.

Diversification: A Misunderstood Concept

For the sake of comparison, we begin with "simple" diversification—the ownership of shares in more than one company. There is no flow in simple diversification; in fact, it makes perfect sense to spread capital among many different risk/opportunity stocks. And even within a particular market sector or among stocks sharing similar economic characteristics, simple diversification is a wise, basic way to begin protecting your portfolio.

Simple diversification provides several advantages:

1. *Ease of tracking and comparison of the fundamentals.* When you own several stocks sharing similar or identical market characteristics, you can easily track and compare the fundamentals. In that respect, you become an expert. For example, if you like retail stocks, you become familiar with the seasonal cycles, the effects of economics on buying patterns, and the profit or loss profiles of the leaders in the retail sector. As a result, you also come to know the strengths and weaknesses of the corporations in the retail sector.

2. *Convenience of keeping up with relevant economic factors.* Complimenting the ease of following fundamental indicators, when you specialize you also become familiar with the various economic factors affecting market strength in one sector. For example, if many of your stocks are interest-sensitive, you will be able to gauge how the sector reacts as a whole to interest news (and more to the point, how a particular company's stock reacts in comparison with other stocks sharing its characteristics). The economics that affect a sector tend to affect all stocks in that sector in the same manner; however, one company with stronger sales and profits and with different levels of capitalization is likely to react differently than stronger or weaker competitors. When you own several stocks with the same characteristics, you become familiar not only with how economics affect market value, but also with those companies that are likely to withstand negative news more aptly than their competitors.

3. *Identification of a range of stocks compared to the market as a whole.* One of the most difficult tasks for investors is identifying how a single issue performs in relation to the market as a whole. The *beta* of a stock would be a useful technical tool if it were dependable over a period of time. Beta, however—the measurement of a stock's price performance relative to the average market—tends to change with time. It is a useful comparative technical indicator, but it is not particularly useful in individual portfolio management. When you review a sector as a whole, however, the tendency to perform in comparison to the larger market is more easily identifiable. A particular sector goes in or out of favor, which is one element in price strength. Economic cycles also have an effect, more so

on some sectors than on others. Investing in a sector that you believe has greater-than-average potential makes sense, especially if you identify the stocks within that sector that have the greatest potential for growth. This procedure is possible when you review the entire sector relative to the market.

The idea of buying similar stocks goes back to the old problem every investor has: wanting to concentrate on the greatest opportunities while avoiding the greatest risks. While risk and opportunity are tied together and cannot be separated, it brings up the primary advantage in simple diversification: If you identify a population of stocks (for example, a sector) that you believe has exceptional growth potential, then buying stocks in several companies within that sector provides you with simple diversification—in other words, you spread capital among several different stocks that share the same risk exposure, but you also place your capital in the path of the opportunity that comes with that risk.

Of course, even though simple diversification has several distinct advantages, it also has its limitations. The obvious one, of course, is that stocks with similar characteristics tend to suffer in the same manner when the market for those stocks does not perform well. So the opportunity might not materialize as you thought, meaning that you are exposed to similar risks. Simple diversification means greater risk in that respect. Two other disadvantages include the following:

1. *Potential lost opportunities elsewhere.* Just as some sectors overall perform well above market averages, others fall out of favor and fall behind. This situation is a cyclical trading pattern partly tied to economics and the natural economic cycle and partly a matter of investor sentiment. The patterns are easy to spot in hindsight but nearly impossible to see in advance. So, specializing in one sector exposes you to a specific risk: that all of your capital will be committed in stocks falling behind while other sectors rise in prominence and become greater opportunities. The only way to take advantage would be to sell current holdings at a loss and move your capital to the new sector. Not only does this action create a capital loss, but it also transfers your capital to a new set of issues that— like the old set—share the same risk/opportunity characteristics. This problem makes the point: simple diversification might not be adequate to avoid the most common risks: those arising from market and business cycles.

2. *Risk of a narrowing point of view of the market.* Whenever you specialize, you tend to become very familiar with the characteristics of the sector, but you can easily lose sight of the larger market. There is a particular tone and mood to the overall market, and when you concentrate on a handful of stocks and a single market sector, it is easy to fall out of that tone and

mood—to lose touch with it. Just as being out of the market altogether means it takes quite an effort to get back into it, losing touch with the broader market can create a problem of its own. This statement does not mean that you need to foster a pack mentality and react to the chronic rumors and chaos of the Wall Street culture. That tends to be very short-term in nature, and the market at large overreacts to news; however, it does mean that you need to monitor the tone of the investment community (if only to identify momentary buying opportunities as moods shift).

The purpose of diversification, of course, is to spread risk so that you are not exposed excessively to one particular form of risk. Simple diversification can mean you are exposed to *more* risk rather than less risk. This situation is fine as long as you are aware of that exposure, notably when you are seeking the corresponding opportunity that you perceive to be there. All too often, however, this exposure is unintentional and the investor is unaware. It might be that a particular investor likes retail stocks or technology or any other focused grouping of stocks. It is essential to be aware when you expose yourself to a set of risks, however, because you are diversified among different stocks, but you remain invested in such a way that you are exposed to a narrow field of risks.

When this situation occurs, it only becomes a problem if your estimates were wrong. As long as the stocks in your portfolio are performing well, simple diversification is a good plan. All things change, however, and market risk is cyclical just as sectors are themselves. In other words, today's acceptable risk could become tomorrow's unacceptable risk. This statement is especially true in sectors with especially sensitive features. Utility companies are sensitive to interest rate changes, for example. In one period of time, interest rates trend downward, so public utility companies might be performing well as a group. That situation can change rapidly, however, and you need to monitor the economic cycles just as you monitor a company's fundamentals.

When you watch fundamentals, you look for signs forecasting a gradual change in a company's prospects. As a sector leader begins to see its market share erode, for example, that can work as an early signal that you need to take profits and move capital to an emerging sector competitor. By the same argument, you need to watch for signs of changing economic trends. If interest rates have been moving downward for many years and seem to have arrived at a bottom, when will they begin to rise again?

The fundamentals of the entire market might act as early signals of changing economics. Many investors believe it to be the other way around, but that is a technical point of view. If you believe that market price leads the market, then you are a technician. The fundamental point of view is far different, however. The economy, after all, is really nothing more than the sum total of the fundamental strength or weakness of listed companies and their markets. So, as sales and profits begin leveling out and even falling, you might expect signs of recession to show up elsewhere as well. For example, when sales and profits drop, there is a tendency for companies to reduce inventories and employment levels. So, weakness in profits foreshadows reduced inventory levels, production of goods, and changes in unemployment statistics—all crucial economic indicators that in turn affect market sectors. Ultimately, falling market prices *follow* economic trends. And the more sensitive an industry to those factors, the greater the reaction will be in terms of market price a few weeks or months after those early signals appear.

Broad Forms of Diversification

While simple diversification serves a purpose—specifically, the concentration of capital in an area perceived to offer greater-than-average growth potential—it also exposes you to similar or identical risks. With this knowledge in mind, broader forms of diversification probably are appropriate for long-term investing.

Some financial advisors prefer the term "asset allocation" over diversification. It is intended as a more descriptive term than diversification (although it contains the same syllable count). It is really nothing more than a technical term for sector diversification, however, or for an even broader form—diversifying between stocks and other alternatives.

Conventional wisdom calls for spreading of capital among several different investment types, with the idea that you don't want to expose all of your money to singular risks. Before considering investments outside of the stock market, however, it is appropriate to review how you can distinguish features of one sector from another.

The primary risk features of different sectors should be based on a study of the fundamentals. Once you understand the primary features of a corporation for its primary lines of business and how markets respond at different cyclical times, you will be able to identify features. Fundamental attributes should include the following:

1. *Identification of the primary product or service.* What does the company sell? Is the product manufactured, and if so, is it domestic or international? Is the corporation or sector primarily involved with a workforce that is unionized, and if so, what are the effects of worker strikes? Each product or service is accompanied by a specific set of features, including the probability that a narrow range of return on sales is going to be achieved. A specific company holds a position within the sector in terms of market share. So, as a fundamental question, you also should ask: Is a particular company the leader? Is it on the rise in terms of growth? Or, is the company a long-time established leader that is likely to begin losing market share in coming years? The answers to these questions might lead to identification of ways to diversify, both within a market sector and among different sectors as well.

2. *Identification of the primary market for goods or services.* Who buys the product or service? Every market is limited (some more than others). In addition, the sector-specific competition for market share will further limit the potential growth in the primary line of business. With this knowledge in mind, diversified corporations present a good potential for long-term growth, assuming that market share for a primary line of business can grow only so far and that likely buyers are finite as well. The fundamental test of markets is essential; a company can grow in only one of two ways: by picking up a greater market share within its primary sector or by diversifying successfully into other sectors and product or service lines.

3. *Sensitivity to interest rates.* Among economic indicators that affect operating profits, the sensitivity to interest rates is among the most immediate and severe. This effect is apparent by the market's overall reaction to interest news and even to rumor about interest rates. Some sectors are especially sensitive, notably those whose capitalization is largely debt rather than equity. When companies fund growth through bonds to a greater degree than equity, it usually means that new bonds are issued from time to time. If interest rates are going to be higher next month than they are now, that will affect profitability because an interest-sensitive industry will need to pay more to raise debt capital. In some sectors, notably public utilities, interest rates are perhaps the single most significant and important feature affecting profits.

4. *Business cycles.* Most business cycles are easily identified, although the timing is not always as easy to pin down. Retail concerns have a specific cycle tied to the calendar. High sales volume is expected during November and December, and companies are judged by how well they perform in this period of time. In fact, holiday season sales often characterize the market's overall opinion of the retail sector for the rest of the year. Everyone who is familiar with small retail operations knows that virtually all of the profits in a year are earned in the holiday season. To an extent, the same is true for larger operations as well. In other sectors, the business cycle tends to be more subtle. Manufacturing cycles are characterized and identified by volume of production, inventory levels, workforce employment, and backorder levels. An analyst specializing in manufacturing corporate fundamentals can identify and predict cyclical changes based on trends in these areas. In high-tech industries, business cycles might be more erratic and changes can occur more quickly. When an industry is dependent upon trends in international labor markets or raw materials, the business cycles are vulnerable to changes beyond domestic control. As a consequence, one feature of such market sectors is a more rapid business cycle.

There are differences between economic and business cycles, of course. The debate within the market is whether prices lead cycles or cycles lead prices. This argument is ongoing between technicians and Dow Theory proponents on the one hand and analysts and economists on the other.

It makes more sense to believe that the fundamentals lead the economy; however, in some respects, it is easier to believe that prices lead the market. To some, the current market price *is* the definition of the market. It does not really matter which element leads; in fact, to a degree, there might be a cause and effect between the two forces, and the pendulum effect witnessed in the market tells the real story. It might not be a matter of which side *leads* the other. The economic and business cycles affect prices, and in turn, price changes might affect economic and business cycles.

Fundamental Diversification

With the great emphasis on price and price risk, real market risk often is over-looked. The distinction is critical: Price risk is really a reflection of short-term trends and can be measured by trading range. Most people refer to relative degrees of volatility to describe and compare price risk. Market risk, though, is really quite separate and is based on fundamentals.

For this reason, we make a distinction between the technical (price) risk and the fundamental (market) risk. Fundamental diversification is essentially where you truly achieve the goal of avoiding having common risks at play in a single portfolio. When you study the *features* of market sectors, you are aware of the effects on many levels:

The economy (interest rates, unemployment, inventory and backorder levels, for example)

Business cycles (tendency of similar markets to experience change at the same time)

Market opinion (attitude among investors favoring one sector over another)

Price trends (volatility of stocks in a sector, for example)

All of these are important insofar as they affect price volatility. These features are most often used to judge stocks on their technical merit, however, and rarely are they equated in terms of their financial side: the fundamentals. In fact, to really diversify your portfolio, it makes perfect sense to seek methods based on the fundamentals. In the long term, this feature is what is going to matter (and it is where you will define growth potential).

Fundamental diversification is based on varying characteristics among stocks that you are considering buying or that you already own within your portfolio. It should be based on whatever fundamental attributes you consider revealing for long-term investments. At the very least, you should diversify in terms of no less than four areas:

1. *Sales trends and market share.* As a general rule, you can define companies by their sales attributes in three groups. First are those companies that are in obvious growth patterns. They are relatively young, and sales are increasing from one year to the next. Aggressive growth is also characterized by growing market share within the sector. Second is that group of companies that are well established, either as leaders in their sector or in a comfortable second or third spot in terms of sales and profits. Third is the broadly diversified corporation, with many subsidiaries and divisions in other sectors. In this group, growth is possible without needing to increase market share in any specific sector because expansion is achieved through merger and growth outside of the primary sector. When you own shares in companies across the spectrum of attributes by sales patterns, your portfolio can grow in many different patterns.

2. *Earnings per share consistency.* Although some Wall Street analysts and market watchers would disagree, it is not necessary for the return on sales to increase each and every year; in fact, it is simply unrealistic to believe that. In practice, a particular type of company is likely to earn a return on sales that is consistent from one year to the next, even when sales are expanding. You diversify by the fundamental return expressed in earnings per share by selecting stocks for your portfolio that have dissimilar characteristics. First is the best-known group that earns a consistent return on sales from one quarter to another and at an impressive rate. Second is the inconsistent earning company whose earnings per share vary considerably during growth periods, perhaps due to the cost of expansion. In this case, a lower-than-expected return on sales could be caused by the expense associated with expanding market share. Third is the interesting set of companies whose earnings are respectable or even above expectations but that are out of favor among market watchers and analysts (the sleepers). These stocks tend to have exceptional PE ratios, a very narrow trading range, and little interest among institutional investors (mutual funds, for example). Their return on sales is impressive, however, given the sector and growth pattern for the company. When you own shares in companies with varying return on sales features, this form is a sensible form of fundamental diversification.

3. *Dividend rate and history.* Companies often are judged largely by the consistency of their dividend declarations and payments. Investors expect dividends to increase gradually over time, and if they do not, then the company might fall out of favor. Some investors, though, consider dividends an outmoded form of compensation—and they would rather see profits invested in creating larger profits (and, as a result, more rapid

growth in market price). There are obviously several different ways to look at the dividend question. You diversify your portfolio by selecting stocks with differing characteristics. First is the group with a strong dividend payment history, periodic increases in declared dividends, and enough earnings strength so that it's unlikely dividends will be reduced or missed. A second group includes companies with relatively small dividend yield but exceptional growth potential. And a third group would include companies earning profits (but ones that do not declare and pay dividends). By diversifying according to dividend policies and history, you are covered for several points of view about dividends. For those stocks that do yield dividends, it also makes sense to participate in a dividend reinvestment plan if the company offers that feature. By enabling stockholders to purchase additional partial shares rather than taking cash payment for dividends, the company keeps its working capital without missing dividend payments—and stockholders are able to earn compound returns on their dividend yield.

4. *Capitalization ratios.* One of the most overlooked tests of a company's financial strength is in the area of capitalization ratios. A corporation funds its operations and growth through raising equity (shares of stock) or debt (bonds and notes). The two together represent capitalization. The higher the debt capitalization, the higher interest payments are to bondholders. So, out of total operating profits, less capital remains for payments of dividends to stockholders. Many companies use a balance of equity and debt, depending on the level of the interest market. For example, if rates are exceptionally low today, issuing bonds could be less expensive than paying dividends—so the company might fund growth through a bond issue rather than more shares of stock. By the same argument, when interest rates are high, it makes sense to capitalize growth and operations through equity and to avoid the relatively expensive bond market. The point, though, is that when the debt ratio begins to increase over time, that could serve as an important danger signal—a sign that the company is depending too much on debt (meaning the erosion of future dividend payments). This situation will show up eventually in slower growth and consequently in the market price of shares as well. Diversification by capital structure is one way to select companies with differing attributes. Some corporations have to depend more heavily on debt capitalization because their capital costs are high compared with other sectors; so picking stocks with a higher-than-average debt ratio is one of the groups of stocks you could select. A second group would be a set of corporations that maintains a *consistent* ratio between equity and debt. And a third group would be large, well-capitalized companies that have little or no debt on their books and are capable of funding growth and operations strictly through larger-than-average profits. The attributes

for these different groups are going to define the diversification in your portfolio in a fundamental way so that potential future growth and profits can also be derived from a variety of possible outcomes.

Mutual Funds as the Vehicle

For many investors, studying the fundamentals in order to achieve diversification or simply buying stocks in different sectors does not satisfy the need for broad diversification. Some people believe that to truly protect a portfolio, it is necessary to achieve a form of diversification that spreads across a wide spectrum of the entire market. For these investors, mutual funds are the most practical choice.

You achieve instantaneous diversification from the moment you buy shares of a mutual fund. This statement is true because funds need to spread their capital among many market sectors. Even highly specialized funds remain broadly diversified. It is possible as well to combine stock and bond investing in a single fund because many "balanced" funds allocate their capital between high-yielding bonds or stocks paying exceptionally high dividends and growth stocks. Other mutual funds are designed for income alone, for aggressive or conservative growth, for particular sectors or in companies sharing similar attributes, and in international stocks. These are all forms of diversification. Using mutual funds can serve as a way to diversify your portfolio, because it is relatively easy to move available capital in and out of mutual funds for little or no cost when you sell stock and do not want to purchase other stocks right away.

Even though mutual funds are convenient and offer a broad range of investment exposure, they usually remain just another form of simple diversification. This statement is true for those funds that specialize in stocks sharing similar characteristics. In other words, the fund is going to invest most of its capital in stocks of companies likely to grow in the same manner and likely to react to economic and market news in the same manner. A balanced fund might try to overcome this problem by spreading its risks so that similar exposure is limited, but the majority of mutual funds actually are widely disbursed but narrowly diversified.

This observation might surprise many people who view mutual funds as the ultimate diversification vehicle. Remember, though, that while a fund can be diversified because it owns shares in dozens of different companies, it can still be the simple form. If those companies are likely to share market and price risk attributes, then the fund does not offer broad diversification.

Fallacy: Mutual funds are the best way to diversify.

Some investors use mutual funds to diversify their portfolios, of course. Some capital is placed in mutual funds and other capital is invested directly. An equally practical way to overcome simple diversification associated with mutual funds is to invest in shares of several different funds. For example, some money can be kept in a money market fund and other money can be invested in aggressive growth, income, balanced, or international funds. This method achieves broad diversification as well as a wide spectrum of investment in different types of equity and debt. These funds would react in different ways to economic and market conditions, as well. It is still true, however, that mutual funds do not really present the best diversification vehicle. Even selecting several funds with different characteristics might still not achieve the mitigation of risk that every investor seeks, and you might simply be placing capital at risk in different ways (but still, without the broad risk coverage you seek).

One problem with mutual funds is that collectively, they represent such a large share of the overall market that they can be expected to average out as a group at market rates. More than $7 trillion is invested in funds today.[1]

Because mutual funds represent such a major share of the total market, they cannot be expected to perform very far above the market average. In fact, the latest available figures reveal that only 39 percent of all funds performed above market averages.[2]

That record indicates that mutual funds do not offer the best way to diversify your portfolio. If less than half even match or beat the market average, then buying shares of mutual funds works against the very purpose of diversification: avoiding losses. In fact, if the purpose is to create a portfolio that performs *above* the market average, then mutual funds clearly are not the best way to diversify. We need to replace the fallacy with a different point of view: Mutual funds invest so broadly that they cannot possibly protect your capital position. If anything, they are so overly invested over a spectrum of stocks sharing similar characteristics that this form of simple diversification can work against your primary goal: to out-perform the market averages.

Because stocks sharing similar attributes are likely to act in a similar manner to economic and market trends, mutual funds also tend to move with those averages. Everyone who has invested money in individual stocks knows that the key to profit is finding companies whose growth potential is far greater than average. Mutual funds work *against* that principle. When funds invest in a spectrum of growth funds, the actual growth they achieve is going to be about the same as market averages at best. In this respect, when a fund provides a form of simple diversification it can work against the goal of creating growth, because exceptional growth in some stocks will be offset by lackluster growth in others. The result is a mundane average.

History shows that funds underperform the market averages for the most part, so the observer of fund investing has to wonder why funds are viewed as such excellent vehicles for diversification. This situation goes back to the widespread belief in simple diversification. As long as you own shares of many stocks, you are diversified. This concept is the mutual fund approach. To beat the market averages, however, you need to look beyond the mere ownership of as many different stocks as possible. It makes more sense to diversify in the broad sense, based on sectors, fundamental characteristics, and other features that distinguish stock groups from one another. It is equally important to recognize that diversifying over many, many stocks is going to have an averaging effect rather than creating exceptional opportunities.

Clearly, dozens of mutual funds grow far above market averages and create profits for their shareholders. Many others perform under the averages. Over the long term, mutual fund investors need to compare realistically in trying to understand how fund share value grows. One of the historical advantages to mutual fund investing was the ability to reinvest dividends and interest, creating ever-growing shares. Under the traditional methods of investing in stocks and bonds, investors simply received cash payments for quarterly dividends or semi-annual interest on bonds, and had to decide how to invest or use that money. Today, however, it is not necessary to employ mutual funds to keep earnings at work. By selecting stocks that offer dividend reinvestment, you can achieve compound growth even with relatively small dividend payments four times per year. This method offsets the traditional advantage mutual funds offered over direct ownership of shares of stock.

This statement brings us to another widely held belief about mutual funds as diversified vehicles: the belief that funds perform better than individuals in virtually every case.

Fallacy: Mutual fund performance history is impressive.

The observation that mutual funds perform for the most part below market averages might appear puzzling to anyone who has seen the sales brochures showing mutual fund performance over many years. The typical claim reads, "If you had invested $10,000 in 1951, it would have grown to $102,857 by 2001." This claim is often accompanied by a chart showing the sharply climbing rate of return.

What does this information really mean, however? Over a 40-pear period, the return based on reinvesting all income represents only an average of 6 percent per year. No one would call that rate of return impressive by any standard. That consists primarily of reinvested dividends and capital gains without growth above market averages whatsoever. So, making $10,000 grow to over $100,000 over a 40-year period is not an impressive rate of growth whatsoever. Given the effects of inflation and taxes, it certainly does not offer much growth for your capital. If your combined federal and state effective tax rate is 34 percent and inflation averages 4 percent per year, that 6 percent return over 40 years represents slightly more than break-even return. Most people believe they can do better than that by investing money directly.

In fact, investing in mutual funds not only should be troubling in terms of how investments are diversified but also in terms of how well the mutual fund is likely to perform. How do you pick those that do better than average? Looking at recent history is not dependable, because a fund's management might have changed. In addition, there is no guarantee that past performance will be repeated in the future. Certainly, funds offer one form of diversification and are convenient places to park capital between other investments. It is not adequate to depend upon the diversification of mutual funds to diversify your entire portfolio, however. The chances that your return will exceed the averages are going to be slim, and you might be able to do better by managing your money on your own.

This statement brings up a final point of concern about mutual funds: the cost. Every fund charges a management fee, which is how overhead and compensation to fund managers is paid. Beyond that, however, you face an array of possible fees and charges. Because fees are deducted from your capital, the real cost of investing in funds often is not as apparent as it first seems.

Fallacy: All mutual funds are the same in terms of how money is invested.

Because many mutual funds charge fees to their stockholders just for making a transaction, your money will not work at the same rate in every mutual fund. For example, if you have to pay an 8.5 percent fee up front, that means that only $91.50 out of $100 invested actually finds its way into the investment. So, with less capital at work, your return on investment will be far less than it would if you invested in a fund that did not charge the up-front fee.

The best known of these fees is called the "load," which is nothing more than commission to be paid to a salesperson. If you believe you are able to pick your investments on your own, there is no need to pay a sales load. In fact, there is no distinction between load funds and no-load funds in terms of performance. The argument that a salesperson somehow is able to pick better-performing funds is vacant. You should always limit your selection to a no-load fund, because in fact, you are not paying for better advice when you are charged a sales load.

Some funds disguise their load fees by charging nothing when you purchase shares but charging a back-end, or deferred, load. This charge is assessed at the time of sale. The same argument applies here: You should not pay a fee for so-called advice that does not help you locate a better investment when that fee does not actually place your money in more profitable mutual funds. Another charge is called the 12b-1 fee, which is a charge to cover the cost of advertising. In other words, you are expected to pay for the fund to advertise and raise capital from other investors. You should also avoid mutual funds charging a 12b-1 fee because it is simply an added expense that you don't need to pay. To the extent that you diversify using mutual funds, limit your search to no-load funds that do not charge a 12b-1 fee.

The Securities and Exchange Commission provides a useful tool for comparing the real cost between funds based on the fees they charge. Check their Web site to go through the cost calculator at www.sec.gov/investor/tools/mfcc/mfcc-int.htm. Because there is such a range of fees that could be charged, calculating the real cost of investment is not an easy matter. The belief that all funds work at about the same level has to be replaced with a more accurate observation: The distinctions between funds are largely a function of the fees that they charge. To make valid comparisons in seeking to diversify among different funds, you should limit your search to only those funds that charge neither a load nor a 12b-1 fee.

Diversification by Market Risk

Whether you invest through mutual funds or by buying shares directly, the price risk is separate and distinct from market risk. Price risk tends to be a short-term problem, although price ultimately determines whether you make a profit or suffer a loss. Market risk really refers to the characteristics of the company as opposed to the immediate price of its stock, however. You can diversify your portfolio by selecting companies with different market risk attributes.

The well-established "blue chip" company is a long-standing favorite among investors. Part of the appeal is the obvious capital strength and part is the familiarity. A glance at the list of stocks on the DJIA makes this point. Virtually everyone has heard of most of the companies on the list. Investors are more comfortable investing in the familiar and well known. When you use a company's products, recognize the name, and know that it has been around for 100 years or more, you have a high comfort level with that company—making it easier to buy its stock.

Comfort level and risk profile are not the same, however. Just because you are familiar with a company and it has managed to hold onto its market share for many decades does not always mean that company is the best candidate for long-term growth, given *your* criteria for selecting investments. The rules still apply, and picking a company should be based on relative fundamental strength. For example, there might be more growth potential in a smaller competitor within one sector than in the firmly established sector leader. It could be that the period of strong growth is over for the giant blue chip you know so well and that a similar period of growth is about to take place for another younger corporation. Thus, if you want to include a firmly established company in your portfolio, you probably take comfort in the safety of your capital—but you still need to assess whether or not the fundamentals support that company as a worthwhile candidate for a hold decision. The market risk is that as well established as an older company might be, the growth rate might not be as strong as that for a smaller company hoping to take away some market share from the older giant.

Another range of possible investments that can be selected would include stocks on the far extreme—the very young corporation. *Initial Public Offerings* (IPOs) are the most extreme among this group, and the market risk and opportunity is extreme as well. Without a history of growth to review as a publicly listed company, you invest in an IPO or a relatively young company because you believe in the growth potential of the product or service, the quality of management and customer service, market timing, and of course the current strength of the sector. Smaller corporations tend to expand rapidly, however, and while expansion often leads to profits, it sometimes leads to disaster as well. When small-capitalization companies outrun their resources, they can suffer high losses and resulting losses in the market. If a newly issued stock runs up beyond a price supported by the fundamentals, a shakeout can occur as well. The consequences of such a market were seen in the dot.com phenomenon, where many newly formed companies ran up in price in a true frenzy only to fall rapidly—causing many severe losses among investors. The market risk of the newly formed and young listed company is twofold: first, the short-term price risk is a reflection of the lack of fundamental history, and when prices rise unreasonably, wise investors should be troubled by it. Demand is the sole cause for price rises when the fundamentals do not support the runup, and demand alone cannot sustain too high a price. Ultimately, the market risk can be in buying stock at inflated values. The second form of market risk is that the company might not be able to acquire and hold a reasonable market share adequate to create a healthy long-term growth pattern. If a company cannot expand over many years, then its stock price will not continue to grow. Sudden, rapid expansion is troubling because it gives no indication about whether the company is going to be able to grow over many years. In fact, if sales grow too quickly, it could be a sign of pending trouble. If capital is not adequate to support growth through staff, facilities, asset acquisition, and of course strong top management, then the sales growth—like the rapid increase in market price—could end up being a negative rather than a positive.

In between the two extremes of blue chip and IPO is the third range of market risk and perhaps the most promising for most investors. While blue chip companies have a firm hold on their market share and might be comfortable with moderate growth, and IPOs are expanding rapidly on all fronts, the mid-range investment could prove to offer the greatest growth potential without the risk associated with smaller startup corporations.

Middle-range stocks in terms of capitalization, market share, and history have several attributes that mitigate market risk. First, there is a fundamental history available for your review. You can see the trends evolving with five years or more of earnings reports. Second, the company has probably established its growth rate and position within its sector, so chances for survival are established as well as prospects for continued growth. Third, the fundamentals probably have settled into a pattern so that sales and earnings growth is relatively predictable and stable. Fourth, you can spot the status and trends relating to market share. It's likely that a strong middle-range company is not the leader but is acquiring market share from smaller companies. The growth pattern is controlled but strong. This growth is a sign that the company is a viable long-term growth candidate. While blue chips have capital strength and significant market share, their potential for rapid growth is limited, often intentionally; when you are already the leader, it makes no sense to take chances by venturing into new fields. While IPOs tend to grow quickly and emerging success stories reward stockholders with triple-digit returns, most IPOs do not do so, and spotting tomorrow's stars is a difficult task. Investors like to speculate about how much they would have today if they had bought 1,000 shares of Microsoft when it was first listed. But at that time, there was no way to know that Microsoft would succeed where so many other similar newly listed stocks in the same sector would fail. Certainly, each IPO has its followers and believers, and Microsoft probably had more than most companies. Even so, the opportunities come with higher risks, and moderate or conservative investors usually are unwilling to expose themselves to those risks unless they have specific reasons to believe in a newly listed company.

As many investors have discovered, market risk is elusive. Some newly listed companies are well managed, strongly capitalized, and offer excellent products. Even so, they do not succeed. They end up losing money during expansion and are incapable of holding onto market share, and ultimately they fail to continue growing at acceptable rates. Prices fall as a consequence. This all too common outcome is puzzling when investors begin with a review of products and management. Lacking a long history of fundamentals, it is impossible to judge how a company will do relative to its competitors. In some cases, it is not the best product idea or management that makes the difference but whether or not the market accepts—and then buys stock in—the newly listed company. So, to a degree, this situation requires that mutual funds believe in the company enough to invest in shares and that the retail segment (individuals) follow suit. The reason why middle-range companies probably present the best opportunity with reasonable risks is that unlike the IPO, there is a fundamental history *and* a record of performance under the scrutiny that every publicly listed company lives.

The newly listed company might have difficulty establishing a record that fundamental investors can use when sales and profits are not yet stable. In initial growth phases, sales tend to be erratic. One year could report exceptionally high sales and profits and the next year disappointing sales and large operating losses. With a record like that, how do you judge a stock's growth potential?

If you return at that point to a study of the product and its potential, you are taking a chance. A company needs to stabilize its fundamentals so that long-term investors can recognize trends, see emerging growth patterns, and project potential growth into the future. Ultimately, rising sales and stable earnings per share translate to higher market price. Using the same premise, when sales and profits are erratic from one period to the next, there is no fundamental way to judge future growth potential. So, any corporation whose sales and earnings are inconsistent presents a problem for the analyst. Also, in other words, market risk has to be viewed as high because you cannot know what earnings are going to look like next quarter, not to mention in 5 or 10 years.

Diversification by Markets

There is little doubt that it makes sense to diversify in terms of overall markets. Given the tendency of the stock market to undergo price risk trends that sometimes last for many years, it would be unwise to place all of your investment capital into the stock market without regard for the price risk involved.

When price trends are generally downward, it tends to tie up capital to an unacceptable degree. You cannot afford to liquidate holdings because it would create a loss; even so, prices continue to fall. So, what should an investor do? Is it wise to buy more shares, thus averaging down the price? Or should you sell now and cut your losses? The tendency is to sell at or near the bottom when apprehension and even despair are at their height, just as it is to buy at or near the top when optimism and frenzy are maximized. So, in recognition of the fact that price risk is an evolving and changing matter, a well-selected long-term hold will remain so based on the company's fundamentals—even when the price is depressed and the stock is out of favor with the market as a whole.

Even given the reality about price risk versus market risk, it remains a problem that being overly invested in stocks can present serious difficulty. For this reason, it also makes sense to invest in markets like real estate, where you have the combined advantages of yearly tax benefits and protection from inflation. Well-selected real estate beats inflation over time as a rule, so owning real estate is a smart form of diversification.

Buying your own home is the most obvious form of investing in real estate. You are able to claim annual itemized deductions for interest and taxes. Most of your payment in the earlier years of a 30-year mortgage go to interest, so the tax benefit discounts your cost while property is likely to gain equity just from growth in demand for housing over time. When you sell your home, you are not taxed on your profits up to $500,000 as long as you have lived in the property for at least two of the past five years. This benefit can be claimed over and over as long as you meet the two-year rule.

Augmenting the value of owning your own home, you might also consider buying rental property. In addition to writing off interest and taxes as investment expenses, you also are allowed to claim insurance, advertising, utilities, maintenance and repairs, and other necessary expenses related to the rental property. You also are entitled to depreciate the buildings (but not the land). Depreciation is a paper deduction; however, it often enables you to completely shelter rental income while still maintaining break-even or better in terms of cash flow. If you are able to manage relationships with tenants, rental property is one of the few legitimate tax shelters; you are allowed to deduct up to $25,000 per year in losses on real estate investments.

Losses cannot be deducted for passive activities other than directly managed real estate. So, buying units in limited partnerships or real estate management companies is not going to provide the tax benefits that make rental properties so attractive.

Diversification between stocks and real estate serve as two of the three feet of the typical investment tripod. The third area where you need to build is in ready cash reserves. You need some degree of liquidity to cover unexpected cash demands. These arise from the unexpected: everything from car repairs or maintenance to systems in your house to the more severe loss of a job. Cash reserves include all savings accounts and investments in the money market— either through money market mutual funds or money market accounts. In practice, many investors have not built up an emergency reserve that would be adequate for the loss of a job. Some advisors say that this reserve should equal six months' income, but for young families struggling with a family budget, *any* savings are difficult to create and maintain. In practice, many families consider their credit cards as their emergency lifeline. The lines of credit can be used to continue meeting obligations when the need arises, with the idea that balances will be paid off later. This process can lead to long-term financial problems, but it also is a reality that many people take this approach because they have not been able to build up a six-month's income reserve and are unlikely to do so in the near future.

The three primary markets—which provide growth (stocks), inflation protection combined with tax benefits and long-term equity (real estate), and liquidity (savings and money market investments)—represent a realistic form of diversification that is both appropriate and attainable for most investors. Another point worth keeping in mind is that you need to protect the equity you are building over the years through owning adequate insurance protection.

Life insurance should be high enough to cover your current debts and income for the next five to 10 years. If you are a breadwinner, you need insurance especially if you have minor children living in your home. If you are part of a two-income family and either income would be adequate to sustain the family budget, then you probably do not *need* life insurance—especially if you have no debts beyond your home mortgage.

Health, disability, and other forms of personal coverage often are provided by employers but might need to be supplemented with individual policies as

well. And assets with considerable market value have to be covered with casu-
alty and liability protection. Your home and any investment real estate are the
most obvious in this group. If you also invest in collectible coins, stamps, gem-
stones, precious metals, and other so-called "tangible" assets, however, they
are only minimally covered in the typical homeowner's policy. You need to
acquire additional insurance to protect these assets against loss.

Diversification in terms of markets is not limited just to participating in different areas. It also requires protecting your net worth through insurance.
Certainly, the combination of stocks, real estate, and the money market is a
wise method for diversifying. As to how much of your capital should go to each
might depend upon market conditions or is a matter of personal choice.

The point to remember concerning diversification is that risk and opportunity are always found together and cannot be separated; however, diversification alone does not always increase your chances for more profits with less risk.
In some cases, simple diversification only serves to increase your exposure to a
similar or identical set of risks. Thus, buying shares in a mutual fund that in
turns buys similar stocks could present a lack of diversification rather than the
intended purpose of expanded risk spreading. You really diversify when you
identify the forms by which diversification actually works: based on differences
in fundamentals (IPOs, mid-range companies, and blue chips), market risk features (fundamental trends), and overall markets (stocks, real estate, and the
money market).

Notes

[1]Source: Investment Company Institute (www.ici.org).

[2]Source: Morningstar, Inc. latest available data, 1999 (www.morningstar.net).

CHAPTER 6

Liquidity in the Market

Advisors and investors tend to overlook the importance of liquidity, in part because it is one of those concepts often discussed but not always well understood.

You probably have heard other people say, "Liquidity is very important" or "I have to maintain part of my portfolio in a highly liquid position." To some, this concept means having some cash put away; to others, it means putting money in stocks or mutual funds where it can be withdrawn quickly, as opposed to a certificate of deposit. In fact, liquidity has several different meanings, and you are likely to hear the term used by various people to mean dissimilar things. There are no fewer than seven separate definitions, perhaps even more. These include the following:

1. *Cash availability.* This term refers to your ability to get your hands on your funds. Most investors want and need some degree of liquidity, usually meaning cash in savings accounts, on hand, or invested in stocks that can be sold quickly if the need arises.

2. *Conversion between investments.* A variation on the idea of cash availability is the ability to sell one asset and purchase another. In the stock market, for example, you can easily sell shares of one stock and buy shares of another at current market value without delay. In other markets, this procedure is not always as easy because not every market is a liquid market. For example, it might be easy to buy units in limited part-

nerships, but to sell you usually need to take a discount and go to the secondary market (if it even exists).

3. *Market trading condition.* This condition is the "liquid market" in which trading is easy because volume is high and any disparity between the number of buyers and sellers is absorbed by stock exchanges or boards.

4. *Investment objective.* When financial advisors work with clients to define what types of investments they need and want, one so-called goal might be stated as "maintaining liquidity." This phrase simply means that you do not want to tie up all of your capital so that you cannot get it out without a large loss. For example, if you invest in a 30-year bond at a relatively low rate, that bond will be discounted as rates climb. That leaves you with a choice: accept lower than market rates or sell your bond at a discount. This condition contradicts the stated goal of maintaining liquidity in your portfolio.

5. *High trading volume.* A market is generally described as being liquid when it is experiencing exceptionally high trading volume. This situation is especially true when, even though a lot of trading is going on, the market value is not changing significantly.

6. *Cash value in the case of sale.* The process of "liquidity" applies when a business or other asset is sold (liquidated), also meaning converted to cash. In this use, liquidity is the current cash value of those assets upon sale.

7. *Business working capital.* Finally, liquidity refers to a company's working capital, the funds available to pay current expenses (salaries and wages and other overhead). Assets are said to be liquid when they are convertible to cash within one year. These assets, also called "current" assets, include cash, accounts receivable, and inventory at cost. The current assets, when compared to current liabilities (accounts payable, taxes payable, and notes payable in the next 12 months), define working capital. The assets should exceed liabilities in order for the business to maintain adequate liquidity.

With all of these definitions in use, it is easy to understand why confusion arises. If someone refers to "the need for liquidity," it could mean several different things. For the purpose of this chapter, "liquidity" refers to your portfolio as a whole. This liquidity is the level of flexibility you enjoy in buying and selling shares of stock when you want without having to take losses and without having to sell before you are ready. The worst consequence of an illiquid portfolio is the lost opportunity cost. If all of your capital is tied up and cannot be freed without loss, then you would not be able to take advantage of those opportunities when they arise.

For example, if you are watching a particular company and you think the stock is a good value today but you have no capital to invest, you miss the chance. If the market then has a sudden correction and that stock becomes even more affordable, it would be the best time to buy. Again, lacking liquidity in your portfolio, you lose that opportunity.

The purpose for studying liquidity is to devise strategies for ensuring that your portfolio is situated so that you can make fast decisions and change course if the need arises. That could mean selling shares in one company and picking up shares in another or accumulating shares in a company whose stock you already own—steps demanding liquidity. So, within that definition, "liquidity" actually means "flexibility"—your ability to move money around without loss. This idea—flexibility in your portfolio—is essential because the market is changing constantly. It is an easy attribute to overlook or underestimate, and many inexperienced investors fail to think about it until the problem exists. In fact, the trading decisions made by inexperienced investors create the very illiquid situations that lead to lost opportunities. These problems are discussed in detail in the following pages.

Portfolio Liquidity: The Profit-Taking Problem

The typical situation that investors find themselves in follows this course of events. First, a series of stocks is selected based on initial criteria (these can include fundamentals, technical tests, both, or just an unspecified preference for particular companies). It's also likely that the range of selection and diversification is dictated by the amount of capital available. Some investors also limit the per-share value of stocks they pick so that they can diversify further.

For example, an investor might decide to buy stock only if its current market value is at or below $30 per share. In this way, $12,000 could be spread among four different stocks. If that investor were to pick $60 stocks, only two could be picked as long as the desire is to own 100 shares.[1]

So, the investor ends up with a portfolio containing a mix of stocks. It might be well diversified in the sense that different sectors are represented; or it might be diversified only in the simple sense that shares of several companies are included. In either case, market values are going to change for all of the stocks included in the portfolio. Had an investor picked stocks with the idea of investing for the long term, the approach should have involved keeping an eye on the emerging fundamentals and ignoring short-term price fluctuations. A hold decision would change to a sell only if and when the fundamentals changed. In that case, one company would be replaced with another as the indicators emerged.

In practice, however, investors easily fall into the common trap of forgetting to keep their view on the long term. Instead, they find themselves involved in the favorite Wall Street game: price watching. The harmful effect of this practice is that it moves investors away from the fundamental approach and turns them into speculators. Remember, proponents of both major market theories agree that short-term price change is unreliable and should be ignored. Whether you follow the random walk hypothesis or the Dow Theory when it comes to the pricing of stocks, you *should* be ignoring short-term change for the most part.

One exception applies when you are willing to accumulate. As you watch a stock and desire to pick up more shares, a dip in price could be an excellent buying opportunity. By minimizing your basis in the stock, you stand to profit more in the future.

If you forget to emphasize the fundamentals, however, a sudden increase in a stock's price means that you can take profits right away. So, the investor who is watching prices daily cannot avoid seeing such opportunities. If you buy 100 shares at $30 and the stock climbs to $33 within the first month, that's a 10 percent profit (if shares are sold) before trading costs. That is tempting, but selling shares presents several problems:

1. If the trend in price is upward, selling now could mean you lose out on further price increases.

2. With trading costs, a small number of shares—100, for example—minimizes your profit so that it is not as attractive as the unadjusted price seems.

3. By the time your order is placed and executed, a relatively small price change could disappear so that profits are minimal or even non-existent.

4. You will be taxed on your profits. If you have held shares for only a few months, you will pay tax on short-term gains—meaning no tax break like you would get by holding shares for one year or more.

5. The decision to sell shares contradicts your goals if you bought shares as a long-term hold and the fundamentals have not changed.

6. You next have to decide where to invest the capital you receive by executing a sell order. If your stock rose as part of a generalized up trend, then most other stocks are going to be inflated in value as well. That leaves you in the position of having idle capital without knowing where to invest it.

In that situation, most inexperienced investors buy shares at inflated value only to see the share price drop rather quickly. In other words, they end up back where they started, or worse, with only brokerage fees and a short-term capital gain to show for it. In long-term perspective, it would have been better to simply hold shares of the original company. Of course, because the investor bought shares at an inflated price, the current price represents a paper loss. So the idea now becomes getting back to the starting point. This position is illiquid, because if those shares are sold now, they will create a loss—offsetting the profit-taking step taken previously.

In this scenario, working with a few market points of change, it is very difficult to maintain profitability given the trading costs and minimal profit levels. In addition, if this step is repeated with all of the stocks in a portfolio that become profitable, consider the consequences: You would end up with a series of current-year short-term capital gains, which are taxed, and your portfolio would be full of stocks valued *below* your basis.

This series of events occurs far too often because investors lose sight of their initial idea—selecting stocks based on strong fundamentals and ending up making decisions as a speculator. If those shares were held as long as the fundamentals remain strong, market values would rise gradually over time. That is far less exciting than making a lot of trades, but also far more profitable.

The greatest problem for new investors to overcome is impatience. The desire to be a player and to make trades can overwhelm common sense, and some people want to make decisions as a matter of just being an investor. The idea that a lot of trades represents being part of the action on the market is a serious and expensive error. A periodic review of a company's fundamentals is the basic requirement for deciding whether or not to hold shares, but for the new investor, making actual trades—especially when those trades result in very fast profits—is a difficult thing to resist. The market is a very exciting place, and having money at risk is far more exciting than just stepping back and watching it grow.

The solution is to actually limit your trading activity. There is no sound reason for high-volume trading in most market conditions. If you have selected companies with strong fundamentals, that action translates to long-term growth opportunities. So short-term price changes are just that, and they do not affect growth potential. It is easy to forget that market price and the fundamentals are unrelated for the most part. Supply and demand is driven by forces that have little or nothing to do with a company's capability to create and hold market share, grow through diversification into different sectors, maintain profits and dividends, and pass the other important fundamental tests. Market price is a reaction to a broad collection of perceptions, rumors, fears, and expectations. A sudden and unexpected change in price often is an overreaction to fundamental news such as earnings reports. To a degree, decisions made by mutual funds affect a stock's market price. If a fund buys up a large number of shares, that action drives the price up; and if a fund decides to sell its holdings in a company, that creates more supply or shares and the price is likely to fall.

These changes, however, are short-term and temporary. The way to study a company's price is by reviewing long-term moving averages. To make this study as reliable as possible, any exceptional "spikes" in price—sudden diversions away from the normal trading range—should be removed for the purpose of the analysis. These spikes only distort the real picture. Whether a company's stock trading range is relatively narrow or broad, if the fundamentals are secure the price should be rising gradually over time. Ultimately, the factor causing growth is itself fundamental. Growth in sales and profits makes the stock more valuable, so as a company continues to expand profitably, its market price will follow suit. This situation occurs even in situations where a stock is highly volatile and the day-to-day price changes are significant. This situation occurs for several reasons (see Chapter 7 for a more expanded analysis of volatility). As a general rule, stocks that are more on the minds of investors, and whose fundamentals fluctuate widely, are also likely to have a more volatile market price history.

The volatility, however, is a short-term problem or opportunity. Certainly, the speculator can make good use of the price waves seen in many stocks as long as his or her timing is good. Speculators tend to experience a mix of higher-than-average losses along with their higher-than-average profits, however. If you consider yourself a long-term investor and a believer in the fundamentals, then volatility in short-term price should be largely ignored.

Market price is, of course, the real test of value. The application should be over the long term, though, and not from one trading period to another. As long as the stock's value is rising over time, then the selection of companies on the basis of fundamental strength matters more and the changes in price in the short term have no lasting effect on the investment value of that stock.

Alternatives to Selling at a Loss

As you study the fundamentals, you become accustomed to ignoring current price changes and concentrating on longer-term trends. Remember, as long as the fundamentals continue to show strength, current price does not affect the viability of that investment. The test of viability includes a range of criteria: growing sales in expanding markets, consistent return on sales and earnings per share, a reasonably stable debt capitalization ratio (in which debt capitalization is not increasing over time), and other basic indicators. As these tests continue to show strength, there is no reason to consider selling stock that you hold. When fundamentals begin to change, however, that acts as an early sign that it is time to sell and find the new emerging leader in the sector.

Typically, sales flatten out and profits might begin to decline somewhat as the company loses market share to more aggressive competitors. Debt ratios might begin to edge upward and dividend payments flatten out as the corporation begins to feel a squeeze on its working capital. In this situation, fast action enables you to sell at a strong current price, before a decline in the fundamentals becomes a decline in market price as well.

This sound approach—based entirely on fundamental analysis as an ongoing process—makes a lot of sense. Where some investors go wrong, however, is in following price only or making decisions based only on technical and short-term indicators. As a consequence, they forget to look to the fundamentals to identify strongly capitalized companies with good growth potential. If you have such stocks in your portfolio, replacing them with stocks of companies whose fundamentals have been studied and tested makes perfect sense.

Even when your selections include companies that pass your fundamentals tests, however, it remains possible for the market price of stock to decline even without any sound basis. Some industries and sectors go out of favor in the market, sometimes for reasons that have nothing to do with a company's specific fundamentals or with its potential. While such companies might continue to represent good long-term growth candidates, a sharp decline in current market value delays the time until your profits can be realized. Of course, this situation also makes your portfolio illiquid because you cannot afford to sell shares at their depressed price. With this knowledge in mind, it makes sense to develop a policy for limiting losses in your holdings by selling if and when a price decline appears to be continuing—and when you believe your capital will grow faster elsewhere.

This decision is difficult. It is possible that a price decline will reverse after you sell, meaning that you take a loss in your investment and miss out on the growth that led you to that company in the first place. Selling shares at a loss makes sense only to preserve liquidity in your portfolio and when it appears that it will take many years for the company to turn around its current market value.

The selection of the price level at which to sell is an individual decision. For example, you might decide that it makes sense to sell if and when the price drops 10 percent or more. Fearing a further decline, you might sell shares and look for companies with stronger market price history. This process usually means finding a stock with a strong support for its current trading range that you believe has strong long-term *and* short-term growth potential. Ideally, this growth potential should translate into short-term price growth as well as long-term potential. It might require moving capital from an out-of-favor industry to equally strong companies (in terms of fundamentals) in sectors currently in favor among the investing public.

Setting price limits preserves liquidity while also creating losses. These losses are small compared to larger losses that could occur if you were to continue holding; however, the decision has to be based on what you know today. As an alternative to selling shares when prices are on the decline, consider two other possible solutions (both involving options).

First, if you believe the current depressed price situation is temporary (meaning you believe it will correct within two to three months), you can provide down-side protection by buying puts on the shares. One put protects 100 shares of stock. If the stock's price falls below the put's strike price, the put's market value will rise one dollar for each decline in the stock's market price. The put is a form of price insurance when used in this manner. The problem with puts is that they expire in the near future. The longer the term until expiration, the more expensive the put.

If the price of stock does not decline, then the money you paid for the put (the premium, which in many cases is not going to be that high) is a short-term loss. You discount this loss to a degree by claiming it as a capital loss on your tax return. If the price of stock does decline, you have two choices. First, you can exercise the put and sell your shares (100 shares per put) at the strike price. For example, if your put's strike price is 35 but current market value has fallen to $29 per share, you can sell your 100 shares for $35 per share through exercise. The second choice is to sell the put at a profit. At the point of expiration, that put will be worth $600 (intrinsic value represented by the difference between strike price of $35 and current market value of $29 per share), and if you sell you will receive $600 (less the brokerage fee). This choice covers your loss between strike price and current market value.

The put is a useful method for protecting your position when stock is on the decline. There is a cost involved, but it is a worthwhile strategy when you wish to continue holding the stock and you want to preserve liquidity through the period of price decline.

A second idea is to sell covered calls. The call is a second type of option; when you sell, you provide a buyer with the right to call away 100 shares of your stock. Sellers have the advantage because time works for them and against the buyer. When you sell a call, you receive the premium value and commit 100 shares of stock that can be called if the stock's price rises above the strike price. If the stock's market price does rise above that level, it can be called away and you will be required to sell 100 shares at the strike price. (When selling calls, a good rule is that you would be willing to sell shares at the strike price, which also should be greater than your basis in those shares; exercise creates a profit from sale of stock plus a profit from option premium.)

If the stock's market price remains at or below the call's strike price, it will eventually fall in value and expire as worthless. In this case, you have two choices. You can keep the short position open and allow it to expire, or you can escape the exposure by closing the position. When you take this choice, you buy the call for less than its original sales price—and the difference is profit. This action also serves to reduce your basis in the stock, thus providing down-side protection.

As long as your sold calls are covered—meaning that you own 100 shares of stock in the company for each call sold—this strategy is conservative. The stock either is called away at a profit or you pocket the option premium, reducing your basis in the stock.

Both option strategies, when used prudently, are conservative strategies that protect your liquidity. They are preferable to selling shares in a company you continue to believe will work as a long-term growth candidate. The ultimate goal is to keep such stocks in your portfolio *and* to preserve liquidity. The advantage of the covered call strategy is that it can be used over and over again as long as you limit the short position to one call sold per 100 shares of stock owned.

Placing yourself in this short position makes sense when you believe the stock is undergoing a short-term price depression. Such periods often are characterized by market-wide softness, and many fundamentally strong stocks' prices are depressed over a broad spectrum—just because the market mood is fearful. If you have a good sense of this mood, meaning that you read the financial press and watch the financial TV programs, you will be able to estimate when that mood begins to change. If you think stock prices are going to start climbing again, close out your call short positions and await the rise in prices. If you have an open short position and your stock's price does begin to rise, you risk being required to sell shares at the strike price, which would be below current market value. That is really the only risk element to selling covered calls—the loss of potential future profits between the date you open the position and the call's expiration. If you watch the relationship between the option's premium value and current market price, however, you can recognize the emerging signs, time your decision to close out option positions, and avoid exercise.

Liquidity and Fundamental Attributes

Most investors—even those with a sense of adventure—will shy away from options because that is a highly specialized market. No one should venture into that field without first understanding the rules of the market, the special terminology, and the various strategies available to the options investor or speculator. The previous section makes the point that not every option strategy is high-risk; some uses of options are very conservative. As with all specialized markets, however, you need to first understand how options work.

Your liquidity requirements always relate to the fundamentals. Use of options and other techniques are meant to preserve your liquidity, not to replace sound selection judgment as a means for building and preserving your portfolio. The fundamental attributes that will affect liquidity include any test of emerging financial trends that weaken or soften the company's capability to grow. In that respect, the liquidity tests (referring to the company's management of working capital) are related directly to long-term effects on market price and the related market liquidity (the price per share and its growth over time). These fundamental tests include at least the following four indicators:

1. *Current ratio trends.* The current ratio is a comparison between current assets and current liabilities. "Current" refers to the period of the coming 12 months. Current assets include cash, accounts receivable, inventories, and other assets that are likely to be converted to cash within 12 months. Current liabilities include all debts payable within the coming year, accounts and taxes payable, and the current portion of all notes payable, for example.[2]

The current ratio is the relationship between the current assets and liabilities. The ratio is computed by dividing assets by current liabilities. This formula is summarized in Figure 6.1.

For example, if a corporation's current assets are \$4,256,007 and current liabilities are \$2,099,264, then the current ratio is:

$$\frac{\$4,256,007}{\$2,099,264} = 2.03 \text{ to } 1$$

As a general rule, a ratio of 2 to 1 is considered a standard; you would expect a well-managed company to maintain a current ratio at or above that level.[3]

The current status of a corporation in terms of its current ratio is not the ultimate test. Rather, it is the long-term trend that deserves watching. In some very well-capitalized companies, the current ratio might be so far above the two to one minimum that it seems illogical to even apply this test; however, the trend and change in current ratio reveals far more. As the ratio changes, it demonstrates how well the company manages its working capital (that is, the net difference between current assets and current liabilities). This number is the net amount available for paying current obligations and funding any growth, such as expansion of facilities and staff, acquisition of capital assets, advertising and promotion, and research and development, for example. As you spot changes in current ratio, that deserves further investigation. Changes should be expected to occur when a corporation merges with another; adds or drops major product or service lines; or otherwise changes the makeup of sales, costs and expenses. If the current ratio begins to change without these major adjustments present, however, then you need to determine the causes of those changes. This criterion is the basic liquidity test on the business level, and it should be relatively stable over time.

2. *Debt ratio trends.* A corporation funds expansion through its capitalization, which consists of equity (stock) and debt (bonds). The relationship between these two forms of capitalization is a critical test. The way to

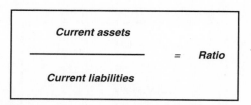

FIGURE 6.1 Current ratio.

compare capitalization is to check the ratios between several corporations in the same industry. The debt capitalization for public utilities should be much different than that for the financial services industry, so comparing the two is not a valid form of comparison. There is no universal standard. You can determine a lot about a company's relative capitalization strength by comparing its debt ratio to that of similar corporations, however.

The debt ratio, also called the debt-equity ratio, is expressed as a percentage. It is computed by dividing total debt capital by total capital. This formula is summarized in Figure 6.2.

For example, if a corporation has $16,584,607 in outstanding bonds and its total capitalization (outstanding stock, retained earnings, and so on) is $37,003,523, then the debt-equity ratio is as follows:

$$\frac{\$16,584,607}{\$37,003,523} = 44.8\%$$

As with all trend analysis, the singular result is not meaningful until it is compared to something else. In the case of the debt-equity ratio, the comparison should be made between companies in the same investment sector and between today's ratio and the same ratio for the past.

If your company's debt ratio is exceptionally high compared to other companies in the same business, this reality is troubling. In other words, more operating profit has to be paid to bondholders in the form of interest, thus less left over for dividend payments and funding of future expansion. In comparison to competing companies, the subject company is relatively weak in terms of liquidity because it depends more than its competitors on debt to capitalize its operations and growth.

The second comparison is equally important. As you spot changes in the debt-equity ratio, you can draw conclusions. If the ratio is falling over time, that is a good sign that the company is retiring debt and building up equity capital. In other words, there is more operating profit left to pay dividends and fund growth. If the debt portion of total capitalization is on the rise, however, then it is a troubling sign. As bondholders receive

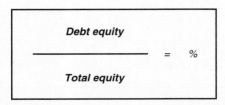

FIGURE 6.2 Debt equity ratio.

an ever-growing share of operating profits in the form of interest, shareholders are going to be left behind. The net return on sales is going to fall as well, because interest payments rise along with the debt. Ultimately, this situation spells less growth in the future.

Exceptions apply, of course. A corporation might make a decision to capitalize growth with what it considers inexpensive bond capitalization. When interest rates are low, this situation could make more sense than paying dividends indefinitely. When the debt-equity ratio changes, it should be investigated further. Why is the ratio changing, and what does that mean for you as a stockholder? If the corporate management has made the decision to use debt capital, you need to find out why. Analysts study this trend and report on it, and the shareholder relations department of a company will also be able to provide more information. Finally, the footnotes and comments accompanying audited financial statements might include an analysis of capitalization. All of these sources are worth studying to determine the underlying reasons for changes in the long-term trend.

3. *Return on sales.* The favorite indicator for market watchers everywhere is the return on sales. That's the percentage that net profits represent when divided by sales. This ratio is one of the misunderstood ratios among investors, however.

It is not realistic to expect the percentage to rise indefinitely. The test of management is its ability to maintain a consistent return on sales, even when sales are on the rise. The tendency during periods of expansion is for the dollar amount of profits to rise but the percentage to fall. That is a troubling trend and a danger signal. Each industry should be expected to produce a return on sales based on the attributes of its product or service. Compare your company to other companies in the same sector to get an idea of what level of return is normal.

When a company is expanding, it tends to relax its internal controls so that expenses rise. This situation translates to a lower return on sales. The trend is difficult to spot just looking at the numbers, because a cursory glance shows increasing sales and profits. This trend appears to be positive until a more detailed examination is undertaken. If the percentage represented by return on sales does not maintain at previous levels, it is a sign of internal problems—usually in the control of operating expenses. An exception, of course, is when expansion includes a mix of different products or services. For example, if a company merges with another and moves into new markets, that changes everything. The analysis has to be done on a divisional basis. If the return on sales falls in the primary product area, that can be masked when a merger takes place. So, the analysis has to be segmented to monitor what is really going on.

The analysis is further complicated by any extraordinary items. Corporations report and highlight extraordinary items, which are non-repetitive events affecting profit and loss. These include write-off of obsolete inventory, one-time judgment payments from lawsuits, adjustments and changes in accounting methods, and other events that are not related directly to operations. Extraordinary items have to be excluded for the purpose of consistent analysis. Remove the items to track return on sales from one period to the next.

4. *Diversification among products or services.* Growth is always the test of success in business, even when it does not always best serve the interests of the company or its stockholders. In practice, ever-continuing expansion can mean a decline in customer service and even the loss of market share in the long run. Some companies do best when they reach a healthy level of growth and then stop. In the view of stockholders interested in seeing the market value of their shares grow, however, a non-expansion policy would never be acceptable.

With that in mind, it is also important to realize that in any given sector, every market is finite. Only so many sales dollars are going to be produced for a specific commodity or service. Corporate expansion is possible through diversification, however. Well-managed companies expand and diversify in terms of sectors and markets. One well-known and highly successful example is the decision by Phillip Morris to expand into non-tobacco industries. Expansion in this manner lets a company grow through subsidiaries and divisions. By also segmenting its management, a diversified corporation is less likely to suffer from internal expansion so that profits suffer. If a company tries to manage too many diverse products from one location and with a single management mentality, it can be disastrous. When Sears tried to expand into a range of financial services, it was not successful. The company was described by some as a source for "socks and stocks" (which, in effect, is a way of saying that it made little sense for a retail giant to try and run a stock brokerage firm as well). Diversification works as long as the specialized management is allowed to continue running its division with the right background and experience to compete within that sector.

You can spot continued growth as you watch a broadly diversified corporation expand its sales *and* return on sales through expanding into different sectors. This move is wise, and it serves to continue adding to dividends and earnings per share over time. In the long term, companies have to expand in one of two ways. Either they need to become leaders in an industry whose market is growing or they need to branch out into different market sectors and increase sales while maintaining or improving its overall return on sales.

Knowing which corporate liquidity tests to apply is the cornerstone for monitoring stocks in your portfolio. As an overall observation, you expect ratios to maintain or improve over time. When they begin to decline, that is the sign that you need to get more information. If the corporation is losing market share or profits are falling as debt capitalization rises, it is time to move capital out of that company's stock and seek a better-managed alternative. For long-established sector leaders, the alternative often is the second-place competitor who is rapidly picking up steam and moving toward taking over the leading position.

Emergency Fund: The Traditional Approach

The idea of liquidity to most investors means being able to get money out of an investment without trouble. On a more realistic level, it might also mean getting money without suffering a loss. On a financial planning level, it has most often come to mean having a reserve of ready cash for emergencies.

All of these variations are closely associated yet distinct. The first is a reference to a "ready market," the idea that trading is easy even when the balance between buyers and sellers is far off. The second refers to market and price risk. The third is a matter of managing a family and personal budget, the planning of cash so that you do not run short unexpectedly when expenses arise for which you were not planning. The typical argument involves matters like major car repairs, broken-down systems in your house, and other unexpected expenses. On a more serious level, the sudden loss of income, such as termination of a family breadwinner, requires some contingency planning.

The traditional approach to planning for the unexpected has been to save an emergency reserve in a bank account, money market fund or account, or some other liquid reserve. Some traditional-thinking people even suggest hiding away precious metals, fearing the worst—the collapse of the American currency. That, however, would be so extreme that segmentation of one's portfolio wouldn't be necessary. If the currency were to fail, there is little doubt that all investments, notably the stock market, would witness huge losses as well. The more reasoned approach has called for the establishment of a reserve fund, however—often described in terms of monthly income. For example, the thinking goes that you should have six months' income put away in a savings account. This action is not practical, however, nor is it always necessary.

Fallacy: You should have a portion of your capital put away in an emergency fund.

If you think about what it means to have a half-year's income in a savings account for emergencies, you realize that it represents a large sum of money—capital that is not available to put to work in higher-yielding investments. For the past several years, liquid savings have not yielded enough to make this idea practical. Even certificates of deposit, often requiring commitment of funds for six months or more, rarely match the average returns you expect from investing in stocks.

For many families, saving six months' income would represent a major problem. It is difficult enough to meet monthly obligations, and many people are barely able to put aside a relatively small portion of their earnings in long-term investments. Many families put small monthly deposits into mutual funds and supplement this amount with an IRA and through employer-paid retirement programs. A half-year's salary put into a savings account or money market fund is, for many families, an idea that is more luxury than reality.

The fallacy goes beyond the practical problems of accumulating that kind of capital. It also presents a problem in terms of return on investment. For example, if you expect to earn an average return of six percent just as a break-even point to keep up with inflation and taxes, you need to earn the average over your entire investment portfolio. If you have a relatively large sum of money sitting in a savings account or money market fund yielding 2 to 3 percent per year, you need to offset this percentage with relatively high rates of return on other investments. The requirement to put aside a large sum of money in a low-yielding account can mean, overall, that your investment capital would not keep pace with inflation and after-tax break-even. So, protecting yourself with an emergency reserve could be translated to mean that over time your equity loses purchasing power.

An alternative is to invest a portion of your capital in areas of the market where it can be removed with little or no delay. For most investors, this sentence describes the entire stock market and mutual fund arena—you can remove capital within a week in most cases, even depending on the postal service for the delivery of a check. Wire transfers are common as well so that your capital can be removed and credited to your bank account within less than a full week. Few investors would want to tie up capital in illiquid investments to too great an extent, at any rate. For example, putting your entire investment portfolio into real estate would not make sense because it can be removed only through refinancing or sale—both of which take time and could also be untimely.

Another idea for the unknown emergency, replacing the traditional but low-yielding savings account, is the use of lines of credit. The modern trend is to use and depend on credit cards and home equity lines of credit as a means for managing a budget, and as long as you manage your money well, this situation makes sense. Those with a good credit rating can easily acquire a significant line of credit through several credit cards, and it is not unlikely for people to have six-figure lines of credit available through their credit cards and home equity. Many lenders also offer the home equity line of credit in which you pay interest only on the amount you withdraw from the line itself. The funds are available instantly in most cases, often through simply writing a check against the line of credit.

The use of credit can be thought of as a form of "contingent liquidity," which means that funds are available for use in the case of emergency and unexpected expense, but those funds should *only* be used in those circumstances. The misuse of credit can lead to disaster for a personal budget, and it requires planning and discipline to avoid the pitfalls of readily available money. The popular idea that "a penny borrowed is a penny earned" can destroy your otherwise well thought-out personal plans. So, the use of lines of credit, either based on home equity or credit cards, has to be controlled well. When used, the amount withdrawn has to be planned for repayment within a reasonable time to avoid accumulating debt and allowing it to get out of control.

The advantages of using lines of credit as a fund for contingent liquidity include the following:

1. *Interest costs are lower than with the traditional loan.* When you borrow on your home equity, the interest rate can be considerably lower than it would be through the traditional bank loan. Because it is secured by your equity in most cases, the rate usually is very competitive. In addition, you only pay interest on the funds you withdraw, and interest stops as soon as you repay the amount used. In other words, *you* control the amount of debt and the interest costs.

2. *Tax benefits might apply.* The home equity line of credit generates interest expenses that are deductible as itemized deductions in most situations. This procedure discounts your cost of borrowing. For example, if your interest rate is 8 percent but your effective tax rate is 25 percent, that discounts your after-tax interest cost to 6 percent (reduced taxes equal 25 percent of your interest, so .25 x 8 percent = 2 percent savings).

3. *You can go in and out of debt repeatedly.* The flexibility of home equity lines of credit and credit card-based funds is that you can use that money for as long or short a time period as you desire. You can repeat the process of borrowing funds many times without having to apply for financing and usually without a processing cost. The use of lines of credit provides you with convenience, and as long as it is controlled carefully, it means greater financial freedom for you.

4. *Prudent use of lines of credit gives you flexibility in your budget and portfolio.* Without having to tie up funds in a low-yielding savings account, you can put more of your capital to work in stocks and other higher-yielding investments, which provides you flexibility in family budgeting and within your portfolio. If unexpected expenses arise, you do not need to liquidate investments to get through a few weeks of tight cash flow. Instead, you can use the "contingent liquidity" of a credit card or home equity line of credit, thus preserving your investments and leaving them in place.

5. *You avoid committing investment funds to low-yielding accounts.* Using lines of credit enables you to avoid the use of traditional low-yielding savings altogether. In recent years, the insured account—whether demand accounts or money market-rate accounts—has yielded dismal rates in comparison to the stock market and mutual funds. So, the more money you have in a traditional account, the lower your overall portfolio yield. A counter-argument is that savings are a form of diversification and lower risk. If your overall rate of return is so low that it does not match the double effects of inflation and taxes, however, then it does more harm than good to maintain a liquid insured account. Most investors need to struggle just to maintain break-even with inflation and taxes, and today the majority of savings accounts do not meet that test. It makes more sense to keep funds in relatively liquid investments that yield more, accept the higher risk associated with them, and consider lines of credit as the best source for emergency funds.

The use of debt to manage emergencies requires careful controls, of course. It is all too easy with many lines of credit to lose control over your budget and to experience ever-growing debt on those lines of credit. As long as you limit their use to emergencies and tighten up other spending until the debt has been repaid, you are likely to avoid the problems of taking on more debt than you can manage.

Just as a large corporation can get into trouble if it uses debt capitalization so much that too much of its operating profit goes to interest, families can experience the same difficulties. When a corporation cannot continue paying dividends to shareholders and further expansion is inhibited by ever-growing debt, this situation often spells long-term disaster. For the family trying to manage its budget, a similar problem has to be managed carefully. If you accumulate too much debt, then monthly interest and principal payments could mean you can no longer afford to invest money in your portfolio. With this fact in mind, the contingent liquidity available from lines of credit might replace traditional savings; but it has to be used carefully because it can also jeopardize your long-term equity-building plans.

Coordinated Portfolio Management

The potential pitfall associated with too much use of debt cannot be emphasized too greatly. It is perhaps the greatest risk for those with good credit. The better your credit, the more lines of credit you can obtain and the greater the potential for danger. The risk in its worst form is that your portfolio can be reduced by ever-mounting interest expenses, and rather than achieving financial freedom through your investment program, you could end up deeply in debt by retirement.

This situation can be avoided by coordinating the various aspects of your family budget and your investment portfolio. These are not separate entities, but are part of the overall plan for building wealth and avoiding debt in later years. The family budget should allow for a regular plan of money put into your investments so that it becomes part of the budget; at the same time, debt and your portfolio both require careful and diligent management.

In the management and selection of stocks with the idea of maintaining adequate liquidity, the potential need for quick cash can be managed through the availability of credit; the handling of your portfolio with liquidity in mind as well as the desire for long-term growth is also possible through the coordinated approach. When you consider your portfolio, it makes sense to think about it in its entirety rather than looking at each part. Just as a family budget has to be planned and expenses prioritized, the portfolio also works best when the balance and diversity of holdings are constantly on your mind.

Some traditional approaches to the selection of stocks involve emphasis on the attributes of the company alone. This traditional approach using fundamental analysis as the means for stock selection makes perfect sense; however, the range of decisions should be made with the whole portfolio in mind and not on a one-by-one basis. The belief that each stock buy, sell, or hold decision has to be made on an individual basis can create an imbalance in your portfolio and the loss of liquidity.

Fallacy: The decision to buy and sell each stock has to be made independently.

Why is this idea ill advised? If you begin with a nicely balanced portfolio in terms of type of stock, fundamentals, growth potential, and sector, it also makes sense to maintain that form of diversification. There is a tendency as stocks are sold to reinvest capital in the stock of companies similar in character, however. If you are pleased with the performance of a stock with one set of attributes, you are inclined toward wanting to repeat that experience by buying stocks that share the same attributes. Because that is a backward-looking point of view, however, it can gradually eliminate the diversification of your portfolio but in a subtle way. As you replace various holdings with an increasing number of stocks similar in character based on past performance, you become ever more vulnerable to cyclical changes. If a major portion of your portfolio is invested in stocks that will all move in the same direction when market sentiment turns, you could lose your diversification *and* liquidity very suddenly.

If the market mood turns and a majority of your stocks lose market value in a relatively short period of time, you cannot sell shares without taking a loss. Thus, a large portion of your portfolio ends up invested in stocks with depressed prices. Some investors do not realize that their decisions have led to this problem until it is too late. As they gradually remove some stocks from their portfolio and replace them with other stocks that are similar in nature, they enjoy the strengths of the mix of issues they own as long as they maintain market value or rise in value over time. When the opposite is true, however, they discover that their broad diversification plans were converted to a form of simple diversification, exposing the portfolio to overall price risk.

Even when the mix of stocks represents strong long-term growth prospects, it remains a problem that the portfolio at large is going through a depressed price situation. In other words, capital cannot be moved without taking a loss or at least without losing the profits that were there before prices corrected. Investors tend to think about price in terms of where those prices were *before* they fell. So, if you bought stock at $20 per share and it rose to $45 and then fell back to $30, how do you view the change? In effect, your holdings have risen 50 percent (from $20 to $30 per share). The way that many investors view this situation, however, is as a substantial loss (from the high of $45 per share to the current price level of $30).

A good rule of thumb is as follows: Paper profits are only real if they are taken when they exist. The tendency to look back at what could have been if your timing were only better is the primary flaw of every investor. Just as you know you should have sold when the price was high, you can also look at stocks you do not own and realize that you should have bought shares when their value was far below today's market price.

You cannot perfect your market timing; you can only hope to reduce risk and maximize long-term growth through intelligent analysis and selection. The desire to maintain liquidity in terms of price and value also requires great care in the replacement of stocks, however. To avoid the consequences of sudden changes in the market—which we all know will happen from time to time—you need to ensure that you maintain broad diversification in many aspects: sector, fundamental characteristics, market share, and profitability of the company.

The fallacy that each buy, sell, or hold decision has to be made independently can be replaced with another point of view: The diversification in your portfolio beyond the simple ownership of many different stocks is the key to maintaining liquidity. When one stock is sold and replaced, it requires the study of the mix in the entire portfolio. The need for diversification limits the selection of a replacement stock to avoid duplicating too many market attributes. Maintaining portfolio liquidity makes it necessary to reduce the risk that too many of the stocks you own are going to act or react in too similar a matter to sudden changes in market mood.

Tax Planning and Liquidity

The tendency for stocks with similar (or identical) attributes to act and react in the same manner is a problem for those whose portfolios are not fundamentally diversified. It would make perfect sense that such a portfolio will tend to rise or fall in unison, because the similarities between stocks also become similarities in terms of market and price risk.

The need for liquidity in your portfolio makes diversification by risk elements as essential as ever. In this respect, liquidity refers to your inability to sell without suffering a loss. This factor is one of two aspects concerning tax planning. The second aspect is profit taking. Creating situations in which you have unplanned profits *or* unplanned losses will defeat your good intentions in managing your portfolio.

A short-term capital gain (the profit on a stock transaction in which the holding period was one year or less) is taxed at ordinary rates. In other words, no reduced rate applies as it does for long-term capital gains. So, if you allow yourself to take profits just because a particular stock has risen in current market value, you create two immediate problems. First, you need to decide where to reinvest those funds; and second, you will be taxed this year on the profits created when you sold. As long as you held the stock for less than one year, it will be a short-term capital gain.

If you have a number of stocks in your portfolio and you turn them over by taking profits whenever you can earn a few hundred dollars in the short term, it will add up to a considerable profit by the end of the year—an unplanned profit that ultimately will be discounted by the consequences of taxation, both federal and state (in some areas, by local income taxes as well). Of course, if you sell off only those stocks that become profitable in the short term, you also end up with a portfolio full of stocks that have either not moved upward or that have actually lost value. This situation is the second problem—ending up with an illiquid portfolio. The stocks cannot be sold without suffering a loss.

If you do sell a number of stocks at a loss, then you accumulate a series of short-term capital losses. Some people will shrug off the losses with the argument that they create a tax write-off. This thinking is not only inaccurate but it also enables the acceptance of losses that could be avoided simply by continuing to hold shares of companies whose long-term growth potential remains positive.

The short-term losses you write off in a year can offset short-term capital gains. They remain as losses, however. The real tax "benefit" of the loss is the discount value it provides. The write-off does not erase the loss. For example, if your effective tax rate is 25 percent, you discount the loss by reducing your tax liability. So, if you have a $1,000 loss, the after-tax loss will be $750, or 25 percent less than the full dollar value of the loss. The $1,000 loss is actually an after-tax loss of only $750; however, the write-off should still be a troubling aspect, especially when it was created prematurely. If you act as a speculator by taking short-term profits or losses rather than holding shares so that they season in the market, then you have to expect a larger number of losses than the long-term investor would experience. Many people who think of themselves as long-term investors act as speculators, without realizing that they are damaging their portfolio and violating their own carefully designed long-term plan.

Another problem of taking short-term losses is that they are severely limited. For federal tax purposes, you can claim up to a total net capital loss of $3,000 per year. Any losses above that level have to be carried over to future years. So, you cannot shelter other income indefinitely when you take losses; they need to be timed and balanced against gains so that the excess is not left to idle for another year or more before they can be claimed.

The combination of unplanned tax consequences and the illiquidity in your portfolio can damage your long-term intentions. This common problem should be avoided, not only because profit-taking makes no sense as long as the company is a valid long-term growth candidate, but also because it does damage to your current year's tax planning as well as to your personal investment program. There is another solution to the problem of profit taking in which you maximize the short-term fluctuation in price with reduced risk. That is the writing of covered calls.

Most investors do not understand options, and for this reason they should not use them. Covered call writing can work as a solution, however—especially if you own stocks whose prices tend to swing up and down from week to week. The long-term investor recognizes that intermediate price volatility does not have any significance over the long term and might ignore those price swings, viewing them as opportunities to buy more shares on the down swing rather than as profit-taking opportunities on the upswing. Another approach is to use price volatility to increase short-term profits with covered calls.

The covered call is a conservative option strategy. You receive cash when you sell, and one of three possible outcomes will take place:

1. *The call will be exercised.* If the price of stock rises above the call's striking price, the call will be exercised before expiration. In that event, your 100 shares will be called away at the striking price. So, your "risk" is losing profits that have not materialized at the time you sold the call. As long as the striking price is higher than your basis, however, you profit in two ways: from the sell of stock and from the option premium you were paid when you sold the call.

2. *The call will expire as worthless.* Because time works for the seller and against the buyer, it is necessary for the stock's price to rise above striking price in order to exercise the option. If that does not occur, the call expires as worthless and you keep the profit. Once expiration has passed, you are free to tie up the same 100 shares by selling another call, and this pattern can continue indefinitely.

3. *The call position will be closed at a profit.* Some people write covered calls with maximum time value and then wait for the time value to decline. At that point, they close the short position by buying the call, and the difference between sell price and buy price is profit. You can

trade in calls in this manner indefinitely, and you remain covered as long as you do not sell more than one call per 100 shares owned.

Time value is that part of the option's premium that has no tangible value. As long as the striking price is higher than current market value, the entire option premium is represented by time value. When the market value is higher than striking price, intrinsic value equals the number of points of difference between current price and striking price. The key for option sellers is to trade with maximum time value, because that will evaporate as expiration becomes closer.

The conservative investor might want to avoid options altogether, especially those who recognize that the real value is found in holding stock for the very long term. Even if selling covered calls were well understood, many investors would prefer to keep their shares and avoid the risk of having them called away—even when such a risk would be minimal. The point here is that there are ways to take profits, especially when a stock's price tends to overreact to immediate market news, without ending up with illiquidity problems in your portfolio. If the only alternative is to sell and take profits now, then where is the risk in selling a covered call? The real advantage to this strategy is that it enables you to take profits while still keeping your shares in the majority of option scenarios. This scenario assumes, too, that you would follow the sensible guidelines for option sellers:

1. Deal only in covered call selling.
2. Sell for maximum time value.
3. Close positions when they are profitable, or leave them open and allow options to expire as worthless.
4. Avoid exercise but only if you can do so without taking a loss.
5. Only sell calls when you are willing to have shares called away at the strike price.

Liquidity and Timing

Just as the option seller needs to time transactions to maximize profits, every investor has to deal with the problems of *when* to buy or sell shares of stock. The problem of maintaining liquidity in your portfolio often is really a matter of timing rather than one of proper selection. If you choose shares of a company whose capital strength and growth potential is promising, it is still possible to buy shares at a relatively high price.

The relativity of price is determined by subsequent price movement. If you buy shares at $48 per share and the market price then falls to $42, it means you bought at a relatively high price. This situation does not mean that the decision was a poor one, however; you were the victim of timing. There is no solution to the timing problem; every investor has to live with the reality that some decisions are going to be poorly timed. Stocks might fall in market price right after you buy, and they might also rise in price right after you sell. That is simply the reality of the market. In fact, timing is what makes stock market investing so interesting. Many success stories have little to do with good analysis and a lot to do with lucky timing; the same is true of many market disasters.

So, how do you overcome the problem of market timing? In fact, the only solution is to go back to the advice to invest based on fundamental diversification. In addition, it is not necessary to purchase all of the shares of a company at the same time. By investing in increments, you might miss some short-term opportunities, but you also will overcome the problem of poor timing. For example, if you intend to buy 100 shares of stock, you might do so in a single transaction or you might make a series of trades. If the price rises or falls by five points or more, that is a signal to purchase more shares. So, if you buy 100 shares at a time and only buy an additional 100 shares when the market has moved a number of points, the effect is to average out your cost per share.

An example of price averaging in a falling market, assuming 100 shares are purchased at each price change listed:

Price per share	Average price per share
$85	$85.00
83	84.00
82	83.33
79	82.25
78	81.40

Note that even though the total range spreads over seven points on a downward trend, the average cost of shares as of the last transaction is only $3.40 above current market value. Using this technique evens out the price differences in a falling market and minimizes the illiquidity. This technique works when you believe that the subject stock remains a viable long-term growth candidate. In such a case, you would expect the stock's market price to turn around and swing in the opposite direction.

An example in a rising price situation:

Price per share	Average price per share
$85	$85.00
87	86.00
88	86.67
89	87.25
92	88.20

In this example, the average price per share is always below current market value, but this price is paid for minimizing the risk of illiquidity. Remember that price averaging tends to reduce both risk *and* profit opportunity. Some combined techniques call for buying more shares when the price goes up and fewer when the price goes down. This strategy is of limited value if you have only a small amount of capital to invest, however. The trading cost of several transactions might offset much of the advantage gained through this technique.

Price averaging is only one technique to overcome the short-term price risk that leads to illiquidity. Remember that an illiquid position in a single stock is not a problem as long as your portfolio is in a strong position overall. Not every stock will gain value; at least, not right away. In some situations, you will have to wait out the market.

One error some investors make is attempting to offset losses with short-term gains. For example, if you own two different stocks that were purchased within the past year, they can be used to even out the illiquidity in one of the stocks. For example, if one stock has lost four points and the other has gained five, you would sell both and accept a net profit near zero after trading costs for the entire transaction.

This example presents problems yet again. Once more, you end up with an amount of capital that has to be reinvested somewhere, so the decision to off-set profit and loss only exposes you to yet more market risk. Second, there would be no reason to sell shares of the profitable company except to offset the loss. Third, the capital gain and loss also offset one another. While you cover your short-term capital gain, you also get no benefit from writing off the loss.

As an alternative, it would make more sense to sell the losing stock and invest that capital in additional shares of the winning stock. Thus, you place capital in a company whose prospects seem more promising while giving up some fundamental diversification in exchange. Second, you keep shares of the successful company and actually increase your holdings in that company. Third, you get the current-year short-term loss, which discounts that loss by reducing your tax liability.

The problem of how to deal with paper losses in your portfolio is a troubling one, especially if the market is down broadly. It is likely in that situation that the entire portfolio is depressed, and you cannot afford to move capital around. Even if you did, what are the chances that you would do better elsewhere?

Some suggestions are as follows:

1. *Wait out the market. Everything, even price depression, is temporary.* The picture will look different in the future. If you have selected strong growth stocks, they will work out over time.

2. *Pick strong growth stocks with good dividend history.* You enhance your growth potential by picking high-yielding stocks. Don't forget to include dividends in your calculation of returns. If your company offers a dividend

reinvestment plan, take advantage of it, and gain compound growth on your dividend income.

3. *Use options to protect market value.* Remember, you discount your basis in stock when you sell covered calls. The premium you receive per 100 shares of stock is yours to keep, and a depressed stock price could be a break-even point when call premium is taken into account. You can further protect stock price by using puts as insurance. When you buy a put, in increases in value dollar for dollar with a falling stock price.

Notes

[1]The traditional 100-share purchase has been a trading norm in order to minimize trading costs. The trend today, however, is to enable investors to buy odd lots without additional cost, either through organized plans (such as www.foliofn.com, referred to in the last chapter, or through dividend reinvestment plans). This concern might be less of an issue in the future as markets become increasingly flexible.

[2]Ratios are valuable tools for financial analysis. They translate dollars and cents to simple, lower forms so that we can better understand the real relationship. We can more easily grasp the significance of ratios that way. Ratios are expressed as a single number (as in the number of *times* inventory turns over); as a percentage; or as the relationship between two related values (such as 2 to 1 or 3 to 1).

[3]In some industries, exceptionally high inventory levels or wide fluctuations in inventory due to the business cycle make the current ratio vary widely. In these cases, an alternative is to exclude inventory from the current assets side of the equation. This process is called the "quick asset ratio" or the "acid test ratio." As a standard for comparison, the minimal requirement is a 1 to 1 or better for this variation.

CHAPTER 7

Volatility and Its Many Meanings

When stocks are compared to one another, they invariably are defined in terms of their price volatility. More than any other measurement, volatility helps investors determine the relative degree of risk involved in buying and owning shares of a stock. That approach, however—because it is limited to a conclusion based on price—can be very misleading and can even point you in the wrong direction unless the relative conclusions you reach about volatility are analyzed with all of the facts in hand.

Volatility as it is usually reviewed consists of a study of price trends over the past year. This study is used to decide the following:

- Whether a stock's current price is stable or not
- How broad a price range is involved in trading in that stock
- Whether a stock's price is near its current high or low for the year
- The degree of price risk (not to be confused with market risk)
- Whether a trading range is expanding or leveling out

As important an idea as volatility is, however, it usually is applied only to study and predict price trends in the immediate future. The market places great emphasis on short-term prediction even though it is widely recognized that such trends are not reliable in the analysis of the market. Under the Dow Theory and the random walk hypothesis, the unreliability of short-term indicators is agreed upon, and it is perhaps the single area where these divergent points of view do meet.

As an alternative to using volatility for short-term price analysis, it makes more sense to look for the reasons why one stock's price will be highly volatile while comparable stocks are fairly stable. There are valid answers, and they are found by tracking a stock's price history back to the fundamentals.

One Aspect of Price History

Volatility, most people will agree, is a relative matter. If one stock has traded during the past year in a five-point range and another has traded in a 50-point range, the differences between these two company's stocks is significant. The former usually is considered a safe investment in terms of price stability, whereas the latter will be viewed as far more volatile.

What does that mean, though, in terms of *market* risk? With all of the emphasis on price, is the information reliable? Volatility reflects *current* price range, meaning only the past year. In fact, that alone tells you only about one aspect of the price history. Concentrating only on the recent history of market price is not entirely useless, because it does provide you with raw material for further investigation. If you are looking at two corporations in similar market sectors with the same growth patterns and capital strength, relative volatility is a good form of analysis to start with—especially if it is different between the two. Your first question should be, "Why is one stock more volatile than the other?" A study of recent fundamental information should be the next step. Have sales and profits changed over the past year? Are predictions different for each company? Are there rumors of a merger or takeover for one company?

The study of relative volatility is useful to the extent that it leads you to other information. Another way to use volatility is through a study of the price pattern itself. Chartists—technical analysts who study price patterns—watch price trends regularly. Support and resistance is a valuable study for identifying the nature of relative volatility.

Support is the price below which a stock is unlikely to trade, and resistance is the price above which the stock is unlikely to trade. The area between support and resistance is called the trading range. Volatility of a stock can occur in several ways, and the key to understanding the actual trend is found in a study of support and resistance. For example, consider the trading pattern in Figure 7.1.

In this study of a 26-week pattern, the trading range is established in the first half between 49 and 53 per share; a breakout occurs and the trading range is re-established between 52 and 56 per share. Now, consider a second chart (shown in Figure 7.2).

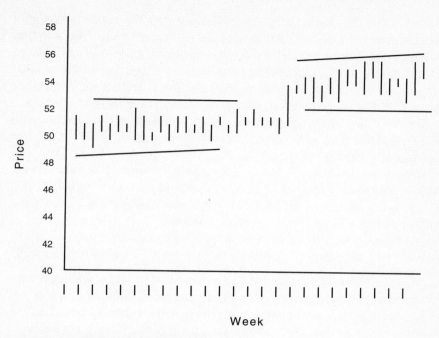

FIGURE 7.1 Chart pattern with breakout.

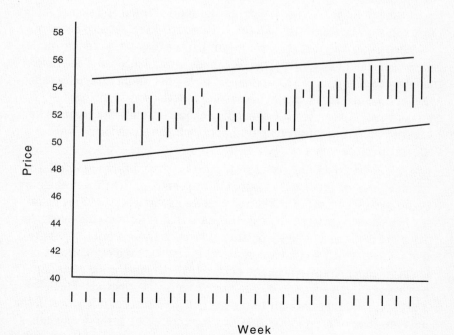

FIGURE 7.2 Chart pattern without breakout.

In this case, the trading range is established over the entire period on a gradually increasing basis, with a 26-week low of 49 and a high of 56. Note that the 26-week trading range in both of these examples is between 49 and 56; however, the significance of that trading range is quite different given the two patterns and in the fact that one example had a breakout pattern while the other showed a trading range that was moving over time. These recent histories are significantly different than one another. Such comparisons can take place on the down side as well, with breakout going down in price or with a trading range that is declining over time.

The point worth making here is as follows: Volatility by itself does not always tell the whole story. Merely comparing one stock to another in terms of price volatility is not going to reveal a valuable conclusion until you also compare the actual price changes, patterns, and current status.

Using this information to predict future price changes—the usual reason why charts are used to analyze stock prices—is a troubling idea for several reasons:

1. *Price is a short-term indicator.* The recent price history of a stock is not a reliable indicator for long-term growth prospects. While the study of price over many years might indicate the long-term trend in a stock's price, the immediate price study is far from reliable. Price is not only a technical indicator not directly related to the fundamentals, but it can be deceptive, as well. Many companies with exceptional long-term growth prospects are likely at various times to go through a one- to two-year price slump. In such cases, their short-term price trend and recent history will appear dismal. In such times, these stocks might also be more volatile than usual; that does not mean that the long-term fundamentals have changed. In fact, price studies can distort and mislead if the fundamentals are not followed as well. Short-term price trends are *not* a reflection of fundamental change. They might point the way to further fundamental study; however, depending on price trends and changes in volatility alone is a purely technical approach and should serve only as a starting point for more study.

2. *The recent past does not necessarily show how the future will look.* The chronic problem for chartists is that most people realize the unreliability of the technique itself. The chartist spends a great deal of energy pointing to past price patterns to make the case that certain events (such as price breakout, head and shoulders patterns, or trading price gaps) predict immediate price changes. In practice, though, predicting what is about to happen proves far more elusive than demonstrating what happened in the immediate past. The price trends that chartists offer, even if accurate, would refer only to the immediate future; in other words, the next few days or even weeks at best. These trends do little to indicate long-term growth prospects, because price trends as studied today and

yesterday reveal nothing about those long-term trends. So, the long-term investor who believes in the fundamentals needs to recognize the technical nature of price trends and accept them as only short-term in nature.

3. *Forecasting of price is different than forecasting in business.* One of the flaws in stock market analysis is the attempt to equate price forecasting with business forecasting. The stock market is dominated by businesspeople who understand the nature of forecasting and budgeting on the corporate level. It is a science used to monitor trends in business and to spot emerging changes that require corrective action. It is a *science* because good forecasting is based on studies of marketing trends and on those markets themselves. In comparison, forecasting of price in the market cannot be based on the fundamentals because price does not reflect the month-to-month changes in sales and profits. It cannot, because those results are not available every week or month. So, price changes are a factor of supply and demand, meaning that the auction marketplace affects stock prices. These forces cannot be predicted in the same way that a marketing department can predict sales levels based on customer base activity. The desire to approach price in the same manner as business forecasting can blind investors to the realities of price and price trends: They are truly random, at least in the short term.

The long-term benefit of owning shares in a company should be based on strong fundamentals rather than on short-term price trends. The approach of buying stock when the price is at a 52-week high or low is a hit-or-miss method, because that price trend really reveals nothing about the fundamentals or about where that price is going to move next. The value of a volatility study is found in what it reveals about the company itself. It is interesting to observe that two similar corporations will have vastly different price volatility; this observation can be used to further study the fundamentals with the premise that the market is efficient—even with its short-term, random nature. The efficiency of the market relates to the idea that investors will trade in a different pattern when the fundamentals change. So, if there is a higher-than-average level of uncertainty about a company's immediate future, its trading pattern is likely to be more volatile as well. So, with changes in management, acquisitions, expansion into new sectors, and changes in earnings predictions, stock prices will react in the short term. If two seemingly identical companies have varying levels of volatility, there will be reasons why.

In this respect, price volatility can serve as a symptom of other problems or advantages. Because uncertainly might cause higher-than-average volatility, potential good news might cause high volatility. It is not only the negative. There is a tendency to view high volatility as a sign of problems, because volatility translates to greater price risk. The other side of that reality, however, is that there also might exist a higher level of profit opportunity. So, if a company is branching out into new product areas, bringing in a more aggressive management team, investing capital in the development of new products, and taking other bold steps, the possibility of price volatility will accompany these changes. If the new moves are successful, value rises and so does price; however, if these investments fail, the opposite will also be true. So, changes in volatility have to be studied in terms of how the fundamentals are changing; what kinds of long-term risk those changes represent; and whether or not you want to own shares in the company, accepting the risk as the cost of the opportunity it also presents.

A widespread point of view about volatility is that a volatile stock price history is a sign of instability, thus a greater risk for investors. In the earlier example, however, where a company is investing in expansion moves, the volatility could represent change of a positive nature that ultimately will benefit shareholders. The market, though, does not like unpredictability and change; it wants predictability, which is why it thrives on analysts' reports. Even though those reports might be wrong, investment decisions are made in anticipation of outcomes. The emphasis on PE ratio (which reflects perception about potential growth in the future) and volatility (which defines relative short-term price stability) makes this point. While the fundamentals serve as the basis for identifying viable long-term investments, the real market *interest* is going to be found trying to anticipate what will happen tomorrow and next month.

So, volatility often reflects investor apprehension rather than actual evidence. A company expanding in intelligent ways, into secure markets and with properly planned investment levels, presents a promise of future growth and should encourage long-term investors to buy and accumulate holdings; however, those same changes might cause higher volatility because change itself—whether positive or negative—worries the market. The market, by definition, is more prone to worry than to study. The short-term price trends described in terms of volatility can mean many different things, and changes in volatility should lead not to immediate conclusions but to further analysis.

Translating the Raw Material

The actual raw material developed from the typical study of volatility can be used to lead to more studies as well as conclusions about price stability. Remember, a stable price—meaning a narrow trading range—makes for a "safe" investment in terms of price risk but could also represent little or no market opportunity. So, you need to understand not only how volatile a stock's price is today, but also what that means in terms of potential for future growth. This knowledge requires further analysis of the fundamentals.

The volatility conclusions drawn from financial reports involve studying the 52-week high and low range of a stock. The idea here is that the broader the trading range, the more volatile the stock. If volatility is the same as "risk," however, then the analysis of the trading range can mislead the analyst unless the study is taken further. Because business expansion means going into areas of uncertainty, accompanied by business risk, it is likely that a growing company will also experience a volatile price history. That growth is exactly what investors want, however. So, the instability in price reflects the desirable growth activity. In fact, a volatile stock price can be caused by any number of fundamental factors (some positive and some negative).

A positive fundamental activity usually involves expansion, investing capital in new sectors, the introduction of new products or services, and other forms of risk-taking. This period of expansion can also be accompanied by net operating losses and instability in sales, even though the long-term outcome will reward stockholders. Investors with a long-term view understand that the expansion process is likely to be a rocky one, and only the inexperienced, nervous investor will sell off shares just because short-term price is more volatile this year than the year before.

In a simplistic approach to investing, the concept of volatility is seen as a negative. Not liking price risk, investors will tend to sell off shares at the beginning of expansion periods. The same investors are likely to reinvest capital in shares of companies whose expansion has peaked because their price risk is low. That is to say, the volatility level is low and price is relatively stable. This situation also means, of course, that the potential for long-term profit has passed and performance of that stock might be consistent but mediocre.

The typical calculation of volatility does not take these important variables into account; it only uses high and low prices over the past year. This flawed form of analysis is comparable to averaging only the highest and lowest elements in a field and calling that *typical*. No statistician would call that fair or accurate; yet, in the stock market, that is exactly how volatility is computed and compared.

The formula for price volatility is shown in Figure 7.3.

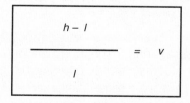

$$\frac{h - l}{l} = v$$

h = 52-week high price
l = 52-week low price
v = Volatility (percentage)

FIGURE 7.3 Volatility.

Volatility is expressed as a percentage by using this formula. It is a popular measurement of stock prices because it is easy to compute, and it makes side-to-side comparisons easy. An example of the calculation: A stock's high price during the past 52 weeks was $47 per share, and its low price was $34. Volatility is calculated as such:

$$\frac{\$47 - \$34}{\$34} = 38\%$$

If this outcome were being compared to other stocks, it would be easy to conclude that a stock with a volatility of only 19 percent would be half as volatile, thus half as risky, as this one and that a stock with a volatility of 76 percent would be twice as risky.

The problem, though, is that this formula is far from accurate. In previous examples, a trading range was described in terms of volatility; and two different stocks with identical trading ranges were shown to be vastly different in their price characteristics. The trading range taken at face value might lead to some conclusions, but it does not necessarily mean the same thing in every case. Some further examples follow to make the point that the mere study of volatility cannot be taken as a reliable indicator.

Example: A stock begins the year with a price of $47 per share and has declined gradually so that the current price is at the 52-week low of $34 per share.

Example: The stock began the year at $34 per share and has traded consistently between $34 and $38 with one exception: a spike in price up to $47 on a rumor that the company was going to be taken over, which proved to be false.

Example: The stock normally trades between $40 and $47, but its main product recently was pulled from the market after several class-action suits were filed. Profits have evaporated, and analysts' predictions are very pessimistic. During the past week, the stock fell to a new low of $34 per share.

Example: The company has been expanding aggressively by acquiring smaller competitors and most recently acquired a company in a different sector, diversifying its product base. Sales are up, and predictions are that profits will reach all-time high levels as well. The stock began the year at $34 per share and has risen steadily, ending the year at $47.

Each of these examples demonstrates that volatility, by itself, does not tell the story underlying the market price trend. In all of these examples, volatility is 38 percent—but that obviously means different things based on different price patterns. The causes of those price changes, even if based solely on market perception, cannot be used to decide what is going on in the company or even whether volatility and price patterns are positive or negative. Given the fact that price, as a short-term technical indicator, is likely to change due to immediate perceptions, volatility in price does not help you to pick good stocks for long-term investments or even for short-term gain. For example, if the market were to fall several hundred points, it is also likely that many stocks whose trading range is usually quite narrow would experience a sharp price decline as well. If the overall market levels recovered within the following week, individual stock prices would also be likely to return to previous levels.

Perhaps the greatest flaw in the volatility formula is its failure to exclude price spikes. The fact that it is based on the rather primitive method of the two extremes of high and low price makes it far from scientific, and it should not be treated as conclusive. Anyone who reviews the daily stock listings, however, finds the 52-week high and low prices, making trading range quite visible without explanation. An alternative would be to calculate price volatility by using a moving average for closing prices, at least at the end of each week. While this method also can be distorted if the end of the week is untypical, the moving average at least offers the advantage of evening out the distortions. Even so, it remains a problem that volatility can mean several different things. So, even with the more accurate moving average method, you still need to look at the trading pattern for the year to discover not only the range of trading, but also the trend itself.

Interpreting the Patterns

Given the fact that trading range is simply listed along with the rest of the stock listings each day, it is easy to make a series of assumptions about a stock—none of which are reliable given the potential for variation in trading patterns. Some investors like to compare the current price of a stock with its trading range. Some of the following conclusions could be reached easily. For example,

The stock is trading near its one-year high:
>It is a good time to buy shares because the stock is showing an upward trend.
>It is a good time to hold and take no action; wait to see how the trend moves.
>Sell shares now. The stock's price has peaked, so you want to get out at the top.

The stock is trading in the middle of its one-year range:
>This is a stable company and a safe investment.
>The stock is not moving and should be dumped.

The stock is trading at the low end of its one-year range:
>The stock is at a bargain price and should be bought now.
>The stock is exhibiting a downward trend and should be sold.

Obviously, any of these conclusions could be right or wrong. It is impossible to actually make an intelligent conclusion based on high and low price in comparison with current price; yet, this method of judging stocks is common and popular. It is not only unreliable, however, but it also contradicts the tenets of fundamental analysis in that it completely ignores the financial facts. Price is a technical indicator and cannot be used as a sole method for picking stocks. In fact, the high and low price as well as current price are all short-term in nature and are collectively unreliable. Even those who use the volatility statistics to pick stocks need to look closely at the trading patterns to discover what they mean before making decisions in the market.

In analyzing the trading pattern of a stock, study more than a single 52-week period. Look for the long-term price history of a stock. Examine trading patterns, recognizing that long-term growth is typified by a trading range gradually moving upward over time. When a price breakout occurs—the movement in price above resistance or below support—what does it mean? It might be worth investigating the underlying causes of breakout, notably for companies whose stocks have demonstrated consistency in trading range over many years.

Breakout often is caused by market overreaction to news or rumor, perhaps relating to new products, pending litigation, government anti-trust actions, unexpected earnings reports or outcomes, mergers and acquisitions, changes in management, insider trading, and many other fundamental events. The real test of breakout is not the event itself (in spite of what chartists claim) but the subsequent price activity.

A breakout based on rumors that prove to be false would typically be resolved by a return to the previous trading range. In this case, the breakout should be ignored and discounted entirely. It is nothing more than a distortion, and the astute chartist would know that the *typical* trading range is far more revealing that an aberration caused by unfounded rumor.

A breakout followed by the establishment of a new trading range is far more significant, even to the fundamental analyst. This breakout usually is based on significant news changing the fundamentals of the company. For example, when the subject company merges with another and the new concern has a broader product and customer base, sales and profits will be expected to reflect the stronger new company. Thus, with more growth potential and a diversified market share, the trading range might re-establish itself at a higher level. On the down side, a company that is forced to stop selling its most profitable product following a class-action lawsuit or a negative action by a regulatory agency can be expected to lose sales and profits. A breakout on the down side could be permanent in this case, requiring the company to consolidate its remaining products and change its marketing strategy—which could take months or even years.

So, breakout by itself cannot conclusively reveal a change in the price pattern—despite what chartists insist to the contrary. You need to examine the underlying causes for sudden market reaction that leads to a surge above resistance or a drop below support. The chartists are correct in their belief that long-established support and resistance (even if gradually changing over time) are important "lines in the sand" and that a violation of those levels is a significant event. The significance is questionable in some cases, however.

One point of view about breakout is that a strongly capitalized and well-established company should see gradual growth over many years with low volatility. Thus, even the unexpected rumor about that company should not cause a breakout. This area might be a valid starting point for understanding price risk and for defining what low volatility *should* mean. Even so, what does it mean when a breakout occurs and almost immediately retreats? Is that a test of support or resistance, as some chartists claim? Is it a sign foretelling sudden price movement in the opposite direction? Or, rather than assuming that price movement has significance just in its pattern, is it necessary to try to understand the causes for market reaction? It often is the case that the price change is the result of short-term worry (on the down side) or euphoria (on the up side), which are temporary and extreme. In cases of more serious problems and permanent changes in the fundamentals, breakout is the predictable result of the underlying problem. In the majority of such cases, investors were aware of the potential problem (thus, market risk) well in advance of the conclusion. So, the breakout should not have come as a surprise.

For example, it should not have surprised investors when Amazon.com experienced a sudden and extreme drop in market price. It had never shown a profit, after all, so the market price was based on market perceptions only and eventually had to correct. On a more fundamental level, investors with shares of Microsoft knew for many months that the federal government would try to prove the company was a monopoly and break it up; the lawsuit was not a surprise, although the initial outcome and subsequent reversals might have been. In both of these cases, investors who were not willing to be exposed to the market risks involved should have sold shares and sought companies whose market risks were less extreme.

In many cases of price breakout, investors should not have been surprised. A permanent breakout usually can be traced back to well-known and well-publicized causes. When breakout follows surprises, such as earnings reports that are inconsistent with analysts' predictions or a company's own predictions of a slower-than-average year, the tendency is for price to return to previous levels once the news has been absorbed. This process could take only a few trading periods or many months; the point is that real surprises in the market tend to be short-term in nature. Most fundamentals are well known in advance, and investors who want to study the facts can discover them easily.

Price Volatility as a Technical Indicator

The study of price—in fact, the emphasis on price trends in the market—should itself be highly suspect. Does price volatility reveal anything of value? Is recent price history an indicator that you can use, or is it misleading?

The price of a stock is invariably a starting point, especially for inexperienced investors. It is only a means for measuring the overall value of capital, however. If a company has one million outstanding shares at $10 per share or 500,000 shares at $20 per share, the total capital value has not changed. Even so, investors tend to view a $10 and a $20 stock in different ways. Some prejudice about price levels is inevitable, but they are worth examining and resisting.

Many investors who start out with limited capital want to buy 100 shares, so they are forced to look only at stocks at or below their capital level. If they have $2,500, they need to look for stocks at or below $25 per share. So, they might develop the opinion that high-priced stocks are too expensive. In reality, everyone knows that the price per share is not a reflection of actual value; it is really a reflection of a corporate decision to issue a particular number of shares with the initial price a consequence of that decision. Subsequent changes in market price are the result of investor supply and demand plus stock split decisions and issuance of new shares—not to mention the effect of mergers where stock is traded between companies and market values change rather suddenly.

Even given all of these facts, investors tend to depend heavily on price history and to view stock price levels with some conclusions that make little sense. For example, consider the case of a stock that is trading today at $50 per share. An investor might avoid buying shares of that stock because he or she can remember when it was selling at about $70 per share only a few years ago. In the interim, however, the stock might have split two for one so that the $70 stock became a $35 stock with twice as many shares and the market value then rose to $50 per share—a significant increase in value that is easily misread by investors.

Price history, even when adjusted for splits or mergers, cannot predict likely future price changes. A company with strong fundamentals, a diversified customer base, and smart management that knows how to create growth remains a viable long-term investment prospect; however, the current and recent price history for that company's stock might not reflect these characteristics in any manner. Some long-term growth prospects reveal a rather mundane price movement over the past year, just as some very questionable long-term investments might exhibit an impressive history of price increase (as was seen with many stocks in the dot.com phenomenon), which can be subsequently adjusted.

Investors who depend too much on short-term price trends, notably on the typical calculation of volatility, are likely to make mistakes in the timing of their decisions to buy, sell, or hold shares of stock. Price alone cannot be used for such decisions, but sadly it often is the sole determinant in those important decisions. Investors are easily misled so that they make their decisions based on short-term and unreliable technical indicators while continuing to believe that they are investing based on analysis of the fundamentals.

Most investors recognize that volatility is a technical indicator. The mistake is not in relying upon it too heavily, however, but in misapplying the very concept that it represents. A study and comparison of volatility, as we have demonstrated, is unreliable if limited to trading range and current price alone. The statistical flaws involved in limiting a study only to the highest and lowest levels—without defining what those levels mean in fundamental terms—should cause investors to avoid comparisons of volatility between companies. Rather, the real key to using volatility is to first identify the trading pattern and look for surprises and then follow those indicators to the fundamentals and search for the actual causes. If a breakout pattern is temporary, it can be largely ignored. Even though a company with historically low price risk should not experience rumor-based breakouts, it does occur. The breakout that does not last is far less interesting than the one that leads to the establishment of a new trading range, whether higher or lower than its prior range.

If you follow the fundamentals for the corporation, then you probably already know the causes of such breakouts. Permanent changes in trading range for stable companies are invariably the result of predictable change that anyone paying attention would have been able to anticipate. The market risk involved with litigation, labor relations, government oversight, product regulation, mergers, and changes in management (to name a new of the potential factors) define the nature of change, and such market risks ultimately become reflected in price and volatility. Thus, market risk can be said to lead price risk in the respect that the well-known market factors defining the level of long-term growth potential have both opportunity and risk and that those factors will show up in price risk, as well.

To the extent that volatility points to a level of investor confidence, you should examine what that actually means. Are you confident in the company's long-term growth prospects? If so, then short-term price volatility can be largely ignored except to the extent that it signals a change in the fundamentals. A lot of emphasis, perhaps too much, is placed on the idea of confidence in a company when the real price volatility could be caused by decisions made by institutional investors. When a mutual fund decides to invest in shares of a company or begins selling shares that it held previously, that itself can change the supply and demand temporarily. Does this situation mean the confidence of the market has changed as well? The widespread belief is in the market as a singular entity. It either has confidence in a company and its stock or it does not. The mood of the market is singular in its direction under this belief system, but in practice the market is a collection of many conflicting beliefs, risk tolerance levels, and philosophies about investing. So, the idea of confidence probably is overrated—especially for those who want to invest based on the fundamentals. Confidence is related to price strength in the immediate future and is a speculative term at best.

The exception for the fundamental investor is when volatility signals a significance change in market or capital strength or other financially-based factors that change long-term growth prospects. Some of these elements are not clearly visible in financial reports, so changes in volatility—notably breakouts of a significant level—could foretell changes in the fundamentals that could change everything. In these cases, price volatility foretells the announcement of the change in the numbers instead of the other way around. In such cases, you need to study the fundamentals to find the underlying causes and take action, if necessary, to protect your portfolio. If a buy or hold indication should change to a sell decision, then the study of volatility can be a useful way to get an early sign of bigger changes to come. This situation is usually seen in a broadening volatility, which reflects investor uncertainty or insecurity about the fundamentals. The tendency to recognize such instability often takes place too late to do anything about it, because that volatility means a lower current market price. The trick is to recognize the causes that are going to lead to that uncertainty before the market reflects the problem in lower prices.

Volatility in Earnings

To identify emerging problems in price stability—in other words, price volatility—a study of sales and earnings trends can be most useful. For example, a stock whose price has been within a narrow trading range might begin to expand its range. This situation occurs whenever price begins moving upward or downward; change is disruptive to a nice, narrow trading range; and even good news (expanded earnings, for example) is likely to create greater price volatility.

Price stability by itself is not a desirable attribute for a stock. By definition, a stable price range also means that the value of that company is not growing. The price remains within a narrow trading range until growth begins, and then the range needs to expand. Ultimately, stockholders are rewarded when the stock's price range increases, so an expanded trading range and greater volatility are going to act as symptoms of growth. Of course, the same arguments apply to the opposite direction. When a stock's price is falling, it is equally volatile but for different reasons. The fact that rising and falling price ranges might exhibit the same kind of volatility points out the flaw in traditional price-only volatility study. Because rising and falling prices are caused by vastly different fundamental causes, any unexpected changes in volatility should act as a signal to investigate further. The questions are complex. Volatility is not a simple matter in spite of the fact that when isolated to price and trading range, the typical comparative study is simplistic. In fact, identifying the underlying causes of volatility requires considerable analysis of the fundamentals. Even though short-term price changes reflect an uncertain market that overreacts to virtually all news, significant changes in volatility can have a more permanent meaning.

Fallacy: Volatility is easy to understand; it is nothing more than the history of recent price change.

In reality, changing volatility can mean many different things. Even when prices are moving in the same direction for two or more different companies, it is not enough to limit your study to the relative volatility between a particular stock and other stocks with similar characteristics. Volatility should be studied on a company-by-company basis, including historical information and current, new information.

As long as volatility is limited to a study of price during the past year, it will always be of limited value. It is far more meaningful to review price history over a span of many years. From this study, you can identify price patterns, whether or not there has been growth, and if so, to what degree. Within the multiple-year pattern, you will also identify whether price trends tend to occur within a narrow band of trading or with broader swings in price (the pattern of price change). Whether stock values are rising or falling can be thought of as a reflection of historical market perception about the company. You should ask, however, "Why do some stocks trade in a broad range while others trade in much more narrow ranges?" In some cases, companies that appear identical in other respects have much different trading patterns.

The answer contradicts the commonly held fallacy that volatility is easy to understand. In fact, it is not simply the history of recent price range in a stock. Of far greater significance (and value in your analysis), volatility is a symptom of the fundamental attributes of a company. The fallacy should be replaced with a different statement: Volatility is, in fact, a reflection of the market's confidence in the fundamentals of the corporation.

In comparing corporations that have certain similarities—the same sector, similar capitalization structure, approximately the same sales levels—you will find that price volatility might be far different, even given those similarities. Why? The answer, again, is that the market tends to be confident in a reliable forecast and tends to be nervous about less-certain fundamentals. So, when a particular company experiences sales and profits that grow steadily from year to year, whose profits are consistent and whose dividends are paid regularly, the market as a whole takes that as a sign of stability in every respect—and this confidence is reflected in lower-than-average volatility. This situation is true even when growth is occurring. The average market price might rise, but trading continues to take place in a fairly narrow range with that range gradually increasing over time.

In comparison, when a company's fundamentals are less reliable, the market tends to have less trust in its long-term prospects, and that also is reflected in the degree of price volatility. Some companies exhibit wide swings in the fundamentals. Sales are likely to be widely different from one year to the next, and unusually high profit years might be followed by unusually high losses. When the fundamentals are so volatile from year to year, you are likely to see a corresponding volatility in the price.

This tendency can be called *fundamental volatility* because it is far more important in your analysis than any price volatility. Given the fact that price in the short term is not a reliable indicator of future investment value, it should be abandoned as a primary indicator. Its only real value is as a starting point that should lead to an examination of the fundamentals. So, when a stock's price volatility changes suddenly, it is a smart idea to discover why. Price changes can lead to other information and cannot be ignored altogether. As the means for making actual decisions to buy, sell, or hold, however, price volatility is unreliable. If only because short-term price change can be caused by so many contradictory root causes, it cannot be taken seriously as an analytical tool; but to use an automotive analogy, price volatility can serve as a red light on your investment dashboard telling you to look under the hood and check the fluids.

Recent price volatility, because it is limited to the short term, reveals nothing in and of itself about fundamental value. The two major market philosophies—the Dow Theory and the random walk hypothesis—agree on that singular point because it is so obvious. In virtually every financial paper, however, stock listings include the 52-week high and low price range, which is a summary of volatility in its simple but popular form. Remember the important flaw in popular analytical methods: They are popular because they are simple and easy to understand. It often is also the case that those same forms of analysis are misleading and inaccurate, however. Price volatility is a good example. The 52 weeks in the reported range are short term by nature. In addition, because those 52 weeks go backward from each reporting day, you have no way to identify what occurred in price in the 53rd week before. You also have no way to track the reported period in terms of the company's fiscal cycle or market cycle. The timing of the 52 weeks is rigid, whereas the cyclical considerations could change the entire picture. With these limitations in mind, the real test of volatility should always go back to sales and earnings. The past year's price history tells you nothing about fundamental value, and in fact it can give you misleading information and steer you in the wrong direction.

The market as a whole likes predictability. So, a company whose growth pattern is slow and steady will also have lower volatility in its price history (either short-term or long-term). The real value in a study of price history (meaning several years and not just the past 52 weeks) is in how that price relates to fundamental predictability. As long as a company's sales rise steadily over time and the profit yield on sales is consistent, stockholders take great comfort in that growth pattern. Far more exciting but less predictable is the company whose numbers jump upward and downward all over the board. How can you forecast the growth prospects for such a company, however? Of course, it is impossible based on the unreliable history itself. When sales and profits (or losses) change drastically from one year to another, you have absolutely no basis for forecasting future growth patterns. Fundamentals are likely to be more complex than price, which is why price volatility is popular and widely accepted. Fundamental volatility is the real test of a company's long-term investment value, however.

One problem in a study of the fundamentals is identifying the reliability of current growth patterns. Will these continue into the future, or are they going to level off? Of course, all trends will level off eventually. Nothing rises or falls forever, and it is statistically likely that any trend that is going on today will reduce its rate of change over time. Figure 7.4 provides a simplified view of this tendency.

Note that while this trend is sharply upward, it gradually tapers off. Two things occur in this situation. First, the rate of change slows down, as seen in the illustration; this process is the topping-off or leveling effect. Second, the actual range of change (in the case of stock prices, the trading range) tends to narrow as well. So, in terms of price volatility, the trend would show up as a lowering of price volatility over the long term. This process is called "moving toward the mean" in statistics—a reference to the tendency for trends to average out over time.

This tendency has great significance when applied to fundamental analysis. In spite of what many investors and analysts would like to believe, growth is not unlimited. The characteristics of growth change over time, and growth itself is subject to a few statistical rules. These include the following:

1. *The rate of change levels off and declines over time.* As shown in the illustration, rates of change tend to reduce as time passes. So, an impressive growth rate in a new corporation has to be expected to slow down as time passes for a number of reasons. First, impressive growth rates from a small base are fairly easy to achieve; and with a larger base, duplicating the experience becomes increasingly difficult. With this knowledge in mind, investors should not expect growth rates to remain consistent over time. For most believers in the fundamentals, a steady rate of change

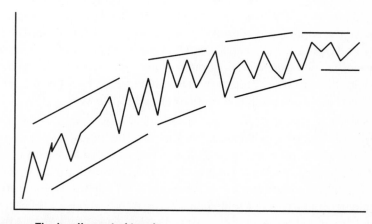

FIGURE 7.4 The leveling out of trends.

over time is adequate, because realistically, investors know about this tendency and they accept it. We are not saying that you will always want to keep your capital invested with one company; you might wish to sell when the leveling off in growth begins to occur and seek out the new emerging-growth candidate.

2. *The degree of change becomes increasingly unlikely as a company expands its size.* One of the problems with expansion, especially if it takes place rapidly, is that the experience itself might inhibit the corporation's capability to repeat its past record. It seems frequently in the market that yesterday's rising star falls out of favor because the numbers level off. So, sales rates are called disappointing even though the slow-down in growth is predictable. And profits, even when consistent and strong, are no longer expanding at past rates. It is a reality, though, that with growth, the rates and degrees of change are going to change. Consider a company that can reasonably expect to generate an additional $1 million in sales each year. Because growth is measured based on past sales, what is the rate of change as sales expand?

BASE	CHANGE	CHANGE
$10 million	$1 million	10.0%
$11 million	$1 million	9.1%
$12 million	$1 million	8.3%

This gradual reduction in the percentage of change, because it is based on ever-growing sales levels of the past year, has to fall over time. This situation does not mean the company is failing to capture new market share; however, it often is reported by Wall Street analysts that sales rates are falling as the company grows. The percentage of growth declines from one year to another, which appears as a negative at first glance. In fact, the dollar value shows that the company is picking up $1 million in new sales every year, which is not a negative at all. There is a flaw in the popular methods of reporting, because it is not realistic to expect that a growing company will be capable of duplicating its *rate* of sales expansion exponentially from one year to another. It should be enough that growth continues, and a troubling sign would be falling or stagnant sales—especially if profits were falling as well.

3. *Trends in a given direction change in a predictable manner but with unpredictable timing.* What makes analysis truly interesting is that change itself is predictable, and change from positive to negative is cyclical. The *timing* of change is far more elusive, however. We know, for example, that corporations experience market cycles and today's strong numbers will be weak at some point in the future. Some cycles have highly predictable cycles, but others experience uncertain timing in their

cyclical change. So, statistically speaking, you have to expect good times as well as bad times for any industry and for any corporation. Knowing precisely when such changes will occur is a different matter. So, analysis depends upon spotting emerging trends before everyone else knows about them and making fast decisions when new information has been discovered.

The importance of recognizing how trends actually work over time points to the advantage of studying fundamental volatility rather than concentrating only on price. It is true that changes in long-term price patterns can serve as symptoms of more subtle changes in the fundamentals. To that extent, watching price trends is valuable. It is really fundamental volatility, however, that defines a company's growth prospects, identifies its expansion pattern, and— most important of all—forecasts the leveling out that certainly is going to occur.

As a long-term investor, it is not enough to purchase shares in a company and then leave them to grow indefinitely. All growth is characterized by change, and eventually today's strongest growth stock will no longer be the same in comparison to others. So, it makes sense to invest in long-term growth companies but then watch the fundamental trends. When growth itself begins to level out, you need to determine whether it makes sense to continue holding shares in that company or move your capital to a smaller company whose potential *rate* of growth is greater. That often means that the investment value itself is also greater. Of course, with greater investment potential comes greater risk. One aspect of the leveling off in the rate of growth is that risk also tends to level off. So, as a long-term investor, you will need to determine whether you want to move your capital to the greater growth potential areas or protect your capital in its appreciated form by keeping it in stock of the more firmly established corporation. Either strategy makes sense as long as you understand the differences.

It comes down to a comparison between companies and a study of the fundamental volatility each will experience. The better-established company will be likely to have a very low degree of fundamental volatility along with a slower rate of growth; and the smaller, emerging long-term growth prospect will exhibit the potential for long-term growth at faster rates but with more risk and a higher degree of fundamental volatility.

Differences between Price and Earnings

The study of trends is essential for every investor, and most successful investors accept the fact that analysis is the real key to consistently beating the averages. The tendency among investors and analysts, however, is to apply the sound principles of trend analysis but to the wrong material. While trend analysis makes sense when studying financial information—sales, profits, capitalization, market share, and so forth—it really makes no sense when applied to the market price of stocks.

It defies logic to believe that market prices can be studied in terms of trend analysis, because volatility and its formula are invariably limited to price movement during the past year. This study is short-term by definition. So, you often find the illogic in the approach itself. An investor might say, "I believe in watching the fundamentals, and I understand how trend analysis can help me make informed decisions." Then, the same person will make an investment decision based on comparisons of price volatility.

This mistake is easy to make. Investors are provided with certain information in the form of stock listings, and the 52-week high and low range is easily found. Volatility as computed is an easy formula, and the conclusions are easily reached. Most investors have the point of view that volatility is easy to understand because it means the same thing when applied to any stock. This belief can lead to problems.

Fallacy: All volatility is the same.

The attributes of price (a technical indicator) and financial information (the fundamentals) are vastly different and cannot be subjected to the same types of analysis. As previously stated, market price is a useful indicator to watch for changes in volatility. As trading ranges change and volatility increases, that might serve as a signal about something changing in the fundamentals; however, because price movement is based on perceptions (and perceptions are more often wrong than right), it cannot be used as a reliable source for making the decision to buy, sell, or hold. A long-term study of price reveals that day-to-day price changes have little to do with the actual long-term trends of a company. The stock price changes with a pendulum effect, tending to swing too high and then too low based on the *facts* about the company. The market, like supply and demand markets, is efficient in many respects. Short-term pricing is not one of those efficient points, however. Speculators recognize the tendency to overreact to just about everything and move in and out of stock positions based on those overreactions. As a long-term investor who believes in the fundamentals, however, using short-term price data is a dangerous idea; it can mislead you into making ill-timed decisions rather than well-informed decisions.

In comparison, the fundamentals have certain attributes and can be studied so that emerging trends are recognized over time. The tendency for long-term growth to plateau is one very dependable factor because it occurs with regularity. Confusing this study is the inevitable merger or acquisition. When companies merge, the trend has to be adjusted so that the long-term field of information reflects the consolidated entity. Otherwise, the whole study loses its meaning and value. When you consolidate historical information, you also discover that the trend itself changes. The previous isolated trend is no longer significant because the combined organization has a different overall growth history.

Just as a sales history tends to move toward the mean, a consolidated history of two merged companies will be more difficult to read. Contrary points average out so that the overall trend is less clear. For example, if one organization is growing at the average rate of $10 million in new sales per year and the acquired company has been growing at the rate of $7.5 million in new sales, the combined record will be difficult to interpret. Complicating the study is the fact that these two entities probably are not the same size in terms of sales, profit, or capital; that they might address different markets and have entirely different fundamental attributes; and that the combined trend is going to move in far different ways that each company moved in the past.

So, trend analysis is not easy when mergers take place. It would make more sense to continue following the trend of each division as it existed prior to the merger, but that presents several problems as well. First, it is difficult to tell how dissimilar trends are affecting the whole organization. Second, the merger itself probably changes the manner in which a trend is going to continue. And third, the value of separating the major divisions of a company is questionable.

The solution is to adjust the overall trend by looking back historically and creating a new trend study, which requires abandoning the prior trend analysis and starting again. In so doing, it also is important to recognize how the merger itself is likely to affect the past trend. For example, if two prior competitors merge, their combined market strength is likely to change the way that the overall organization will operate; thus, the trend will change. If two dissimilar organizations merge, the overall trend will average out the significant factors in prior trends even though they might be entirely different. For example, if the parent company averages a net profit of 8 percent per year and the subsidiary has earned only about 4 percent, the overall profit will be somewhere in between. If both companies had the same sales level, one might expect to see 6 percent net profits; but any variation in the mix of sales volume will distort this expectation. So, if the parent company has sales twice the volume of the subsidiary, the net profit might work out to 7 percent or so.

The complexities of trend analysis are difficult enough for an organization operating within a single market sector. When organizations diversify by branching into different sectors (often through mergers), it complicates the study because the dissimilar features offset one another. It is difficult, for example, to anticipate changes in markets due to business and market cycles when a company has diversified. This situation is intentional on the part of the organization, of course. One purpose in diversifying is to insulate the company from the singular effects of those very cycles. The diversified corporation hopes to achieve expansion by going after market share in several different markets, often with varying and offsetting business cycles.

With these features in mind, it is clear that the methods you use to analyze trends in the fundamentals are going to be far different than the relatively straightforward study of price volatility. For those who are interested in selecting stocks based only on short-term price changes, the study of volatility without detailed analysis is an easy task. The high and low prices for the year define the trading range and thus define relative volatility of the stock. Higher volatility means more risk and lower volatility means more safety (so the argument goes). Even a study of price volatility should include an analysis of the patterns, causes, and exceptions within the price range, however. As previously demonstrated, a volatile one-year history can be interpreted in several different ways.

The commonly held belief that all volatility is the same needs to be examined and questioned. It is more accurate to replace that belief with another: Volatility has several different meanings, and price volatility is far different than fundamental volatility. In either case, the initial conclusion needs to be examined in more detail before any conclusions can be reached. Price volatility is of limited value, because it can act as a signal of change in the fundamentals. That is the extent of its value.

Conclusions Based on Fundamental Volatility

In studying the fundamentals in terms of sales and earnings volatility, it makes sense to question the root causes of inconsistent sales and profits. When a company reports big jumps in earnings one year followed by declines the next, with corresponding variation between profit and loss, that is a big problem for investors. How can anyone forecast the future for such an organization? No one can tell what kind of sales trend is underway because no trend has emerged.

Just as a company that has never reported a profit cannot be analyzed, a company whose fundamentals change drastically from one year to the next is equally as puzzling. When there is no profit, there is no PE ratio, no dividend record, and no way to forecast growth. When a company reports inconsistent sales and profits, it is a sign that management is not in control. You might expect large jumps in the numbers for a year or two of big expansion, but matters should settle down rather quickly after that initial burst. Remember, trends move toward the mean, and in order to be able to forecast future fundamental change, you need to begin with dependable raw material. Thus, you expect sales to come through with some consistency and profits to follow suit. If this process is not taking place for several years in a row, then there is likely to be a problem at the top. Intelligent management often is misunderstood; its function and purpose is not perceived from the outside in realistic terms. Management's task is not only to create bigger market share and expansion. It goes beyond that. Management should also protect and reassure stockholders, who like consistency and dependability. Thus, sales and profits should be reported in a way that makes forecasting possible and fair. In that respect, management is supposed to *control* growth so that it doesn't occur so rapidly that the corporation cannot support its new base. It occurs all too often that uncontrolled growth leads to strains on capitalization, a decline in customer or client service, and lower profits during times of higher sales—all due to management's inability to control the rate and type of growth.

This situation raises a potential problem, of course. If management's primary job is to protect the stockholder (meaning maintenance and improvement of the stock's market price over time), then how much control does management exert over the reporting of sales and profits? The accounting rules for reporting are flexible enough that companies are given some latitude in interpreting its own numbers. Independent accountants will sign off on some management decisions as long as they can find a way to justify management's decisions within the accounting rules. For example, a company that has shown consistent growth might experience exceptionally high sales and profits one year. Management perceives correctly, however, that this phenomenon is a one-time deal that will not be repeated. If the high sales and profits are reported, stockholders will expect a repeat of that change the following year, and when it does not happen, it will be taken as a negative sign. In other words, the inconsistency from year to year rattles Wall Street, so it is more desirable to report sales and profit growth in line with the past trend.

While actual manipulation of the books is illegal and deceptive, the accounting rules do provide for some adjustments in reported sales and profits. For example, a portion can be deferred to the following year as long as there is some justification for doing so. A company might increase its bad debt reserve to reduce sales and profits or change its method for valuing inventory, for example. The practice of putting off sales and profits to future periods, often called "sugar bowling," might not be frowned upon by the regulatory agencies as long as the company is not thought to be deceiving stockholders. It is a far greater problem when a company accrues income in a lower than average year, because there is no guarantee that higher sales will come through in the future. So, the practice of beefing up the sales and profit numbers is seen as a far more serious adjustment of the numbers.

The truth is that management and independent auditors do make adjustments for several reasons in the release of financial information. As long as there is no outright deception in this practice, the rules allow for some adjustments. From the stockholder's point of view, the consistency of sales and profits makes prediction easier. So, in reality, if some sales and profits are deferred during exceptionally high-volume years and the result is more dependable forecasting, then no one has been harmed. Cycles tend to make forecasting difficult, and trends are less reliable when the numbers change too frequently. So, in some respects, changing the reported outcome can be beneficial both to the company and to its stockholders. As long as the independent auditor is satisfied that adjustments fall within the acceptable range, and as long as the *Securities and Exchange Commission* (SEC) agrees, the stockholder is protected. A deception usually refers to exaggerated reports; the relatively harmless practice of under-reporting outcome has more benefits than consequences.

CHAPTER 8

Using Other Peoples' Money

Leverage is a popular idea among investors. On paper at least, the return on investment looks more promising when a limited amount of capital is expanded. There is also the unavoidable question of risk, however, and that is where the idea of leverage becomes more troubling.

As a general rule, *leverage* means using a capital base as collateral to borrow money for investment. For example, when a homeowner puts a down payment on a property, the down payment is collateral—usually representing only a small portion of total value. The balance, the mortgage obligation, is leveraged money because it was borrowed. For most homeowners, this method is the only way that a home would be affordable. Few people can save enough money to pay cash for their homes, so using leverage is normal and acceptable. It is not the same for stockholders, however. With leverage comes more risk and more danger in experiencing a loss.

Leverage can be thought of as a third method to investing, the first two being equity and debt. With equity, you buy tangible value such as shares of stock or real property. With debt, you lend your money to someone else and receive interest payment, such as through the purchase of bonds. These two well-known examples can be achieved through the use of money in hand or on deposit, or the third method, leverage, can be employed. With leverage, you use a small amount of capital to increase your holdings. The theory is that by putting more money in the investment, you will gain more in profits.

The nature of equity investments bought and paid for in full is different than equity that is leveraged. If you pay full price for shares of stock, you exchange one asset for another. If that asset grows in value, you have a profit; if it falls, you lose. But with leverage, a profit is not enough. You will need enough profit to pay interest on the borrowed funds plus a profit that is adequate to meet your investment goals. Your profit has to be greater when you use leverage, and that often leads to problems because equity securities are not always going to behave as you would like.

The same argument applies to debt investments. The interest you receive from a bond issuer has to be equal to or greater than the interest you pay to borrow money. Even then, you are at risk. If interest rates rise after you buy a bond, the market value of the bond could be discounted, so you would not be able to close out the position without a loss. Given the fact that bonds reflect current market rates, it is unlikely that you would be able to leverage capital and buy bonds at a profit. Invariably, the cost of borrowing money will be higher than the interest on a debt investment. A bond paying higher rates would probably be rated so poorly that the risks are not justified.

The risk associated with leverage makes it suitable for only a minority of all investors. If you are willing to accept the higher than average risks, it probably means that you have great faith that the market is going to rise in the very near future. If you are wrong, you will lose; if you are right, you make bigger profits by leveraging than you would by only buying what you could afford to pay for at the time of purchase.

An attitude among stock market investors is that leverage is a sophisticated technique used by all smart investors and that the "real money" is to be made by using other people's money. This high-rolling approach is high in risk to say the least. It might even be foolish given the uncertainties of the market. Leverage, like all forms of speculation, is a dangerous approach to investing and certainly makes no sense whatsoever if you plan to buy and hold securities for the long term. It makes far more sense to buy in increments as you can afford to buy and to leave the use of leverage to the speculator. In respect to the risk itself, leverage is a form of speculation taken to its highest level. It is risky enough to lose all of your money; when the loss leaves you in debt as well, it puts the whole idea in perspective.

The Inaccuracy of Leverage Examples

Anyone who has listened to the sales pitches for leverage knows that the promises are highly suspect, to say the least. If you believe that you hear from the promoters, leverage in real estate, for example, is a sure way to make millions by using no money of your own.

The typical example begins with a false premise and then proceeds, emphasizing the potential for profit while completely ignoring all forms of risk. In the typical sales pitch, you are told that you can buy distressed properties out of foreclosure for nothing down. As good as that sounds, it makes sense to ask, "Why is the property in foreclosure?" If there were any real equity in that property, it is doubtful that an owner or lender would be willing to get rid of it. A distressed property often means that the problems go beyond the mere nonpayment of the mortgage. The property could have structural problems that would cost so much to fix that there is negative equity in the property. The neighborhood could be so dangerous that no properties will grow in value and you will have problems keeping dependable tenants in the property or finding another buyer. Other problems might be less obvious just looking at the facts. If anyone was murdered in the home or committed suicide, for example, that inhibits anyone's ability to sell the property—and, in many states, those events have to be disclosed. So, it could be that a property is distressed because its marketability is at zero.

Beyond the flaws of the initial premise, you are next told that you can turn around and borrow money against the property and use that to buy more properties at foreclosure auction or directly from the government. While some programs exist for moving foreclosed properties in this manner and with minimal down payment, you still need to evaluate the idea realistically. For example, how will you make payments on the property? Will rental be adequate to cover the mortgage? What is the rental demand in the area? Many questions come up when dealing with property and when considering becoming a landlord. To listen to the sales pitch, all you have to do is buy and sell property and take your profits to the bank. In practice, you have to work harder to make distressed properties profitable, and in some cases, it cannot be done. That is why they are being sold for nothing down.

When you get to the point of trying to sell a property, you face yet another problem. Can you sell the property at a profit, or can you even sell it at all? In many cases, owners who cannot afford to meet their mortgage obligations will sell the house. Few people with equity will be willing to just walk away and get nothing. So, when a house is up for sale through foreclosure, chances are there is going to be a problem in selling the property as well.

The programs for leverage make it sound as though you can use equity to pick up more and more houses in this way. In theory, you could own dozens of foreclosed properties and pocket thousands of dollars per month. In practice, you will run into problems getting financing for more than four properties, just due to restrictions placed upon lenders. So, picking up foreclosed properties is naturally limited by the lending market as well as by practical constraints.

Some programs also like to discuss the tremendous tax benefits in owning property. You are allowed to write off depreciation, interest, utilities, property taxes, and other expenses related to rentals. The promoters do not tell you that the maximum loss you can claim in any one year from real estate activity is $25,000, however. The excess has to be carried over and applied to future years. So, even if you could own dozens of foreclosed properties, the tax benefits would be limited each year. It is more likely that you would end up with negative cash flow and minimal profits. When you buy distressed properties, a good rule of thumb is to understand that you also are buying the "distress" portion of the property. Along with the potential for gain come many headaches.

Leverage of that type simply does not work, either in real estate or in the stock market. By federal law, you are not allowed to indefinitely leverage stocks up by borrowing more and more money. If it were possible, there is no doubt that some speculators would be willing to use leverage to get as much stock as possible in the belief that a rising market is going to continue forever. This situation points out the major flaw of leverage and investor thinking: In a rising market, it is easy to believe that the trend will continue forever. Thus, it is easy to fall into the trap of over-committing to a particular investment market. If it becomes possible to use leverage, that over-commitment can be extended even farther. Rising markets never last forever, however, and ultimately the leveraged portfolio is the most vulnerable to reversals. The more you have borrowed to invest, the more disastrous the losses will be.

There is a tendency as markets peak for more and more inexperienced and first-time investors to enter the market. The news that prices are reaching all-time high levels and that investors are getting rich invariably attracts new investors. Many people get into the market for the first time in such conditions. If they are placing their capital at risk, however, that is one thing; if they are also borrowing money and placing it at risk, then they are in far more danger. So, as a general observation, leverage as it often is promoted simply does not work. The opportunity is emphasized, but the realities and the risks are ignored. And finally, the higher risks associated with leverage make it a dangerous strategy. If you use leverage to invest, you should also be fully aware of the potential for loss.

Leverage and the Regulatory Environment

Even with the high risks of leverage, it remains a popular idea among investors. To understand why leverage is so popular, we have to examine the nature of market cycles and how investors react to them. When markets are falling, the market is ruled by fear. Not knowing how far prices are going to fall, many people sell at the lowest strata of the market. When markets are rising, the fear is replaced by euphoria and greed in an unrealistic belief that the market will continue rising indefinitely. As a result, many investors buy at the top of the market just before the cycle turns around. So, the advice to "buy low and sell high" should be followed by a second part: "instead of the other way around."

The old saying is more profound than it might seem at first. In essence, it means that investors should observe the cycles of the market and resist their emotional reactions, investing in a contrary manner. So, when most people are fearful, it means the market is at or near a bottom, and it is time to take the contrary step of buying stock at bargain prices. When most people are optimistic and buying stock as quickly as they can, the contrary person begins selling shares, recognizing the potential for a sudden turnaround.

The idea of leverage usually shows up in rising markets. As prices reach their cyclical top, more and more investors want to "get in on the treasure hunt," so they want to buy as many shares as they can. With their capital resources committed already, one alternative is to commit those shares as collateral and borrow money to buy even more shares. Working through a brokerage account, this activity—buying on margin—involves interest payments on the borrowed funds. That is not a problem as long as prices continue rising. In theory, leverage makes perfect sense as long as the value of invested capital climbs. The trick is all in timing, however. How do you know when the market is topping out? The leveraged investor is continually at risk because prices could begin falling at any time. It often happens that significant paper profits evaporate more quickly than they appeared, and leveraged capital is lost in an unexpected margin call.

Investors attracted to leverage should also recognize the risks of that strategy. The more leverage, the higher the risk. We have all seen illustrations of how the use of borrowed money can increase profits exponentially, and on paper it all looks and sounds good. But fortunes have been lost in the market when the up trend ends and the down trend begins. Risks are always the greatest at market peaks, and those are the times when optimism is most likely to blind investors to the pending change. Of course, the precise turnaround moment is only visible in hindsight, and again, it is the timing that spells the difference between a handsome profit and a complete disaster.

Leveraged investing tends to offset all of the advantages gained through diversification. In one respect, it is fair to say that leverage is the opposite of diversification. With a diversified portfolio, risks are spread among different risk-profile areas—stocks, sectors, fundamental attributes, or markets—and in the event of loss in one area, the balance of the portfolio is supposed to protect your position. Leverage, however, involves having more money invested than you have available. Thus, a leveraged portfolio is entirely at risk of loss in the event of a general fall in prices, even if leveraged capital is invested in a traditionally defined form of diversification. Because market-wide price trends tend to follow the leaders, an overall rise or fall in prices is most likely to be widespread. So, a diversified portfolio that involved leverage is likely to lose value along with the rest of the market. Because a portion of capital has been borrowed, the losses also tend to accumulate rather quickly, resulting in losses the investor cannot afford.

Even with federal regulation limiting the amount of margin leverage you can use, the maximum use of the margin account does place the entire portfolio at risk. At the very least, the risks of leverage should be mitigated by using only a portion of the overall capital resource to leverage (if it is to be undertaken at all).

The regulation covering how much a brokerage firm can lend to a customer to purchase securities in a margin account is called Regulation T. This regulation grows out of the Securities Exchange Act of 1934.[1] The exact margin requirements are covered in Section 220.12 of the Act.

The Securities Exchange Act of 1934 authorized the formation of the SEC and provided it with the authority to regulate the entire securities industry. This act also established rules and standards for financial reporting, insider trading, tender offers, registration of securities, and more. The act forms the basis for most of the regulatory requirements imposed on publicly listed companies and on brokerage firms, including limitations on the use of leverage. This regulation includes oversight of the industry's self-regulatory agencies, such as the *National Association of Securities Dealers* (NASD).

Regulation T is such an important feature of the rules governing leverage because without that regulation, there would be no way to limit potential losses. Market crashes and adjustments are inevitable, and many investors would leverage so far beyond their resources that ultimately, huge losses would result. Many brokerage firms would also allow unbridled leverage without the regulatory restraints, as history has shown. The failure to recognize the inherent risks of excessive leverage is not limited to individual investors; brokerage firms have facilitated losses in the past by failing to self-impose limitations on the degree of risk their customers are allowed to take. So, in respect to the limitations imposed by Regulation T, the SEC, in enforcing the act, provides investors with a valuable service—even if that service means limiting their risk exposure through regulation.

TIP

The entire text of Regulation T, including margin requirements, is provided at the Web site www.bankinfo.com/Regs-aag/reg12220.html.

TIP

The entire text of the Securities Exchange Act of 1934 can be viewed at www.law.uc.edu/CCL/34Act/. A useful overview of the laws governing brokerage firms and stock exchanges is found at the SEC Web site at www.sec.gov/about/laws.shtml.

Were the decision left to brokerage firms and their customers (investors), who would decide how much leverage is safe and affordable? The limitations make sense, because in a rising market it becomes easy to believe that prices will continue rising. The "greed factor" would enable many investors to expose themselves to risk and to profit in the short term and also to accumulate sudden and devastating losses. Given the opportunity to do so, it is fair to say that some individuals would not use good judgment. The same is true for the brokerage firms that would ultimately end up having to pay for the losses that their customers would accumulate through leverage.

Leverage at the Corporate Level

The temptation to leverage as much as possible refers not only to individuals but also to corporations. Leverage is not restricted to the individual, because many corporations use a form of leverage to capitalize growth—often to the detriment of their stockholders.

Capitalization refers to the total capital available to the corporation. It might come from selling stock or from issuing bonds (as well as other forms of debt, such as borrowing from conventional lenders). From the corporate point of view, leverage makes a certain amount of sense as long as the use of borrowed funds is likely to produce profits that exceed the cost of borrowing. For example, if corporate management believes that its net profits would exceed 8 percent after taxes and it can borrow money through issuing bonds at 6 percent, then using leverage is a smart idea. The risk factor should be considered, however. How certain is management that 8 percent growth is possible? Is the risk worth the margin of 2 percent?

The danger to the corporation is that the cost of interest as well as repayment of the obligation will be unaffordable if the expansion plans are not as profitable as was hoped. If the interest cost exceeds additional profits, then the whole idea turns out to be a loss. It does not show up as a loss, however, and this point is where the astute investor can evaluate corporate performance unrealistically. Net profits might be higher than in the past but at a lower rate; thus, at first glance it looks as though the corporation is performing at a higher level of profit, when in fact more of those profits are going to interest payments. This situation means less profits left over for further expansion or for dividend payments to stockholders.

As you analyze corporate performance, one combined trend worth watching is the net profit trend along with the debt ratio. If the dollar value of net profits expands but the return on sales falls, that itself should serve as a red flag; however, it can be caused by any number of problems, some short-term in nature and some internal to the company. Some forms of expansion also mean higher costs and expenses, so net profits could be affected during periods of significant growth. When lower returns are accompanied by a growing ratio of debt to total capitalization, however, the signs are more troubling. If the corporation is coming to depend more on lenders, that means ever-growing payments of interest and shrinking profits.

The net operating profit (or profit from operations) is the profit before payment of interest to bondholders and other lenders. Tracking the operating profit is revealing in some aspects, and it reports a trend that is valuable for long-term growth forecasting. Net profit, however—the profit after interest and taxes—is equally important. The trend that shows up in the net profit number might be of more immediate concern to you if you want long-term growth prospects to continue strongly. If the company is replacing equity capitalization with debt capitalization and the result is lower returns on sales, however, that trend is highly negative.

Corporations should use leverage only when the additional profits it creates exceed the cost of leverage. As an analyst of your own portfolio, the ratio between equity and debt capitalization should be monitored carefully to spot subtle shifts in profitability trends. Even when profits are marginally higher due to leverage, you should also be concerned if the continued use of debt makes sense. Should the company expose itself to risks of leverage for marginal gains? If a down turn in the sector were to mean lower profits, then the decision to leverage could quickly turn from a marginal gain to a large loss.

As an investor in that company, you might decide to sell your shares and look for a company with a more conservative approach to capitalization. The problems of leverage do not always show up in the numbers but exist in the potential for loss in the comparison between the degree of profit and the ongoing risk of losses. So, even when the numbers are moving in a positive direction, meaning a growing dollar amount of profit with a sustained return on sales, if the debt ratio is climbing your question should be, "Does it make sense to take this risk?" This situation is especially troubling with long-term bonds. If the company's bond debt increases each year, the risk level increases as well.

It makes sense to keep debt capitalization at a moderate level, and the analysis should look for situations where debt commitments are growing each year. If the corporation has to continue issuing new bonds to continue financing growth, that could spell trouble later when the growth curve gets to a plateau and profits level out. At that time, the higher debt service and interest expense could begin eroding profits so that equity investors will suffer as a consequence. In spotting the emerging trend of marginal profits combined with expanding debt capitalization, you might decide to move your invested capital elsewhere. This situation is an example of how corporate leverage can lead to trouble later in terms of investment value for the corporation's stockholders.

The Risks of Leverage

Your awareness of risk defines your ability to invest successfully in many respects. We cannot depend on the regulatory agencies to fully protect us from others nor from our own lack of awareness of risk. Those investors who are taken by surprise when the market declines find themselves in the position of not being aware of investment risks until too late. This situation is true in all forms of investing, but when it comes to the use of leverage, it is critical to be aware of the potential of both gain *and* loss.

The risks associated with leverage are most severe in rising markets. Ironically, when the mood of the market is the most optimistic, the dangers are greatest. Anyone who has not been through all types of markets might think the opposite. And in practice, investors do tend to think that their exposure to risk is greatest when markets are falling because they worry about the loss of value in their portfolios. In a rising market, however, a leveraged portfolio is exposed to greater-than-average danger because the invested capital is not the extent of risk exposure. The real exposure consists of your total capital plus borrowed funds.

As markets rise and portfolios gain value, the tendency is to extend the risk to the maximum and to borrow as much as possible. So, an investor with $10,000 invested would borrow another $10,000 in the belief that the larger sum will produce twice the profits. As long as the market continues to rise, this statement will be true. As experienced investors have discovered, however, a change in the direction of the market happens very suddenly. A rising market becomes a falling market, often not in gradual stages that everyone sees coming but with sudden surprise. One trading day, the market is safe and secure; and the next, it is falling like a rock.

The rising market is a risky environment for any investor who cannot afford to place money at risk plus borrow even more money to increase that risk. Such a market is suitable for speculators who know the dangers and are willing to time their decisions, hoping to get out before the market peak has been reached. Leverage through a margin account is rarely appropriate for investors whose goals are long-term in nature. If you want to find companies whose prospects for long-term growth are better than average, borrowing money to buy shares does not make sense.

When you have capital invested as markets rise, your portfolio value rises as well. When the market turns around and takes a fall, however, that paper profit tends to evaporate quickly. If you have all of your capital invested for the long term, you can afford to ride the waves of the market—secure in the belief that over the long term, your investment decisions will prove to be profitable. If your decisions were based on a study of fundamentals and the indicators remain strong, then you have nothing to fear from the short-term gyrations of the market. You know that even the strongest stocks are going to follow those day-to-day trends, and when severe changes take place, all stocks are affected.

If you have borrowed on margin to increase your portfolio value in a rising market, however, you find yourself in trouble if the value suddenly falls. If the required margin value falls below the Regulation T level, your brokerage firm will issue a margin call. In other words, you will have to deposit additional funds or securities to cover the shortfall. If you do not have extra capital available, the brokerage firm will sell your securities to minimize their risk of loss. Obviously, as values continue to fall, you will be required to deposit more and more cash or other securities to cover your position. So, as a very basic starting point, you would not be able to afford to borrow on margin unless you could cover yourself in the event of a margin call.

That risk alone is not worth exposure for the majority of investors. For example, if you have a $10,000 portfolio and you borrow another $10,000 on margin, you actually risk having to liquidate other assets in the event of market losses. So, if you lose half the value in your $20,000 portfolio, you remain indebted to the brokerage firm for the original $10,000 borrowed. Your margin call will require a deposit of an additional $10,000 or immediate liquidation of the entire portfolio. At that point, your net value will be zero.

So, with half the portfolio borrowed, losses are doubled as well. Losing 50 percent of overall value means you actually have lost 100 percent of your equity. With this knowledge in mind, the truth about margin investing becomes glaringly obvious: You double the potential for profit, and you also double the risk of loss. The degree of change is doubled, given the previous example, for better *and* for worse. Those investors who think leverage is a good idea see borrowing money as a way to double up on their gains, but they can easily overlook the reverse side of that potential—the doubling up and acceleration of losses.

Another risk in margin investing—one that is easily overlooked—is the need for your investments to become profitable more quickly and to a greater degree. As long as you are obligated to pay interest on your margin account, you not only risk loss in the event of a fall in the market but you also have to earn enough profit in your portfolio to pay for brokerage fees for buying and selling (as well as interest on the borrowed portion of your portfolio). Beyond these costs, you still need to make enough profit to justify the decision to invest with borrowed money.

The need to achieve a profit with borrowed funds is significant. In Chapter 4, the break-even requirements with taxes and inflation in mind were explained. This definition has to be expanded for the investor borrowing money for another element: interest. The calculation of break-even in these circumstances deals only with the requirements to keep your after-cost spending power. It does not consider the significant risk of loss, however, nor does the rate of return take brokerage fees into account. So, the real "net net" requirement with borrowed money has to be after inflation, taxes, interest, and trading fees. Collectively, that requires significant growth in your portfolio.

A revised chart showing the break-even for taxes, inflation, and interest at various rates is provided in Table 8.1.

In this calculation, the factor 'i' takes on a greater role. When it represented inflation alone, it was singular in its effect on break-even. When you add inter-

TABLE 8.1 Break-Even Chart Including Interest Expense

Tax rate	Rate of Inflation Plus Interest				
	6	7	8	9	10
22	7.7%	9.0%	10.3%	11.5%	12.8%
25	8.0	9.3	10.7	12.0	13.3
28	8.3	9.7	11.1	12.5	13.9
31	8.7	10.1	11.6	13.0	14.5
34	9.1	10.6	12.1	13.6	15.2
37	9.5	11.1	12.7	14.3	15.9
40	10.0	11.7	13.3	15.0	16.7
43	10.5	12.3	14.0	15.8	17.5
46	11.1	13.0	14.8	16.7	18.5
49	11.8	13.7	15.7	17.6	19.6

est to be charged for borrowing on margin, the demand for break-even becomes even more problematic.

For example, let's assume that you believe inflation will be only 2 percent over the coming year. Your brokerage firm charges 7 percent for margin borrowing. That means that you need to use the value of 9 in the top half of the break-even formula (2 percent inflation plus 7 percent interest). As shown in the table, the break-even varies by effective tax rate. If your combined federal, state, and local income tax rates add up to 40 percent, you will need to gain a 15 percent return in your portfolio *just to break even.*

Considering the exposure to loss in the event that your portfolio loses value (increased as a result of borrowing part of the portfolio value), the risk is tremendous. If your overall portfolio value were to rise by an annualized rate of 15 percent after trading fees, you would maintain value only and would not have any profit whatsoever. So, the question becomes, "Is it worth the exposure to loss to borrow money to invest?" When you consider the required rate of return just to break even, most people would agree that margin investing makes no sense.

There is a popular myth in the market that smarter investors know how to make more money by using leverage and that margin investors are smarter and make more money than the average person.

Fallacy: Sophisticated investors always trade on margin.

This fallacy is widespread. It is also false. The numbers simply don't support the contention that it makes sense to use margin investing. In some circumstances, it stands to reason that someone would want to expose himself or herself to risk for the short term, maximize his or her portfolio value, and take profits quickly. These circumstances would be rare rather than undertaken as a matter of standard practice, however. In addition, an investor who would borrow on margin, even for the short term, should also be aware of the risks involved and of the required rate of return just to break even. If your break-even is 15 percent annualized return, how much potential return makes the risk worthwhile?

For the average investor, leverage in the form of borrowing money in a margin account would be a rare step. The truth is, even the most sophisticated investor would avoid expanding risk exposure. The sophistication that an individual gains through experience teaches that taking on unreasonable risks does not make sense. The belief that sophisticated investors always use margin accounts and invest with other people's money has to be abandoned, and a different fact must be observed: With experience, investors learn how to avoid risk. It is unlikely that experience leads to expansion of risk exposure; if anything, market experience tends to make investors more conservative.

The Realities of Leverage

An inexperienced investor is likely to believe that get-rich-quick schemes make sense if only because that investor has not experienced losses or known how quickly they can occur. The accelerated rate of loss or gain that takes place when a portfolio is leveraged means both greater opportunity *and* greater risk.

One persistent belief in the stock market, even among those with investing experience, is that leverage is the way to accumulate wealth quickly. For some, it is a matter of choosing to believe a fallacy that simply is not true; for others, it is generally assumed that when it comes to accumulating wealth quickly, you have to go into debt.

Fallacy: Leverage is the best way to get rich quickly.

Leverage does not belong in most portfolios for the reasons already stated: the risks are simply too great. Also, leverage places a demand for better-than-average performance just to cover trading costs plus the triple problem of inflation, taxes, and interest on borrowed money.

If the plan is a good one—meaning that the investments picked with leverage will double or triple in value—it still doesn't mean that leverage is a good plan. For example, the assumptions could be right but the timing wrong. Some stocks will grow in value, given other market conditions that are assumed to occur. So, if you use leverage when the market in general is rising, the market condition can only help accelerate the growth in those stocks you buy. If the market peaks and then begins falling after you commit your leveraged portfolio, however, even the best stocks are vulnerable; their market value might fall as well in the short term.

The short term in a market reversal can mean a few trading hours, days, weeks, or months. The timing in the market is perhaps the most difficult part, and for this reason long-term strategies and analysis make sense—whereas most short-term strategies are prone to error. So, the timing of the decision to use leverage makes it a greater problem. Besides having to cover interest costs, you also need to have the outcome take place in a relatively short period of time. Because interest accrues from day to day, you are continuously losing money when you have open positions in a margin account. As long as you owe money to the brokerage firm, you have to be able to afford the interest. This situation usually means that you are depending on the stocks' market value to rise rapidly. That does not always occur.

The mistaken belief that leverage is the path to fast riches in the market is also a dangerous belief. Perhaps a more accurate statement is, "With leverage, you can gain fast profits or fast losses. It is also possible that your capital will be eroded over time by ever-growing interest expense related to borrowing money to invest."

Stock market leverage is far different than the kind of leverage taken by homeowners for a number of reasons:

1. When you borrow money to buy your own home, you are allowed to write off interest and property taxes so that tax benefits discount your actual interest costs.

2. You are making payments to a mortgage lender instead of to a landlord. In other words, you do not necessarily take on an additional obligation, just a change in where the payment goes.

3. Because you live in the property, you take care of it and keep it in good condition, which maintains market value.

4. A well-selected and well-cared for home will increase in value over time based on historical information.

5. The investment in your home is insured with homeowners' property.

In comparison, borrowing money to invest in stocks is always more speculative, even with conservative strategies and long-term growth stocks. Carefully picked stocks will increase in value, of course, but in the short term their value could remain at current levels for many months or even fall when the market is soft. Unlike the necessity of a house, stocks are by nature higher-risk. When you buy a house, you take steps to reduce and eliminate risk. When you buy shares of stock, you willingly expose yourself to risk in exchange for the opportunity presented.

Leverage works to the homeowner's advantage. Waiting until the entire amount is available to pay cash for housing is impractical. With values growing in housing each year, a savings account would not keep pace; so buying a house with the majority in borrowed funds makes sense and works as an inflation-fighting asset.

Housing has traditionally beat inflation, so it also makes sense that the combination of increasing equity and tax benefits will exceed the net cost of borrowing money. A stockholder cannot make the same arguments when part of the portfolio has been borrowed. When you open a position, you are supposed to understand the risks. In some cases, it takes time for current values to increase—and in the meantime, they might also fall in value. As interest continues to accumulate against margin account balances, leveraged investors find themselves in a most undesirable position: having to make interest payments regularly while their portfolios are stagnant, and even worse, having to put more cash or securities on deposit in the event that values fall and margin calls are issued to the investor.

The two types of investments—home ownership and stocks—are vastly different in many respects, including the nature of leverage. Even so, the home ownership scenario often is used as an example of why it makes sense to use borrowed money to invest in the stock market. It is a flawed argument. Some investors have erred when talked into increasing their mortgage debt (through refinancing or use of equity lines of credit) to invest in the stock market. This advice is usually poor. It is a misuse of home equity to place capital at risk. Consider these points:

1. *Conversion of equity is also a conversion from low risk to high risk.* The principal aspect of borrowing home equity in order to invest is the conversion of your capital base from a relatively low-risk investment (your own home) to a very high-risk investment (stocks purchased with the use of leverage). As a general rule, stock investments are considered to be moderate risks as long as investments are carefully selected by using sound methods. Using borrowed money, however, whether through a margin account or with converted home equity, changes everything. In this situation, stocks become high-risk because of the requirement that you earn much higher returns and in a faster turnaround period.

2. *The debt service (mortgage payment) will continue for many years whether or not the investment plan works out.* Remember that when you convert home equity into cash and then invest that cash in the market, you will need to make higher mortgage payments for many years. If you refinance your 30-year mortgage, your monthly payment has to be made for the full 30 years. It often is argued that refinancing also means that your payments go down (if interest rates have fallen), but when you recommit to a 30-year mortgage, your overall interest commitment is going to be higher. Is it a reasonable risk to expose your equity to the stock market? Given the higher and longer-term debt service associated with borrowing money secured by your home equity, this situation represents a significant risk—usually higher than most people realize.

3. *Higher payment threatens the security of your home ownership investment and strains your personal budget.* When you take out an equity

line of credit or refinance your mortgage, you are borrowing money secured by home equity. As long as your payments increase or the term of your repayment is extended, you are placing a strain on your budget and putting your family's equity and security at risk. One purpose in home ownership is supposed to be the accumulation of home equity. It takes a long time considering that most payments in the early years go predominantly to interest; in fact, the typical 30-year mortgage is only half paid off by the 25th year. So, when you refinance and start the term over again, you are making three changes. First, you extend your personal obligation and payment term for more time. Second, you expose your capital in a higher-risk environment. And third, you are at the very least converting your home equity to profit for the lender.

4. *This use of leverage is not as safe as it seems at first glance.* Availability of funds is not the same thing as low risk in spite of promotions to the contrary. The promotions trying to get homeowners to refinance or take out a line of credit often include statements like, "Put your idle home equity to work." It is important to realize that your equity is not idle when allowed to accumulate in your own home, however. It should gain value over time, and borrowing against it only exposes you to ever-growing risks. The ads put out by lenders and the prompting by advisors often confuses the differences between availability of capital and low risk. We are told that we can take our equity out of our homes and put it to work, which sounds simple and virtually free of risk. It is inaccurate to refer to borrowed money as "your" money, however. The only way to take equity out of your home is to sell the home. Any steps involving new mortgages or lines of credit also represent the use of equity, and if that equity loses value, you will end up with a higher mortgage and less equity.

5. *The usual market risk associated with the stock market is accelerated unreasonably when using converted equity.* Investors often are told that investing in stocks makes more sense than real estate because the opportunity to make a profit is greater. The other side of the equation often is forgotten, of course—that losses could occur more quickly as well. No matter how much risk you assume to be related to investments in the stock market, they are considerably higher when you use converted equity. A hidden cost of borrowing equity should be kept in mind, and when you calculate the real costs, you discover that you need to do far better than average just to cover higher interest. For example, if you use an equity line of credit to invest in stocks and your interest rate is 7 percent, that means that you need to earn a minimum of 7 percent after trading costs just to cover your equity line of credit debt service. This situation does not take into account the extra burdens of taxes and inflation. Referring back to the chart earlier in this chapter, if you assume that

inflation is 2 percent and your effective tax rate is 40 percent, then you need to earn 15 percent on your stock investments just to break even. In this situation, you should ask whether it is reasonable to place your equity at risk, given the real problems of getting that kind of return consistently and given the overall exposure to the usual market risks. Using another example, let's say that you refinance and are able to pull out $20,000 while keeping your payments at about the same level. That is possible if interest rates today are considerably lower than when you first committed yourself to the original mortgage. At first glance, it would seem that this transaction is risk-free. You free up $20,000, and your mortgage payments don't change. In reality, however, you begin your mortgage term all over; and in the early years, almost nothing goes to principal. So, by extending your mortgage term, you are also extending your overall commitment and increasing the total interest you will have to pay over the full term.

A calculation of the differences is revealing. Let's say that you had $80,000 that you took out 15 years ago when you purchased your home for $100,000. The interest rate was 8.5 percent, and monthly payments have been $615.14. Today, your mortgage balance is approximately $62,400. Your home is worth about $150,000 today, which is $50,000 higher than when you purchased it.

At today's lower 6.5 percent rates, you could refinance your mortgage to $95,000 and your monthly payments would be $600.47, about $15 per month *less* than you're paying now. So, the mortgage payment goes down but you free up about $30,000 (assuming that you also have to pay some closing costs, the actual cash out of the deal has to be reduced somewhat). Where is the down side? In fact, there *is* a down side. Under your original mortgage term, your total interest for the 30-year mortgage would be $141,450. As of the end of the first 15 years, you have already paid $93,125. The calculation is as follows:

$615.14 x 180 months = $110,725.20

Equity is $17,600 ($80,000 – $62,400), so the difference is interest:

$110,725 – $17,600 = $93,125

By refinancing now, you recommit to 30 years. Although the rate is lower, the interest on this mortgage will be $121,169 over the next 30 years. That added to interest you already paid in the amount of $93,125 increases your total interest to $214,294 over 30 years. The original interest commitment with your 8.5 percent loan was $141,450. So now, the difference is as follows:

$214,294 – $141,450 = $72,844

Can you be sure that the $30,000 you could free up by refinancing would justify the higher interest *and* the additional 15 years of commitment to a mortgage? If you believe that your plans for the use of leveraged money in these conditions will work out, then at least you are aware of the risk factor. Before proceeding, that is an essential step. Problems arise when investors do *not* understand the risks to which they expose themselves. The advantage of leverage in this example is that, unlike the margin account, you are not vulnerable if the market goes through a big down turn. Your mortgage lender cannot put out a margin call on your house.

This illustration demonstrates how interest associated with borrowed money can work contrary to your plans and interests. Your idle equity is indeed an expense to borrow, given the requirements about how that capital would have to be put to work to replace the additional interest costs.

The use of leverage—whether in a margin account or with your home equity—is a problem for most investors. The increased risk comes not only from the uncertainties of the market itself but also from the fact that the debt service places greater demands on performance. The break-even after trading costs, inflation, taxes, and interest has to be so much higher than it is with available capital that for most people, borrowing money simply does not make sense. Sound investing is a matter of identifying and understanding risks, and when it comes to borrowing money to invest, the numbers usually don't work out.

Another Form of Leverage

Most people understand leverage in terms of the use of money. You use your capital to borrow more money, thus increasing the opportunities for profit (and the risks of loss). To the extent that we talk about leverage in this way, your choices are limited. You can borrow on margin or use some other asset, such as your house, to borrow money for investment. But that is not the limit to the scope of leverage.

Fallacy: The only way to leverage is to borrow money.

Most investors begin their analysis of leverage with the idea that their capital has to be invested in shares of stocks. One widely used form of leverage involves the use of options, however. The advantage to options is that they enable you to control a large block of stock for relatively small amounts of capital and risk.

No one should consider becoming involved with options unless they fully understand all of the risks involved. Options investors should be familiar with the terminology, trading rules, and risks of option investing before deciding to proceed with any strategy. This market is highly specialized, so only those who have studied its features can afford to take the risks associated with it.

Options are used to leverage when you act as a buyer. When an option's premium (its cost) is expressed, it is in an abbreviated manner. So, when an option has a current premium value of 3, that means it costs $300. Each option refers to a specific stock (the underlying stock) and represents 100 shares. So, for the premium of $300, an option buyer can control 100 shares of stock.

If the current value of that stock is $55 per share, the option presents considerable leverage. Instead of buying 100 shares and spending $5,500, you can buy one option and spend only $300. Another advantage is that your total risk in this situation is $300; if the option becomes worthless, that is all you lose as a buyer. In comparison, when you own 100 shares, your losses can be considerably higher.

The down side for this leverage advantage is that the option is finite. It expires within a few months, and upon expiration it becomes worthless. The option's value rises and falls with the stock, so when you buy an option, you hope for movement in the stock's price so that your option will increase in value. The option can then be sold at a profit. Of course, if the option declines in value, you can either sell at a loss or wait until expiration.

There are two kinds of options: calls and puts. When you buy a call, you have the right to buy 100 shares at the fixed *striking price*, even if current market value is higher. When you buy a put, you have the right to sell 100 shares of the stock even if the price of shares is lower.

This statement brings up a second alternative to selling the option: *exercise*. As the owner of the call or put, you have the right to exercise the option, meaning to buy 100 shares (if you own a call) or to sell 100 shares (if you own a put). The many variations of these strategies enable you to use options to protect positions in your portfolio. You insure stock that you own by buying a put, so that for every dollar you lose in share value you gain a dollar in put value. It is also possible to hedge a position. For example, if you have sold short 100 shares of stock, you are hoping the per-share value will fall. You insure that position by buying a call so that if the stock's value rises, that will be offset by increasing value in the call.

The problem in leveraging through calls is that time works against you. The closer the time to expiration, the more difficult it will be for options values to become profitable. As an options owner, you are continuously fighting against time. So, buying options as a speculative venture—hoping to sell at a higher level—is a difficult way to profit in the market. As with all high-risk investments, the potential profit from leverage is high, but the corresponding risks are high as well.

An option premium has two parts, and this distinction shows how risk and opportunity are related in the option contract. The first part is *intrinsic* value. That is the point value equal to the number of points "in the money." That means the current market price is higher than the striking price (for calls) or lower than the striking price (for puts). For example, if the striking price is 55 and current market value is $57 per share, then the 55 call is two points in the money. Given the same striking price, if current market value of shares were $52, then a 55 put would be three points in the money.

Intrinsic value matches exactly the difference between the striking price and the market value. If the market value is lower than the striking price, then calls on that stock have no intrinsic value; and if the market value is higher than a put's striking price, then those puts have no intrinsic value. This portion of premium value rises or falls point for point with the stock. So for calls, the intrinsic value will rise dollar for dollar as the stock's market price rises and vice-versa. For puts, the opposite occurs: as stock market value rises, the in-the-money put falls by one point; and as market value falls, the put intrinsic value rises by one point.

The second portion of option premium value is called *time value* premium. That is the value beyond intrinsic value. If there is no intrinsic value, then the entire option premium is time value. As the expiration date approaches, time value begins to evaporate rapidly. This situation is what makes it so difficult for option buyers to make a profit. Time works against them. Even if the in-the-money market value is rising moderately, increasing intrinsic value can be off-set by declining time value. In the last month of an option's existence, it often occurs that time value is replaced by intrinsic value so that the stock is rising but option premium remains the same (or even falls).

As an option buyer, you have specific advantages in the fact that you control 100 shares of stock for each option you own. That means you have the right to exercise your option at any time before expiration. If the stock's market value does not behave in a way that gives you the advantage, however, this control is worthless. The limited risk of buying options is offset by the finite life, a feature that is defined by ever-falling time value.

With this knowledge in mind, a variation of leverage using options is to take the opposite position. Instead of buying options, you can also sell them. Going short on options can either be a high-risk speculation or a very conservative strategy. For example, if you own 1,900 shares of stock and you sell one call, your risks are limited and time works for you instead of against you. As the seller of the option, as time value decreases, the option loses value. Thus, you can close the short position by buying the option at a lower premium than its original sales price.

When you sell an option, you receive the premium value. As long as you own 100 shares, the call sold in this manner is *covered*, meaning that if the buyer exercises the call, you can deliver the 100 shares because you own them already. As long as the strike price of the call is higher than the price you paid for your 100 shares, you cannot lose when you sell a covered call. The effect of getting the premium is to discount your basis in the 100 shares. The only risk is that in the event that the market value of stock were to rise, you would be required to deliver 100 shares at a fixed strike price lower than market value.

Thus, you would lose the potential profits you would have earned had you not sold the call.

Selling calls without owning 100 shares is a high-risk form of speculation. In theory, your risk is unlimited. If the stock's market value rises and the call is exercised, you would be required to buy 100 shares at the fixed strike price and sell them at current market value, paying the difference out of pocket. So, the covered call writing strategy is conservative in the sense that your only risk is the loss of profits that *might* materialize but have not yet shown up. The potential loss is there, but a covered call writing program is undertaken with that potential loss in mind. When your basis in stock is below the striking price, your potential return will invariably be significant. Considering that you continue receiving dividends on the stock even when you have sold an option, the net gain has three components: dividend income, call premium income, and capital gain on shares of stock. Return is calculated in the event of three possible outcomes: return if exercised (you sell the stock); return if sold (you close the short option position by buying it at a lower price than your sales price); and return if unchanged (the option is allowed to expire as worthless, and the entire option premium you received is profit).

When it comes to selling puts, you cannot cover your position. Thus, put selling is a riskier strategy, but by no means as risky as selling calls. The put seller has a limited potential loss, because the worst outcome would be that a put buyer exercises the option and you are required to buy 100 shares at the striking price. If that occurs, you would pay a price above current market value. Put selling is one way to buy shares at a price you consider reasonable, however, while also discounting that price by receiving put premiums. Excessive put selling could result in a portfolio full of over-valued shares; however, if you believe that the long-term growth prospects of the company are high, then put selling could be a smart strategy.

A mistake often made by option buyers and sellers is to forget the importance of studying the fundamentals of the underlying company. If you make decisions to own stock based solely on the activity of related options, you could end up with stocks you wouldn't buy otherwise. The more volatile stocks tend to have higher option premiums because the price volatility makes the entire market in that stock *and* its options uncertain. The volatility is reflected in greater potential for option sellers. That is, you receive higher time value premium and more option profits. When the underlying stock's market value changes in a direction other than what you would prefer, however, you could end up suffering the consequences. If you sell many puts on highly volatile stocks and their market value falls dramatically, you will be required to buy 100 shares for each option at the striking price. So at the very least, put sellers need to have the capital available to buy shares in the event of exercise.

The variations of leverage using options are complex. Various straddle, spread, and combination techniques can mitigate the risks while maximizing the leverage aspects in an options program, whether you act as the buyer or seller.

Options provide you with a method for leverage with varying degrees of risk, determined by the type of option strategy you employ. The options market is efficient even when the number of buyers and sellers does not match. The options exchange is set up to act as a seller to every buyer and as a buyer to every seller. In the event of exercise when the numbers are uneven, the exchange determines whose option to exercise; however, if you have sold at option and it is in-the-money at the time of expiration, it will be exercised automatically by the exchange. So, sellers of calls and puts need to be aware that exercise can occur at any time. To fully understand the risks of leveraging with short options, sellers should be continuously aware of the "worst case" outcome, be willing to live with that risk, and have the capital available to meet obligations that arise when exercise takes place.

You do not have to borrow money in order to use leverage effectively. Using options presents one alternative to that route. The belief should be replaced with a completely different observation: You can leverage by borrowing money or by using options to control shares of stock. Both approaches involve risk, and before determining that either strategy is appropriate, you should fully understand those risks and know whether or not they match your risk tolerance.

Note

[1]15 U.S.C. 78a et seq.

CHAPTER 9

Rates of Return

What is the return on your investments? What seems like a fairly straightforward question is actually quite complex, because the answer has to be, "That depends upon what you mean by 'return.'"

There are so many ways to compute the return that you need clarification whenever talking about the amount or percentage you earn from investing money. To complicate matters further, the return earned by investing in the market is not the same as the return earned by companies, although it is easy to confuse the two. In the minds of some investors, "return" does not have a clear meaning.

The two primary areas of discussion in this chapter are *investment* return, or the profit you earn from investing capital in publicly listed company stock, and *corporate* return, which is the return earned by the companies whose stock you own. When this distinction is made, most people recognize the obvious differences at once; however, it is easy to get the two entirely different matters mixed up, and the result can be misleading as you analyze your portfolio. For example, when you hear that a particular company reported a 25 percent increase in its net return, you recognize a specific meaning in terms of sales and net profit. It does not necessarily mean that the company's stock is also going to rise by 25 percent or that investors who own stock are going to see a direct benefit from the positive news. The two realms—investment profits and corporate profits—are so far removed from one another that they are unrelated in many respects. While a positive history of growing profits certainly translates to an increased market value of stock, the immediate results often are not seen at all. It is possible that a stock's price will remain at the same level or even fall at the same time that corporate profits are strong.

The reality is that the relationship between the fundamentals—sales and profits, specifically—and the price of stock is very indirect. While corporate profits are nuts and bolts numbers based on actual sales, costs, and expenses, market value is more a reflection of how investors in general view the potential for future growth. So, a company's stock price will be set more by what investors believe will happen in the future, whereas a company's fundamentals are based on the immediate past.

Many market watchers would like to believe that corporate earnings reports and stock prices have a very direct relationship and that prices are a reflection of those earnings. This statement is not true for the most part, however—at least, in the short term. Stock prices will rise or fall when earnings reports are released, often responding to a comparative outcome between analysts' predictions and actual results rather than to any fundamental value. So, the market forecasting culture in which analysts report their expectations has great weight on setting prices and on short-term changes in those prices. The market culture and corporate culture are far different from one another, however. Anyone who has worked in a financial capacity in a corporation knows that the preoccupation with sales and profits is a major tool for measuring just about everything and for making all major decisions in the corporation. By comparison, the market culture looks at price potential (usually in the immediate future) to judge a corporation.

So, both cultures are forward-looking but in different respects. In the corporate culture, forecasting is a tool for setting standards and then measuring results, to judge affordability and profitability of market expansion and management, and to test and control internal spending. In the market culture, forecasting is almost always limited to analysis of price movement and attempts to anticipate the direction of price in the near future. These two cultures both relate to forms of "return," but they should not be confused—because in spite of some common beliefs, the two worlds are as far apart as they can be.

The Problem of Comparability

More about the corporate culture and return is presented later in this chapter. First, though, it is important to discuss the problem of *comparison* when talking about returns on investment. In order for an analysis to work logically, all forms of comparison should be accurate and consistent. Perhaps the leading cause of misleading conclusions in market analysis is the problem of making comparisons between dissimilar factual bases.

The most obvious type of problem is comparing fundamental and technical indicators between two or more listed companies that should not be compared. If their primary business involves different market sectors, it also means that they have structural differences as well. Not only will the fundamentals look far different, but economic factors affect different sectors in different ways as well. For example, you cannot expect a large bank to experience the same changes in its fundamentals as a major retail chain. Changes in virtually all economic indicators will have dissimilar effects on those companies, whose profit and price trends will also be different due to their incomparable features.

Even so, a broad assumption often is made that any two listed companies can be compared based on the same standards. Tests such as PE ratio, price volatility, earnings per share, and sales growth are used to judge companies even when their sectors are different and when they market entirely different products or services to vastly different markets. This assumption is illogical.

Another inaccuracy arises when listed companies are compared to one another based solely on patterns in historical price changes. First of all, price patterns from the recent past show a price trend but cannot be used to judge corporate performance. Short-term prices are affected by too many factors not related to fundamentals to have any meaningful value in trying to judge how good of an investment that company represents. It is all too easy to try and identify growth candidates by studying price charts. The comparison between earnings trends and market price, however, is the ultimate form of comparing apples to oranges. Real growth analysis should concentrate on the fundamentals, and short-term price changes reflect only today's market perception about value. Long-term price trends do reflect long-term growth, but the potential for return on your investment needs to rest with the fundamentals.

The confusion between price as a value indicator and corporate earnings comes from the fact that the two are not related directly. The conclusions reached by an attempt to draw insight from such a comparison can be misleading. At the very least, the conclusion is unreliable. So, to clarify what needs to occur, we first need to separate the two broad areas of return and view them separately. The study of price and price trends is a technical indicator, and the study of corporate earnings and other financial results is a fundamental indicator. The return calculated for each cannot be compared, and one cannot be used to make judgments about the other.

Comparing any two dissimilar factors is always inaccurate. Even if we limit the discussion to the question of safety in picking one stock to buy over another, how can we compare stocks in different industries? If one industry has a norm of 4 percent return on sales and another normally sees an 8 percent return on sales, there is no way to compare the two companies based solely on their earnings because they operate in entirely different markets. This situation means that sales and expansion, net profits, dividends, and ultimately even the stock price will all act and react in different ways. The judgment that a particular stock is safe and another is not often leads to unreliable comparisons without qualifying the result.

A valid conclusion about safety should be restricted to a single market sector. Within that sector, one stock might hold the lead in terms of market share and profits while others are on a growth track. A third group might report fundamental volatility or be poorly capitalized. Obviously, these types of distinctions within an industry are valid because the corporations are all involved in the same market. Thus, changes in relative market share, sales growth, and profits can be used to define safety as an investment feature of the companies. All too often, the definition of safety for stocks is based on comparisons without regard to differences in markets and is based on a mix of fundamental and technical indicators.

The term *safety* often refers solely to price volatility, which itself is a poor indicator for judging a stock's value under any conditions or under any definition of real safety for your investment dollars. Price volatility can be useful as a symptom of something else, especially when it changes suddenly. Comparisons between different stocks, however, often completely ignore the one most important safety feature of all: risk.

By most definitions, a safe stock is likely to grow relatively slowly, and a stock that is defined as less safe has the potential for rapid short-term growth or for equally rapid losses. Because such definitions and distinctions rest exclusively with price comparisons, however, they cannot be used by serious fundamental investors to select appropriate long-term investments. Understanding that safety and risk are always related is only one part of the equation. The emphasis on price and the unreliability of short-term price volatility make the point that a real analysis of potential return should be restricted to fundamental analysis and that any study of return based on price trends is going to be inaccurate. No dependable method for anticipating growth potential and defining safety can be based on short-term pricing trends, because those trends are reliable and random.

Comparability in Corporate Rates of Return

The problem faced by every investor trying to find a sensible system for analysis is that so many versions of return exist. How do you know that one discussion of return is the same as another?

In fact, there really is no way to rely on outside information to ensure that you are getting good information. You need to look at the numbers for yourself. For example, if you read that a particular corporation's earnings rose by 14 percent and the stock is expected to be a star in the coming decade, what does that mean?

Who is making the prediction and based on what type of information? Can you simply take the word of the person making this prediction without qualifying the source first? Is the person a market guru or a financial analyst? How often are such analysts right, and why?

To further complicate this series of questions, you need to return to the basic question of what is meant by a 14 percent rate of return. How was that calculated? Is it a return on sales, and if so, does it represent a full year or an annualized partial year? If annualized, does it take into account the possibility that some industries have higher or lower volume at different times of the year? It is not reliable to take a one-quarter result and multiply it by four to estimate the likely outcome for the entire year. For example, if you take the holiday season quarter (the fourth quarter in the calendar year) for a retail concern, it would be highly inaccurate to annualize that quarter and forecast an outcome for the entire year. An accurate estimate of future growth would be made comparing that quarter to a comparable quarter for the previous year; however, it is easy to misread the numbers and make inaccurate reports as a result.

Without knowing the source of information, the basis for conclusions, or the qualifications of the person making the prediction, it is impossible to know whether reports are reliable or not. In addition, if such forecasts are meant to predict short-term price movement, they are even less reliable. A fundamentally based analysis intended to identify long-term growth prospects is one form of analysis that is worth listening to; however, the majority of market reporting is aimed at short-term predictions emphasizing price alone. So, terms like safety, volatility, timeliness, and growth potential invariably are applied to predictions of price change in the immediate future with long-term growth and fundamental return ignored in the process.

A widespread belief in the market is that the rate of return means the same thing everywhere, that the definition is universally understood, and that all calculations of return are done in the same way. The source of this belief might be the corporate world itself. In financial reporting, certain standards are used to ensure clarity in communications. Net return on sales has a specific meaning, as does return on investment and 5 percent annual growth in sales. The methods of calculating these statistics is applied uniformly, and year-to-year comparisons are based on consistency in reporting methods. The same is not true in reporting investment returns, however, or in forecasting returns in the market.

Fallacy: The rate of return is always computed in the same way.

This statement is false. So many different forms of reporting are used, and the basic idea of rate of return can mean so many different things that a report from an unknown source should never be taken at face value without definition and further study. Information from two different sources should never be assumed to be based on the same standards.

All statistical reporting is complex and subject to misinterpretation. The most difficult part of the entire statistical method is validation, that important step in which the analyst ensures that the basic information is reliable, before drawing any conclusions.

An example of how complex statistical studies can be is as follows: Let's say that you hear a corporation has experienced an improvement of 4 percent over the past year, and this figure is reported as a significant change when compared to the previous year. What does that mean? Some possibilities are as such:

Sales increased by 4 percent, but profits fell.

Sales increased by 4 percent, and profits remained at the same dollar amount.

Sales increased by 4 percent, and profits remained at the same percentage of sales.

Profits increased by 4 percent over the past year.

Losses for the year were 4 percent lower than losses for the previous year.

Net losses were *higher* than the prior year, but the rate of acceleration of losses slowly went down by 4 percent.

No sales or profits are involved; the stock price rose by 4 percent.

Obviously, these many variations on a "4% improvement" are troubling. The use of statistics or careful selection of language can make even bad news seem good, so everyone who reads a report about return or change in the numbers has to be very cautious in trying to determine what those changes mean. A negative outcome can be made to sound positive, as in the example of declining rates of increase in net losses.[1]

The belief that computing the rate of return is always consistent should be abandoned and replaced with a different belief: The entire topic of return is complex and varied and subject to many different meanings. It is all too easy to manipulate the numbers to place a positive spin on negative outcomes, and every investor should be cautious when receiving information. Make sure that period-to-period reports are based on the same computation before acknowledging the movement of an ongoing trend.

Investors can easily mistake corporate reporting as the same thing as return on invested capital. The corporation is interested in tracking its earnings, and it seeks increased sales volume with a corresponding higher profit. Investors will experience higher share prices for their shares if more people want to buy (increased demand), however, or lower prices per share when current owners decide it is time to sell (increased supply). The underlying causes for change in supply and demand are interesting as a topic for study, but predicting the cause and effect on stock prices is far more difficult.

Fallacy: You figure return on investments in the same way that companies do.

Corporations compute "return" based on a comparison between sales and profits, which is far different from how investor return is calculated. Even the corporate reporting method is complex in many ways, however. It is easily distorted by changing the base of the report from one period to another.

Some distortions in the real meaning of reported returns are unintentional, whereas others are manipulative and intended to mask bad news by casting it in a positive light. The differences between these two often are difficult to spot. It becomes a serious problem when distortions in reporting are intended to deceive rather than to simply report results. For this reason, year-to-year comparisons are the key. Only through trend analysis can you spot real change and identify real significance in the numbers. As long as a reporting person or company uses the same numbers, the report will have a degree of reliability. When the values being reported are selected to minimize the bad news, however, stockholders can be misled to believe that the bad news is not as bad or that it is actually good news.

For example, if a corporation has been reporting net profits from year to year but one year begins emphasizing *operating* profit, what does that mean? When reports change the base data between reporting periods, you should recognize a red flag if you are an astute investor. In the example given, it is possible that non-operational expenses are bringing down profits to such a degree that the overall trend has turned negative; however, in analyzing *operating* profit, the numbers look good.

The difference between operating and net profits is an important one. Profit from operations is restricted to the recognition of costs and expenses related to running the business. That version of the bottom line is further adjusted for taxes due or paid, interest income and expenses, foreign currency exchange gains and losses, and other non-operational changes to the bottom line. So, the operating profit and net profit can be entirely different values. In the case where a corporation is becoming increasingly dependent on debt capitalization, interest expenses will tend to rise with the debt level. Thus, net profits will fall, too. As more net operating profit has to be paid out in interest to bondholders, less is left over for dividend payments to stockholders.

In this case, you could see a growing trend in consistent earnings based on net operating profit but a declining net profit. So, if the report of profits shifts from one to the other, a more detailed analysis should be undertaken immediately. The source for information on these varying values is the final income statement of the corporation, which is published in annual reports and filed with the SEC. The numbers are easy to find; interpreting them requires study.

This situation is only one example of how corporate reporting can mislead investors with a seemingly subtle shift. Emphasizing operating profits rather than net profits is deceptive, and the purpose of such reporting could be to put a positive spin on otherwise negative outcomes. Whether done intentionally or not, the result is the same: inaccuracy in the report.

The comparison from year to year is more complex when a corporation has a diversified product or service base. As one line of business experiences increased volume and profits, another might be on the decline. The overall outcome will not break down these differences, however, so exceptionally good results (or exceptionally bad ones) often are not visible because the diversified base is averaged out in the overall report. Thus, a precise study of return on sales is itself unreliable. Investors need to study overall trends to gain any meaningful information about consistency in growth over several years; trying to study specific subsidiaries or divisions within a corporation is complex and subject to the whims of journal entries splitting costs and expenses among many divisions. In addition, the outcome itself does not provide any valuable information. You cannot judge a corporation's success by studying only part of its diversified lines. It is the overall effect that really counts in the long term. An audited financial statement provides the basic information you need to study corporate returns; that, of course, is not the same as investment returns.

Even though financial statements are checked by an outside auditing firm and are prepared by using consistent guidelines, their interpretation and reporting is not necessarily objective or accurate. So, each investor should depend not on the message from the president or CEO invariably found in the annual report but on independent analysis of long-term trends. The message from the corporate executive, which invariably places a positive light on the year's operations, is a public relations tool and not an analytical one. So, depending on that message is a mistake. The corporate leader's motive is not to provide you with an objective analysis of the financial outcome, but to attract and keep stockholders in support of the company's stock price—important to remember in the study of return as reported by the corporation.

A second way that investors can confuse corporate reports with investment performance has to do with the profit study itself. When a corporation reports that profits were 8 percent, that is normally computed based on sales. The return on sales simply reflects the comparison between the bottom-line profit number and the volume of sales—a purely fundamental outcome. From the investor's point of view, however, return on sales is not the same as return on invested capital. It is easy to overlook the fact that corporate reporting and investment performance are entirely different forms of return.

A corporation whose annual financial results reflect a steady pattern of growth and expansion under carefully monitored conditions (diversified lines of business, control of capitalization, and so on) translates to strong long-term growth prospects; however, investors should not rely upon these corporate results in expectations about stock performance. If the sector is out of favor, for example, a strong performance by a single company will not necessarily support its market price. If the mood in the market is negative, prices will tend to decline even with strong fundamentals for the specific company. Remember, market price and financial reporting (or return on sales and return on invested capital) have nothing in common in the short term.

Corporations sometimes report net earnings in terms of return on equity; however, that ratio has not become a popular one because it does not necessarily reveal a trend, as does return on sales. A far more popular and useful fundamental statistic is the net earnings per share. That is a useful indicator that can be tracked over time and becomes distorted only when a corporation issues a significant number of new shares during the year. The diluted outcome distorts the earnings per share because the base number changes. The report of earnings on invested capital does not really help investors to understand how their capital is being put to work, so to speak, because the corporate numbers do not correspond to market value. Any attempt to relate these separate realms (corporate reporting versus market price) is going to result in confusion rather than in clarification.

Return on equity is further complicated when the outstanding share value changes during the year. If the corporation issues new shares, for example, then the computation has to be adjusted. So, the return on equity itself is distorted because the base values change. In this situation, the average between beginning outstanding share value and ending share value for the year is usually used. The calculation itself is of little value, however, because it cannot be used to explain why or how the market value of shares changes.

Another form of corporate reporting is the return on book value per share. Here again, the result does not reveal anything of value to investors, so it is a relatively useless form of return. Book value per share is a largely ignored value and for good reason. It does not reflect the actual value per share on the market by any means; in fact, it will be most difficult to find any relationship between book value and market value per share. It would be reassuring if a change in book value per share were reflected in a tracking change in market value per share. But in practice, the book value per share is an ineffective indicator. Just because it would be desirable to track market price changes based on some form of fundamental information, the truth cannot be ignored: Market value per share operates independently from the fundamentals. Book value per share is a remote indicator, perhaps of interest to accountants but to few other people.

One problem with the book value analysis is that the methods used in accounting are by no means fully realistic or accurate. For example, real estate owned by a corporation is always entered as an asset based on its purchase price. It then depreciates over several decades so that as time passes, the book value of real estate declines. In reality, however, the market value of the asset could be rising significantly. You cannot judge a corporation's real value based on its book value, because accounting methods do not take into account the realities of what assets are worth. So much of the real information is likely to be found in footnotes to the financial statements. Even then, if a footnote does deal with the market value of assets, the effect on investors is minimal. The exception is that case where someone realizes that the real market value of assets is far higher than the current market value per share and they are in a position to put together a corporate takeover. The intention, of course, would be to sell off the undervalued assets and make a big profit by taking apart the company; this situation is the inevitable result of disparities between book value, current market value, and *real* value of assets.

What can you conclude from these disparities? In the short term, return on invested capital has to be limited to a simple study between the price that you paid for shares of stock versus what those shares are worth today. The short-term trader or speculator can earn profits by buying up shares when undervalued and waiting out the whims of the market; the successful trader is one who is able to recognize values when they are available.

The long-term investor has to accept the fact that changes in market price are not going to reflect returns as calculated in the corporate world. The calculation of profit and loss affects stock prices to a degree, but only when they are compared to analysts' forecasts; beyond that, the real effect of earnings on market price is minimal and short-term in nature. The long-term fundamental investor needs to track earnings reports to spot emerging changes in the financial strength and trends of the company, because today's strong growth candidate might not be the same company in a few years. So, the fundamentals are the key in the long term, but for those who are more interested in the one-to-five-year outcome, they do not really relate to market price at all.

Clearly, the methods for computing return in the corporate world and those used by investors, are far different. The belief that these two worlds are working with the same base of numbers is misleading and inaccurate. A more informed point of view is one that recognizes the two different systems and that accepts the fact that they do not relate to one another directly. The great desire among investors and analysts to find some correlation between financial results and market value is unrealistic.

Investment Return: Calculation Methods

The inaccuracy of comparing corporate reporting to market value is only one of several problems faced by every investor. Simply computing return on invested capital is complex, as well. The problem begins with the way that market news itself is reported.

Fallacy: Daily stock listings show price changes, which is the important factor you need to compare yields and potential yields.

In the typical news report, several corporate stocks are reported based on the day's change in market price, usually in terms of the number of points that a stock rises or falls. For example, stocks might be reported in the following way:

Stock A	Closed at $55, up $3 per share
Stock B	Closed at $27, up $2 per share
Stock C	Closed at $114, up $5 per share

At first glance, it looks like Stock C did better than the other two because it gained more value per share. But consider the percentage gain of each stock based on the previous day's closing price and the percentage gain in the point value reported:

Stock A	Up $3 from $52 per share, or 5.8%
Stock B	Up $2 from $25 per share, or 8.0%
Stock C	Up $5 from $109 per share, or 4.6%

So, even though Stock C gained more points, its real gain was lower than the gains on both of the other stocks. The persistent reporting of point value changes, regardless of the share value and percentage change, is a chronic problem in financial reporting. The inaccuracy misleads investors and does not clarify the actual results of the day.

The inaccuracy of financial reporting is merely mathematical, but the problem also permeates the methods by which people calculate returns. When people evaluate their own portfolio returns, they can easily mislead themselves in terms of performance and outcome. Consider the following three sales and profit results:

Stock	Purchase	Sale	Profit	Months Owned
Stock A	$ 4,900	$ 5,500	$ 600	4
Stock B	$ 2,400	$ 2,700	$ 300	6
Stock C	$10,100	$11,400	$1,300	14

Looking at these three stocks, it seems that Stock C was the most profitable. The profit of $1,300 is far higher than the profit on either of the other two stocks in terms of dollar value. The percentage of return for the three stocks is about the same based on dividing the profit by the purchase price:

Stock A	$ 600	$ 4,900	12.2%
Stock B	$ 300	$ 2,400	12.5%
Stock C	$1,300	$10,100	12.9%

Making this comparison seems to again support the idea that Stock C performed slightly better than the other two; it earned the highest return based on the simple comparison between profit and cost. This technique is the most popular method for computing return on investment. Unfortunately, it is also inaccurate because it does not take into account the period during which the investment was owned.

To compute return accurately, the comparison has to be made on an annualized basis. That is, a report of the return that would have been earned if the investments were all held for one full year. The formula for annualized return is shown in Figure 9.1.

The two steps involve first calculating return as before and then adjusting it. The simple division of profit by cost produces the percentage return; divide that by the holding period (in terms of months), and then multiply by 12 to produce the annualized return. Using the previous examples, annualized return for each is calculated by using these two steps:

A:

Stock A	$ 600 ÷ $ 4,900 = 12.2%
Stock B	$ 300 ÷ $ 2,400 = 12.5%
Stock C	$1,300 ÷ $10,100 = 12.9%

B:

Stock A	(12.2% ÷ 4) – 12 = 36.6%
Stock B	(12.5% ÷ 6) – 12 = 25.0%
Stock C	(12.9% ÷ 14) – 12 = 11.1%

When the returns for these stocks are annualized, the real comparative return becomes apparent. The stock that had the higher dollar value also has the lowest annualized return. Because it was held for the longest time period, the annualized return is lower than that for the other two.

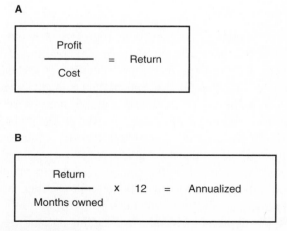

FIGURE 9.1 Annualized Return.

While annualizing return is a useful method for ensuring consistency in how you evaluate your portfolio's performance, it is not necessarily a realistic view about your actual outcome. Because investors buy and sell stock based on price advantages of the moment, there is no guarantee that holding a stock for a full year instead of two or three months would have produced the same yield as that calculated through annualizing the outcome. The purpose is not to reflect an accurate picture of the actual return but to make the comparison between stocks reliable and accurate. These examples show how studying the point value change, or even the dollar amount of profit, can be very inaccurate. The real return has to be calculated in such a way that the comparison between several different investments is accurate. That requires computing the annualized return.

Even though annualization makes your analysis consistent, it should not be used as a reflection of what kinds of returns you experience all of the time. When you keep funds out of the market between investments, it is not earning any form of return, so to truly study the annual outcome of your portfolio you need to study the overall effect of your buy and sell decisions. Should you include the current market value of stocks you own, however, versus their purchase price? Including paper profits can be deceptive, because those are not really profits until the shares have been sold. Every experienced investor knows that paper profits can disappear more quickly than they appeared, so they should not be included in an overall study of portfolio returns.

Annualized return is not an accurate measurement of actual portfolio performance, but it does provide an accurate comparison. For example, an extremely short-term investment can produce impressive annual returns that you cannot count on earning consistently. If you buy shares today at $26 and sell them tomorrow at $27, your one-day profit of $1 per share—or 3.85 percent—translates to an annualized return of:

$$3.85 \times 365 \text{ (days)} = 1{,}405.25\%$$

Obviously, this outcome is not likely to be repeated each and every day, so it cannot be pointed to as your average portfolio return. Annualized calculations have limited value in terms of performance evaluation, so the calculation's real purpose has to be kept in perspective. Speculators going in and out of positions frequently would do better to calculate average monthly returns on their investment, based on closed positions only. The net profits and losses should be divided by invested capital, and the average monthly return is then tracked from month to month as a means for studying the success of the speculative strategy. Options market investors, for example, can use this method if they are acting as option buyers. If their activity is limited to selling covered calls, the return from that activity should be included with overall profits from owning shares of stock, where premium income from selling options serves to discount the basis in the stock, thus increasing returns over time.

The widespread tendency to watch price changes and to judge daily performance on a point basis is misleading, regardless of the market where you invest your capital. The price per share determines the real meaning of the point change, so daily changes should be evaluated on a percentage basis rather than by the number of points. The belief that price change defines a stock's performance on a daily basis is inaccurate. It is far more realistic to track change on the basis of percentages rather than on point value. It is the scorekeeping mentality of the market that leads to so many inaccuracies, and the methods by which financial news is reported—and by which investors receive their information—is more confusing than enlightening.

Compound Returns: How It Works

As long as price is used to determine value (even though inherently inaccurate as a means for judging investment return), it would be better if an *accurate* means for making that judgment were used. Watching point change instead of percentage change is statistically misleading and obviously not useful. Everyone has heard news reports, however, such as: "IBM rose 4 points in heavy trading, and Microsoft rose by only 2."

We cannot know from this statement whether IBM or Microsoft had a better day. If the price per share of IBM is twice that of Microsoft, then these changes are identical. If IBM's price is more than twice that of Microsoft, then the latter had a better day on the market. So, the emphasis on point change does not reveal what is going on in the market, whether reported for individual stocks or on the basis of a larger index.

In a market that is preoccupied with price—and, as a consequence, short-term return—the more profitable long-term gains that can be achieved in the market are easily overlooked. The long-term analysis of growth stocks based purely on monitoring the fundamentals is certainly boring in comparison to the hour-to-hour profits and losses experienced by speculators. It is also less interesting to report on the obscure long-term potential than it is to place emphasis on a 4-point gain for the day. However, the long-term study of rates of return also can lead to higher profits.

It does not matter if your stock goes up today if in the long run its market performance does not continue to meet your expectations. It might be difficult, indeed, to merely preserve the spending power of your equity. Given the double problems of inflation and taxes, just keeping your money at its present value is challenge enough. Profiting beyond that level requires an even more impressive rate of return.

The advice to "keep your money at work" is worth heeding. The way to accumulate equity over many years is through selection of strong growth candidate corporations combined with the reinvestment of earnings. Thus, even dividends should be put back into shares of stock.[2]

The so-called "time value of money" refers to the compounding effect you achieve when you reinvest earnings so that you earn interest on interest (or dividends on dividends in the case of stock). Mutual fund companies like to illustrate the value of buying shares by showing what would have happened if you had invested a lump sum at some point in the past; however, this situation is misleading in many cases because it really does not reflect impressive gains except from the benefits of reinvesting earnings. It is worth evaluating the overall rate of return represented by the gains pointed to by mutual funds—at least to determine whether the fund has done better than market averages.

In fact, the compounding of earnings is one of the best ways to augment returns and to build equity over the long term. Given the historical levels of return from stock capital gains and dividends, it might not even be possible to preserve the spending power of your assets without reinvesting your earnings. For mutual fund investors, this situation simply means that all dividends or interest and all capital gains should be applied toward the purchase of more fund shares. For stock market investors owning shares directly, it means taking dividends through a DRIPs program. Many corporations encourage this practice by offering a discount on the share price of between 2 and 5 percent. Of course, buying partial shares through such a program is also done free of brokerage transaction costs as long as your shares are registered in your name and not in a brokerage firm's street name.[3]

An illustration of how the time value of money works demonstrates the advantage that it provides. For example, let's say that your account (whether a bank savings account or ownership of shares of stock or a mutual fund) is averaging a 5 percent return each year. If you reinvest annual dividends of $25 per quarter, the compounding effect accelerates over time, as shown in Table 9.1.

The quarterly earnings (1 percent, or one-fourth of the average 5 percent per year) are based on the ever-growing accumulation, which includes the earnings on earnings. Thus, the rate continues to rise. Carried out many years, it does not take long for the interest to exceed the pre-interest earnings. In this example, a three-year total of $300 compounded out to $325.52 (8.5% overall) is not impressive by itself, but when carried to the outer extremes, it makes a significant difference.

To compute the compound rate as shown in this example, first multiply the sum by the annual earnings rate:

$25.00 × .05 = $1.25

Because the $25 in this illustration is earned each quarter, the annual earnings have to be divided by 4 (quarters):

$1.25 ÷ 4 = $0.31

For the next period, the sum of $25.31 is added to the new dividend of $25, and that sum of $50.31 is then treated as the new beginning balance. The same

TABLE 9.1 Compound Returns

Period	Amount Earned	Interest	Accumulated Value
Year 1:			
Quarter 1	$25.00	$0.31	$25.31
Quarter 2	25.00	0.63	50.94
Quarter 3	25.00	0.95	76.89
Quarter 4	25.00	1.27	103.16
Year 2:			
Quarter 1	$25.00	$1.60	$129.76
Quarter 2	25.00	1.93	156.69
Quarter 3	25.00	2.27	183.96
Quarter 4	25.00	2.61	211.57
Year 3:			
Quarter 1	$25.00	$2.96	$239.53
Quarter 2	25.00	3.31	267.84
Quarter 3	25.00	3.66	296.50
Quarter 4	25.00	4.02	325.52

computation can be performed by using one-fourth of the annual rate, or 1 percent (0.0125), as a replacement for dividing the annual return by four:

$25.00 \times 0.0125 = 0.3125 (31 cents)

Applying this simplified example to the case of reinvesting dividends, a three-year yield of $300 would grow to $325.52, or an 8.5 percent return on top of the dividend earnings. This profit continues to grow at ever-accelerating rates as long as the reinvestment plan continues. Of course, this illustration does not take into account the effects of taxes. You are taxed on dividends as they are earned, even when those earnings are reinvested in additional partial shares of stock.

This illustration also does not take into account the effect of changing stock prices. The more shares or partial shares that you accumulate, the greater the long-term profits from growth, which is ultimately reflected in higher market value. Of course, when stock prices fall, the accumulated fund of reinvested dividends falls as well. As long as you continue to monitor the fundamental attributes of the company and the signs pointing to continued growth have not slowed down or reversed, however, then reinvesting dividends enhances profits.

The reverse side of the illustration relates to the cost of borrowing, or amortization. If an investor borrows money to buy stock, the interest that has to be paid is based on the outstanding balance due. Thus, a home equity loan of $30,000, repayable in 10 years at 8 percent interest, requires monthly payments of $363.99 for a total of $43,678.80, or more than $13,000 in interest. The interest is higher at the beginning of the loan period because it is calculated based on the balance. So, for the loan as illustrated, the interest for the first year would be calculated as shown in Table 9.2.

The interest payment exceeds principal each month; however, it declines as the balance due also declines. Offsetting that decline, the amount of the monthly payment going to principal increases gradually. The pace of this change accelerates as the loan gets closer to being paid off; however, in the early years, interest is far higher because the balance is higher as well.

This illustration demonstrates how the time value of money works for you or against you, depending upon whether you are investing or borrowing. As an investor, you benefit from the compounding effect, but as a borrower, your cost of borrowing is high during the earlier years in the compounding period. The longer that period, the greater the interest. For example, if the $30,000 were at 8 percent payable over 30 years, the total interest would be $49,247—far higher than the $13,000 payable over 10 years. Borrowers observe correctly that

TABLE 9.2 Loan Amortization

Month	Payment	Interest	Principal	Balance
				$30,000.00
1	$363.99	$200.00	$163.99	29,836.01
2	363.99	198.91	165.08	29,670.93
3	363.99	197.81	166.18	29,504.75
4	363.99	196.70	167.29	29,337.46
5	363.99	195.58	168.41	29,169.05
6	363.99	194.46	169.53	28,999.52
7	363.99	193.33	170.66	28,828.86
8	363.99	192.19	171.80	28,657.06
9	363.99	191.05	172.94	28,484.12
10	363.99	189.89	174.10	28,310.02
11	363.99	188.73	175.26	28,134.76
12	363.99	187.57	176.42	$27,958.34
Total	$4,367.88	$2,326.22	$2,041.66	

the interest rate also affects the total amount of interest; however, because of the way that compound interest is computed, the repayment period has an equally important role in the amount of interest to be paid.

Compounding of earnings in an investment portfolio often is ignored because more emphasis is placed on the market value of stock. To a degree, dividend income is ignored as playing only a minor role in comparison to the more exciting potential for fast profits when stock prices rise. The astute investor, however, should consider both capital gains *and* dividends in the calculation of total return. When shares of stock are owned over many years, the reinvested dividend income can come to represent a significant portion of the total gain. So, a modest 3 percent dividend rate, when reinvested over many years, can grow at a compound rate equaling or even surpassing the capital gain from the increased market value of the original investment itself. Because reinvested dividends are converted into partial shares, the compounded effect of that 3 percent is augmented as well by the growth in the stock's market value.

The Self-Deception Problem

It is not enough to simply look to the past to estimate how the future will look. In forecasting future returns, every investor needs to set specific standards for selling stock. This requisite exit strategy is not limited to a time factor alone. It also needs to include consideration of unforeseen changes in the fundamental characteristics of the company.

A long-term investor will want to base the decision to buy, sell, or hold almost entirely on the trend analysis of key fundamental indicators. As long as the trend continues as expected, the indication would be to hold (and, in some cases, to accumulate) shares. Fundamentals do change over time, however. For example, a company that today is growing aggressively and picking up an ever-growing market share will eventually slow down. At some time in the future, today's strong growth stock will become the dominant company in its primary sector, and other corporations will be trying to take market share away from it. In this situation, the growth-oriented investor should re-evaluate the original purpose in owning shares of that company. It might be that given the change in circumstances, it will be more profitable to exchange those shares for shares in the new aggressive growth company. Even given higher risks, it could be more in line with your goals.

Seeking long-term returns in line with today's expectations requires change along the way. It is not realistic to expect that today's growth pattern will continue indefinitely, so part of your portfolio management task should be to continually compare and evaluate companies whose stock you own with its competitors.

For investors with a shorter-term orientation, the natural tendency is to emphasize price as a means for deciding when to sell. If you seek short-term profits through the old "buy low, sell high" approach, remember that the advice is easier to give than to follow. Many investors who speculate on relatively short-term price change fall into the trap of programming their strategy so that they can never sell at a profit.

For such investors, whether prices are rising or falling, it is never the right time to sell. When prices are on the rise, price-oriented investors might hesitate because they believe the price will continue to rise indefinitely. They do not want to miss out on any of the future profit that can be earned by taking no action immediately. The tendency in this approach, however, is to continually revise the perceived base as the current high price. Once a high has been reached and prices retreat, the attitude is that the price has to return to at least that high level or some profits have been lost. Even when prices do turn around and rise again, however, the attitude returns to the previous approach, that it is not wise to sell as long as prices are moving upward.

As long as prices are falling, the same price-oriented investor will refuse to sell until prices return to the starting point. Unwilling to accept even a small loss, such investors will wait out a temporary downswing, applying patience to a fault. And, when prices do eventually return to the original base price level, the same investor is still programmed to not sell—because now prices are on the rise.

This endless cycle is self-destructive, because ultimately the stock is held well beyond its seasoned price level. Investors who use this approach end up with significant lost paper profits because they can never sell shares unless their patience simply runs out. In some markets, this approach ensures losses. For example, if you speculate in options, the attitude toward rising and falling option price levels eventually runs up against the ever-pending expiration date. When time value evaporates, it takes considerable movement in the underlying stock's price just to maintain original value. So, in the majority of cases, the option will expire as worthless or will be valued considerably lower than the original premium paid.

The failure to set specific goals for when or why to sell shares eventually leads to self-programming for loss rather than for profit. Ironically, the ill-advised approach (essentially a lack of strategy) is contrary to the investor's undefined goals: making profits in the market. Without clear definition, the tendency is to buy when markets are rising, even though astute observers would recognize a peaking-out effect as the price rise begins to slow (so that indications would be to sell) and to sell when prices dip to low points. Thus, the advice to "buy low and sell high" needs to be expanded for a second part: " . . . instead of the other way around."

The solution to this problem is to set specific price-related goals. Short-term investors need to set firm goals for themselves, just as long-term investors do. The latter should sell shares when the fundamentals change significantly, because the companies no longer meet their criteria for holding shares of stock. For the price-oriented investor, the goals define price ranges and when a sale will occur. For example, you might define your sell-point in terms of price by deciding you will sell when one of three price situations takes place:

1. When the value of shares has doubled
2. When the value of shares has fallen 20 percent
3. When six months have passed and neither outcome one nor two have occurred

The purpose in establishing an exit strategy such as this one is not to program your trading so rigidly that you act automatically. It is to overcome the common trap of programming your policy so that it becomes impossible to sell with any specific reason. So, the idea that you will profit if you "buy low and sell high" works as long as you also define the exit strategy. If you buy and continue buying for too long, then you lose the paper profits; if you sell too early because prices have fallen, then you miss the probable turnaround and recovery of value.

When investors replace their original basis in stock with unclaimed paper profits, they also destroy the potential to ever earn gains. If you buy stock at $35 per share but it now is worth $60, it is unreasonable to consider a fall to $55 as a loss. The real paper profit at that point is $20 per share, a return of 57 percent when compared to the actual basis. The problem that many investors face in trying to define their return is accepting the idea that paper profits are not real unless and until they are taken. Remember your real basis in stock, the price you originally paid. So, if the high point has been reached and then the price retreats, it is not a loss. Because price trends, like all others, are cyclical, you can expect a roller coaster effect at least to some degree. It does not matter whether you take profits at the exact moment that prices peak, because you can never time your decisions so precisely. Rather, it is the overall return that you earn on your portfolio by setting goals that signal buy or sell decisions—without allowing yourself to break those rules when the market for your stock changes unexpectedly.

One characteristic of success-oriented investors is to be eternally optimistic. Thus, there is always the tendency to believe that upward price movements will continue forever. Investors put more thought into potential profits than they ever do to potential losses. Thus, when losses occur, it is invariably an unexpected outcome. So, many investors think only about the upside and they really don't know how to cope with the downside; they do not know how to ride out a temporary downturn, nor are they certain that a downward trend won't go on forever in the same way that the upward trend was presumed to act. This situation is especially true of those investors who enter the market for the first time during periods of rising prices. This characteristic defines most new investors; it is rare that people go into the market for the first time when prices are depressed and the mood is negative. Unfortunately, new investors have not experienced a loss, and their capital continues growing at a nice pace—at least for a while. The "easy money" earned on paper during market rises quickly turns into losses when things change. No matter how many cycles the market experiences, new investors are always surprised when their ever-rising stocks suddenly turn and fall.

With this knowledge in mind, it is crucial to set goals for changing a hold decision to a sell. The short-term investor speculates on price, and like the successful gambler, he or she needs to decide when to walk away with the profits that he or she can take today. They might lose out on more potential profits tomorrow, but they also ensure that by taking profits now, they will be able to keep that money until it is again put at risk.

Returns Reported in the Financial Press

Inexperienced investors might unintentionally deceive themselves in the way that they view their return. They use a new high price as the imaginary base, thus ensuring that they can never profit in their minds. As long as prices continue to rise, they make a paper profit and revise their mental base. If prices fall, they view it as a loss and insist on holding until they regain their market value.

While this approach ensures that profits can never be taken, it is a common practice. The problems of viewing investment return unrealistically, even irrationally, is supported to a degree in the way that financial news is reported. The methods and formats of financial reporting present the investor with a series of problems. The complete story is not interesting enough to provide in a news format; thus, investors might approach financial news as the starting point and proceed from there with their own investigation. Finding the essence of a story is not always possible in the brief reports read in the financial papers. While many in-depth analyses are offered in the financial press, it is not always enough to really help the investor. Those new to the market need to be especially cautious in depending too heavily upon what they read in the paper.

Even the basic information about stocks, found in the daily listings, has many misleading characteristics. The problems of judging volatility based only on a 52-week high and low price range were explored in Chapter 7, "Volatility and Its Many Meanings." Augmenting the problem is the way that dividends are reported in stock market listings. Most investors will agree that dividends can represent a major part of the overall profit from investing, so judging stocks by a comparison of dividend yield is going to be an important step in picking stocks. Once you own a stock, however, the dividend yield reported in the financial press can be very misleading.

Fallacy: Dividend yield is easy to find in daily listings.

In fact, the dividend yield as reported can, in fact, be misleading. The value shown in most financial listings is the dividend paid per share, followed by the percentage earned by investors or the dividend yield. For example, a particular stock with current market price of $30 per share shows the following dividend-related columns:

.92   2.9

The first column tells you that the company's declared dividend is 92 cents per share, usually paid as 23 cents per share each quarter. Because the current price is $30.00 per share, this represents a dividend yield of 2.9%:

$$\frac{.92}{30.00} = 2.9\%$$

The actual meaning of these reported values and yields is misleading, however. The dividend yield of 2.9 percent is based on the latest closing price of the stock. Were that stock to rise to $35 per share tomorrow, the dividend yield would change to 2.6 percent, a yield lower than today's yield.

What does this situation mean for investors who already have shares of the company's stock? As the market price rises, the apparent dividend yield falls. Because the calculation is based on current market price, it is of limited value. It does tell someone who does not own the stock what their dividend yield would be *if* they bought the stock at its current price. Consider what occurs when the price of stock changes dramatically:

Market Price	Dividend per Share	Dividend Yield
$30.00	.92	2.9%
35.00	.92	2.6
40.00	.92	2.3
45.00	.92	2.0
$25.00	.92	3.7%
20.00	.92	4.6
15.00	.92	6.1
10.00	.92	9.2

Because a dramatic change in price affects the true yield if you were to buy shares at those price levels, it does matter what the yield is at the time of purchase. The belief that the reported yield applies even after you buy shares is false, however. It is more accurate to say, "The dividend yield an investor earns is always based on a comparison between the dividend per share and the price paid for stock, *not* current price."

The preoccupation among investors with market price per share of stock often means that relatively uninteresting aspects such as dividend yield are ignored. In fact, though, picking up stock when prices are depressed temporarily improves the overall yield because the dividend rate is higher. That factor, even though a relatively small part of the larger picture in the analysis of value and return, can become quite important over time. We have to assume that a growing corporation will continue to pay dividends and even increase the dividend yield over time. Monitoring dividend trends is one of the most important fundamental tests, because it is a reflection of how corporations use their profits. The consistent payment of dividends paid out to stockholders over time tests its ability to manage cash flow and profits. When growing companies depend too heavily on debt capitalization, in comparison, its dividends cannot be sustained because growing levels of operating profits go to interest payments as debt levels increase.

Price Comparisons as the Basis for Decisions

For many investors, the return on investments means the capital gain alone. How much did it cost, and how much did it sell for? Some investors even ignore the transaction fees, preferring to consider the price spread as the true measure of profit.

Price plays such an important role in the evaluation of portfolio success or failure that it also has become the most popular means for determining investment value. In the recent experience of the so-called dot.com industry, this thinking needs to change. Investors saw that prices for particular stocks can be run up to unimagined levels, only to fall even more suddenly. In some cases, prices rose for companies that had never experienced a profit, and even for those that did, the level of price was entirely unjustified by the fundamental realities.

A good lesson to remember in terms of market price and return on investment is as follows: One true relationship between price and fundamentals is that price change has to be supported. The price is determined largely by market perception, so that when investors believe that future growth levels will be strong, the current price reflects that belief. It is best seen in the PE ratio, in which price is expressed in terms of its multiple above earnings. That is the perception of where the company's growth is believed to be heading.

Is it reasonable to determine which stocks to buy, sell, or hold, however, based on price history and beliefs about future price movements? It is somewhat troubling that so many investment decisions are made solely on the basis of price. Just because a company's price trend has exhibited a pattern that looks promising, investors can ask themselves the following questions about price:

1. Is the *rate* of price increase justified by the company's fundamentals? In other words, is the prospect for long-term growth strong enough so that the recent price trends are reasonable? If not, the stock is overpriced.

2. Does the company's history support the continued growth in price, based again on its fundamental record? A company's record of sales and profits should be used as the determining factor about whether or not current price levels are supportable.

3. In the case of a depressed stock, is the low level realistic in terms of equally pessimistic forecasts about the future? Or are the fundamentals strong enough so that the low price makes the stock underpriced?

These are the kinds of analyses that investors can do on their own, just as a means for determining how well price is supported or justified by fundamental history and forecasts. Some causes for price change are strictly temporary and not related to long-term growth prospects. Most investors recognize that the market reacts in the broad sense to news and events that have no direct relationship to economic or to financial realities and that even reaction to earnings reports often are far out of proportion to the facts at play within the corporation. Finally, an otherwise strong stock might experience price depression when a larger competitor experiences falling prices. (By the same argument, a "weak sister" stock's price can be upheld by good news among its competitors.) Recognizing these problems in concentrating only on price, investors can see the need to look beyond in assessing current and potential return.

Price as a measurement of a stock's value is a poor way to make portfolio decisions. By the time a stock's price has changed, the underlying causes are done and gone. In that respect, yesterday's closing price also reflects yesterday's perception. Thus, it is too late to buy shares before the good news is known or to sell shares before the bad news is known by the market at large. Following short-term prices too closely prevents you from seeing the real situation, the market version of the "big picture" where you can spot price aberrations in time to make informed decisions to buy, sell, or hold shares. This situation does not rest only with the fundamentals, although sales and profits play a large role in this evaluation of the company. You might also be able to spot emerging changes in trends by looking beyond the short-term factors, however.

One example is a company that has been growing during recent years and going after increased market share with great success. In that case, the high profile of corporate operations often translates into a high profile price structure as well. The tendency among investors is to make investment decisions concerning stocks in the news, at least to a greater degree than with companies that are not on everyone's mind. Market share is finite, however, so you will eventually see the rate of growth begin to slow down. This situation is not a negative, just a reality about the nature of growth. It is interesting, however, that once investors believe a particular company is a viable growth stock, that label sticks even though its growth might be slowing down.

If you are evaluating long-term trends and looking for a change in the return on investment, you might also recognize the subtle changes in growth patterns that precede leveling out in the stock price as well. This method is one way to time your decisions and to come close to a long-term high in price trend. As sales and profits begin leveling out, the stock's price will ultimately follow. It might be time to look for the *new* long-term growth candidate—another company whose growth trend is still in the early stages.

This situation is an example of how the fundamentals can be used to identify likely long-term pricing patterns and how those fundamentals have to support stock prices. Without that support, the rise in price is false and based only on market perceptions but without a realistic base in the fundamentals. When price does relate to fundamental growth, then price is realistic. The perception of future value has validity when the fundamentals reveal the growth pattern. When that pattern begins to change, you can expect to see the results in stock price, perhaps not immediately, but eventually.

Remember, price is based almost entirely upon perception. So, if perception is based on the fundamental record, then it is logical. But if it is based on nothing but a desire within the market to buy up shares of a company because everyone wants to invest—but the fundamentals simply don't show why they want it—then there is a problem. The market fads come and go, and once investors lose interest, prices drop. When the dot.com run-up occurred and many of those companies had little or no profit to support prices, it was inevitable that those prices would eventually collapse. It happens over and over. Market fads in which some stocks are widely popular often involve the suspension of logic. This situation is where fortunes can be lost. During periods following large run-up and sudden price drops in some group of stocks, a period follows in which investors return to the fundamentals.

Admittedly, the dollars and cents of fundamental analysis are not particularly exciting, nor do the fundamentals command attention in the news like a big price run-up or drop. The real key to market profits, however, is found in the relatively dry financial information published in the financial press, with regulatory agencies, and in annual reports. The analysis of trends that you find in the dollars and cents of published reports reveals the growth prospects for a company and tells you far more than short-term price fluctuation. Remember, too, that recent price patterns can be deceiving because they are based on momentary perceptions, rumors, changes in supply and demand, and unknown other influences that are not lasting. So, prices are literally bounced around at times without any logical reason, and the only evaluation that makes sense has to be to look at the longer-term trend. To those who believe in price as the basis for decision-making, this situation usually means looking at the long-term moving average of price. It might also be expanded to mean far more, however.

When you can relate price history to the fundamentals and establish that the price pattern is justified by the fundamentals, you can take assurance in the conclusions that you reach. This exercise is equally valuable for seeing price changes that have no relationship to the fundamentals so that you can recognize overpriced and under-priced situations as well.

Internal Rate of Return (IRR)

When you analyze returns, compare prices to the fundamentals, and draw conclusions about the success of your portfolio decisions, you need to develop a means for identifying the actual return. The easiest method, of course, is to calculate the return by using the following elements:

1. Purchase price
2. Sales price
3. Dividend income

When the purchase price is subtracted from the sum of the sales price and dividend income received, the net difference is your profit (loss if in the negative). Some investors exclude the dividend income from this calculation, which overlooks an important element of overall return.

To ensure that comparisons of transactions are consistent and can be reviewed on the same basis, your net return should always include the transaction costs. Count only cash actually paid and received. In addition, the return should be annualized so that your comparisons between separate transactions are valid. If you held one stock three months and another for 24 months and they yielded the same percentage return, the annualized comparison will be significantly different. It is not only the percentage that counts but also the time that the investment was held. The time that you commit capital defines return just as much as the dollar amount.

With that in mind, some investors go a step farther and like to calculate what is called the *Internal Rate of Return* (IRR). Also called the average annual total return, this method calculates the return for each segment of the investment based on the time period involved. For example, the annual return of dividend payments would involve annualizing each payment received. Beginning from the first day of a dividend year, payments would be made on days 90, 180, 270, and 360 (for example). Thus, the accurately annualized return for each of these dividend payments would be based on the days involved. If your annual return on dividends were 5 percent, then the actual return on these four quarterly payments would be as follows:

Quarter #1: $5\% \times 270/360 = 3.75\%$

Quarter #2: $5\% \times 180/360 = 2.50\%$

Quarter #3: $5\% \times 90/360 = 1.25\%$

Quarter #4: $5\% \times 0/360 = 0.00\%$

This simplified calculation makes the point that each payment has a time value that adjusts its stated rate of return. The payment at the end of the first quarter has three quarters value based on a full year, and the second payment is yours for only half of the year. Thus, the actual "return" on these dividend payments is not a full 5 percent but a partial percentage based on the timing of payments.

When you annualize your capital gain from owning stock and add in dividends, the IRR will be significantly different for one investment over another if the timing of dividends and the holding period of the entire investment are also far different. IRR is more commonly applied to the calculation of present value and discount rate. It answers the question, "How much do I need to deposit each month to reach a target value, given the interest rate and number of periods?" Thus, for the calculation of total return on your portfolio, IRR is not the most applicable method to use.

The IRR is considered the most accurate method for calculating total return, but it makes a relatively small difference in overall portfolio performance when compared to the simple method of annualizing a single return. Thus, if you make a 5 percent return on two investments, one held for three months and the other for nine months, you can adjust the return simply by annualizing those outcomes:

3-month holding period: $5\% \times (12 \div 3) = 20.0\%$

9-month holding period: $5\% \times (12 \div 9) = 6.67\%$

The simple annualization of returns makes the two investments relatively comparable without going through the complexity of the IRR calculation. The question is made far more complex, however, when dividends are added in as well. For the sake of simplicity, most investors can apply the abbreviated version of annualizing return:

Sales price + all dividends received – purchase price = total return

Annualizing the total return produces a reasonable calculation that also enables you to make like-kind comparisons between separate transactions. The calculation is not different when dividends are reinvested through a DRIP program. These should still be counted in the calculation, even though not taken in cash. To the extent that you profit from holding the stock, reinvested dividends augment total return. This factor is a minor detail, and most investors will find the simplified review over the entire period to be more useful than the precision of IRR.

How do you annualize returns when you have made periodic investments? For example, some investors like to invest the same amount each month, usually in mutual fund shares where fixed dollar amount investing is more the norm than the direct purchase of stock. In that case, a single sale months or years later is more complex, because each monthly deposit would be figured by itself and the overall time period adjusted to reflect the total outcome. Anyone who makes periodic payments into mutual funds recognizes immediately that this calculation could be fairly complex. There is an alternative: finding the average holding period as a starting point.

For example, if you invest $100 per month buying shares of mutual funds and you reinvest all dividends, you accumulate $3,600 over three years. If you then sell, your *average* holding period is 18 months (one-half the period). So, you could annualize the single profit from selling your mutual fund shares by annualizing the profit as though the holding period were 18 months (the average holding period of all regular deposits).

If the timing and amounts of deposits vary, then this method does not work as well. It might be necessary to perform a number of calculations to accurately identify your return on the investment. The exercise should also be kept in perspective, however. How much difference is it going to make in future decisions if you calculate total return using one method or another? For those who are making periodic payments, one fairly reliable method would be to calculate the average holding period and annualize the total return based on that alone— regardless of how much cash was invested on each of several dates. The important point to remember is that there is little purpose in spending a lot of time to achieve absolute accuracy when a fair estimate of total return is sufficient for the purpose of comparison.

The internal rate of return is an important calculation for specific applications; however, the complexity of the calculation makes its value questionable when compared to easier methods—especially because close approximations serve the purpose and precise, detailed measurements of return do not significantly change the outcome. The simple annualization of overall return, if applied with equality to all portfolio transactions, will do the job for most people.

Closely related to IRR is the return calculated in the bond market, *Yield to Maturity* (YTM). This method figures out the actual return on a bond, assuming that the bond is held until maturity. It is somewhat like IRR because it takes into account any premium or discount involved. A bond's face value is the amount that will be paid at maturity. So, a $1,000 bond is worth $1,000 if held through to the end. As current interest rates change, however, a bond becomes more valuable or less valuable on the market depending on the direction of change. For example, if a bond offers a nominal yield of 5 percent based on market yields at the time of issue, that bond will be *more* valuable if market rates fall. This situation occurs because that 5 percent yield is considered high when compared to other rates. As a result, the bond trades at a premium. When a bond has a current value of 106, that means that even though its face value is $1,000, its current market value is $1,060.

The same change in value occurs when a bond is relatively low-yielding. For example, a bond with a fixed nominal yield of 5 percent becomes unattractive when market rates rise. So, if the 5 percent yield is low in comparison to other

TIP

A handy YTM calculator can be found online at the Web site www.cal-cbuilder.com/cgi-bin/calcs/BON1.cgi/financenter.

bond yields, the bond might trade at a discount. When a bond's current value is listed as 92, that means that its value is $920.

The premium or discount gradually evaporates as maturity approaches. (Of course, if maturity is in the far distant future, that evaporation will occur only in later years.) The purpose of the YTM calculation is to reflect the yield that bond investors will earn if they hold the bond until maturity, based on the current yield. This method requires taking the premium or discount into consideration and amortizing (premium) or accruing (discount) from the point of calculation until maturity.

Given these examples, a 5 percent bond selling at a premium of 106 has a current yield of 4.717 percent:

$50 ÷ $1,060 = 4.717%

The 5 percent bond selling at a discount of 92 yields 5.435%:

$50 ÷ $920 = 5.435%

The purpose of YTM is to reflect how premium or discount will affect the overall return of $50 per year (a nominal rate of 5 percent) between now and maturity. This version of IRR requires a complex calculation; however, YTM tables are available for the serious bond market investor. Daily bond listings also include YTM so that it does not have to be calculated by hand.

YTM is a good example of how IRR can be applied. The current discount or premium of a bond cannot be judged alone. Its real relative value depends on the nominal yield and on the time until maturity. So, YTM helps the bond investor study various bonds and make valid value comparisons. A stock investor, in comparison, might find a similar calculation for capital gains and dividends to be more distracting than helpful. While a bond's current market value tends to change very little from day to day, stocks can be far more erratic. This situation further makes the point that a simplified version of annualized return makes more sense for the comparative analysis of stocks.

Return Calculations for Option Buyers

When analyzing return in the options market, there are several different versions and permutations to keep in mind. An option buyer might be speculating or providing a form of insurance against other portfolio positions. A speculator buys an option in the belief that its value will rise. When that does occur, the net difference between sale and purchase is a short-term capital gain.[4]

A second purpose in buying options might be to provide insurance. A put provides downside protection for portfolio long positions in the same underlying stock. In the event that the market price of the stock falls, each put will increase in value dollar-for-dollar when in the money, offsetting losses. A call provides upside protection for short positions. When investors sell short, they face the risk that the stock's market value will rise. In that case, they could lose because they will be required to close the position through buying at a higher market price. A call will match that rise dollar for dollar, offsetting the loss in the short position.

Insuring against losses affects return because it protects against loss. In addition, in the event that values do not move in an adverse direction, the premium paid for options reduces overall profits; it becomes a cost. Investors using options in this manner, however, recognize the importance of protecting against loss and are willing to accept lower potential profits in exchange for the protection. Like other forms of insurance, there is no profit in paying premiums if the loss does not occur. The purpose is to avoid unacceptable losses. This situation might be viewed as a form of avoiding negative returns (losses) through the protection gained by purchasing options. The premium cost can be held down by buying options several points out of the money. In the event of a loss, the loss will be limited to the point spread between basis and striking price so that the investor is partially self-insured. The premium paid for options is the equivalent of protection against larger losses, and the point spread represents the co-insurance risk for the investor.

A call or put buyer can also exercise his or her options. A call buyer can exercise to buy appreciated stock at below-market prices. When the stock's value rises above the strike price, the call owner has the right to buy at that price. Thus, the basis in the stock might be far below current market value. When a call owner exercises, the amount of profit is equal to the difference between current market value and striking price, less premium paid.

For example, an investor pays a premium of 3 ($300) for a call with a striking price of 45. Just before expiration, the stock is worth $57 per share, and the investor exercises his call, buying 100 shares at $45. The immediate profit is:

Current market value		$5,700
Less: Striking price	$4,500	
Premium	300	4,800
Net profit		$900

While this calculation makes sense at first glance, the reality is that the call will have an intrinsic value of $1,200 at the time of expiration. Intrinsic value is always equal to the point spread between strike price and current market value. Thus, the investor could as easily sell the option just before expiration and realize the same profit ($1,200 – $300 = $900), probably with a far smaller transaction fee involved. The decision to profit from the option or to exercise should be made based on a calculation comparison between the two alternatives. In addition, the option owner might not want to actually buy 100 shares in these circumstances. So, the decision also rests with the question of whether the purpose in buying options is to make a fast profit or to pick up stock below its current market value. Buying the stock produces a return of 20.0 percent before annualization ($900 ÷ $4,500) just in market value gain. Selling the option produces of 300.0% ($900 ÷ $300).

This comparison brings up another important point concerning the calculation of return. Is it really valid to compare a 20 percent return to a 300 percent return? It is not. The chances of repeating the 300 percent return by speculating in options is remote. Picking up 100 shares of stock at a 20 percent discount, however, provides a different sort of benefit: ownership of cheap stock with tangible value, dividend income, and no expiration. If the fundamentals of that stock are strong, then this method becomes a reasonable way to buy stock. Thus, the comparison of the two returns is not a like-kind comparison. It is deceptive to conclude that the return from selling the call produces a better yield, given the other considerations.

When a put owner decides to exercise, he or she is able to sell 100 shares of stock at a price above current market value. Thus, an individual who buys a put to protect the value in a long position could take one of two actions in the event of a sharp drop in stock market value. First, the put could be sold and the profit considered as an offset to losses in the stock. Second, if the chances for recovery of market value appear slim, the put could be exercised and the stock sold at the strike price.

When the owner of stock sells the put at a profit, that profit is offset by stock losses. It also has the effect of adjusting the basis in stock, however. For example, if you purchase 100 shares at $45 and also buy a put with a strike price of 45, paying a premium of 4 ($400), what happens if the stock falls to $28 per share? The put could be sold and its intrinsic value would be $1,700 (17 points between strike price and market value). The put could also be exercised and sold at $45 per share, producing the same result. In either case, you are out the $400 premium paid for the put, but in exchange you have bought protection against a very large loss in market value.

If the put were simply sold, that has the effect of reducing market value by 13 points (17 gained at sale, less 4 original cost). Thus, your adjusted basis would be $32 per share, versus a current market value of $28. This situation would be far better than the original basis of $45.

These illustrations show that option returns are not necessarily the typical, traditional profits, the case where you sell the asset for more than it cost. In fact, the insurance aspect of options, whether hedging another risk or insuring against expected changes in market value, really acts to mitigate potential losses. In exchange for the relatively small premium, the option prevents a larger loss. This feature might be as important as a traditional form of return in the sense that *not* suffering losses is just as important as consistently earning profits.

Calculating the return on option investments is so complex because there are so many varieties involved. The relatively simple act of buying an option contract and later selling it for a profit is only the starting point for calculating profit *and* potential profit. Even more complex is the question of how to assess options when used for insurance. How much value should be placed on the elimination of risk? Clearly, the money spent on options used for insurance has to be folded into the overall profit or loss from the stock trade itself; however, even though the option reduces profits, the overall value goes beyond the mere return. The insurance reduces or eliminates risk, so the intangible value of using options in this way makes the black and white analysis of cost and profit more elusive.

For option investors selling covered calls, the estimation of outcomes involves three possible scenarios. Thus, when determining whether or not to sell a call, the writer needs to consider what is going to occur under all possible events. A call seller (or writer) owns 100 shares of stock for each option sold. Because the shares can be delivered in the event of exercise, this transaction is called "covered" call writing. The risk of exercise and the resulting loss is eliminated in one respect because the seller owns the shares. In another respect, however, the call seller continues to face a risk of potential loss. In the event the stock's price rises far above the strike price, the shares would have to be delivered at a price far below current market value. So, the wise call seller sets up the trade at a price that he or she is willing to accept, regardless of what might happen between the decision date and expiration.

Under the assumption that the call seller understands the potential for future lost profits, a call would be sold with the selection of a strike price above the original basis. For example, if you buy stock at $42 per share, and later sell calls at $45 or $50, then exercise would automatically build in a profit. Actually, profit would derive from three sources: capital gain, dividend income, and call premium.

This complexity requires that the covered call writer understands the outcome in three possible ways. When evaluating a covered call trade, the outcomes consist of the following:

1. Return if exercised
2. Return if unchanged
3. Return if closed

The return if exercised refers to having 100 shares called away. The seller owns 100 shares and also sells one call covered by those shares; the stock price rises above strike price before exercise, and the option is exercised. Thus, the call seller is required to deliver the 100 shares at the strike price. In this outcome, the seller profits from all three sources: capital gain on the sale of stock, dividend income, and call premium.

Return if unchanged means that the option expires as worthless. This situation occurs whenever the stock price is at or below strike price upon exercise. The option expires as worthless. In this outcome, the seller keeps 100 percent of the option premium received; however, the calculation is not final at this point. The seller still owns the 100 shares and will continue receiving dividends. Perhaps of greater importance, with the original option expired, the seller is now free to sell another option against the same shares. This action can be done repeatedly as long as the option is not exercised. The 100 percent return on the investment can be treated in one of two ways. It can be considered as a separate transaction from the investment in stock, or it can be treated as a reduction in the basis in stock. For example, if you paid $42 per share and received 3 ($300) for selling an option, your revised basis in stock becomes $39 per share ($42 − $3).

Return if closed refers to the act of trading in covered calls without waiting out expiration. The opening transaction involves selling one call per 100 shares owned. At that point, the seller is paid the premium price less trading fees. If the value falls significantly, the option can be closed with a purchase transaction. For example, if you sold a call at 3 ($300) but its current value is 1 ($100), a closing purchase transaction would produce a profit of $200 (before trading costs on both sides of the transaction). Closing out the position creates a profit and also removes the risk of exercise in the event that the stock's price might rise between the decision date and expiration. It also frees up the 100 shares for a subsequent covered call write; the sale of calls can continue indefinitely in this way, with the seller profiting from evaporating time value over a series of covered call transactions.

Calculating each of these returns has to include the dividend income, if applicable, as well as any capital gain. Examples of these outcomes are as follows:

If the original purchase price was $42 per share and current dividend is $26 per quarter, the three different returns can be calculated based on current strike price and premium. For example, today's current market value is $45 per share, and an option expiring in two months has a current premium value of 3 ($300) with a strike price of $45. If the current option premium value had fallen to 1 ($100), it could be closed out at a profit or held pending expiration. The three calculations under these conditions are as follows:

Return if exercised

Exercise price	$4,500	
Less: Basis in stock	–4,200	
Capital gain	$300	
Dividend (assume 1 quarter)	26	
Option premium	300	
Total return	$626	14.9%

Return if unchanged

Option premium	$300	100% (or $300 reduction in basis of stock)

Return if closed

Option premium	$300	
Closing purchase	–100	
Net return	$200	66.7%

All of these examples include no allowance for the cost of trading. This cost varies from one firm to another; it also is lower on a per-transaction basis when you deal in more than one option per trade. Accordingly, covering 1,000 shares with 10 calls would be less expensive than trading in one call per transaction.

Whether you treat option profits and losses as separate transactions or as adjustments to the basis in stock, tax treatment is not as flexible. You might properly consider using calls or puts to reduce risk and covered call premium as a means for lowering your basis and gaining more downside protection. For federal tax purposes, however, all listed option profits and losses are short-term by definition. Thus, even when you experience a long-term capital gain or loss on stock, all related option transactions are going to be treated as short-term. For those with a complex array of transactions, this point should be kept in mind as year-end tax planning takes place. For short positions, premium received within a tax year is not taxed in that year; it is recognized as income in the year that the option is exercised, expired, or closed.

Mutual Fund Returns

The variations of return on invested capital become even more complex when you reinvest earnings. How can you judge overall performance when a growing portion of your return comes from the compounded effect of reinvestment over many years?

Mutual funds are well known for promoting their historical performance in this way. Sales literature often makes the point that had you invested a lump

> **TIP**
>
> To evaluate mutual funds with their various fees in mind, check the SEC
> Web site, which provides an interactive tool, the Mutual Fund Cost
> Calculator: www.sec.gov/investor/tools/mfcc/get-started.htm.

sum in the past, it would now be worth an impressive dollar value. These illustrations should be reviewed carefully, however, because the real return on investment might not be as good as it looks.

For example, you might read in a brochure, "If you had invested $10,000 in our fund 20 years ago, it would be worth $38,697 today. In other words, your capital would have nearly quadrupled in value. As impressive as that seems, it represents only 7% return compounded over the 20-year term." This approximates overall stock market performance over the long term, so it really means that the fund has done as well as the average. Even so, telling you that you could have gained 387% sounds impressive.

The compounding effect of reinvesting dividends clouds the issue. With mutual fund investments, the *valid* comparison should include not only market performance, but also the costs of buying shares. The comparison between load and no-load funds is significant, for example. If you make your own investment decisions and do not use a stockbroker or financial planner to pick the best possible fund, then there is no need to pay a load fee (which is a sales commission deducted from your investment dollars). So, if the load fee is 8.5 percent, that means that only $91.50 out of every $100 you invest goes into the investment. It also pays to avoid back-end load, which is the same expense but assessed when you sell rather than when you buy. Other fees might apply but are not as apparent. For example, funds are allowed to assess a 12b-1 fee, which is a fee to help pay for advertising costs. If you pick a fund that charges such a fee, you're helping to pay for advertising and promotional materials to attract new investors. You are better off investing in a fund that does not assess a 12b-1 fee.

The elimination of confusion over fees will help to clear the air in attempting to judge and compare mutual funds. The *Net Asset Value* (NAV) of funds is reported in daily listings and is approximately the equivalent of a per-share price for an individual stock. Mutual funds are more complicated, however. They own many stocks or bonds and they also keep some cash in reserve, so the NAV is only useful for comparing day-to-day changes for a particular fund. It is not reliable for judging longer-term portfolio performance. For that, you need to study the longer-term trend of the fund, including all possible sources of income.

Mutual funds derive income from capital gains, the buying and selling of shares of stock. They also pass through dividend income to shareholders. An income or balanced fund will also see income in the form of interest from bonds. The fund reports to its shareholders by way of a monthly report showing current NAV and all current income, whether taken in cash or reinvested. A capital gain distribution refers to the sharing of capital gains among all shareholders at the time of the sale and not necessarily to an actual cash distribution. Your overall income from a mutual fund investment depends largely on the decision to either take profits in cash or reinvest them in the purchase of additional shares.

The long-term building of equity in a mutual fund occurs from the combination of change in NAV and the decision to reinvest dividends. For those investors who want to build equity over time, the decision to reinvest makes the most sense. All earnings from capital gains distributions, however—taxable dividends and interest—are taxable in the year paid or credited, whether taken in cash or not.

Clearly, the calculation of return on investment is complex in virtually all areas. The stockholder who simply buys and holds shares and ultimately sells needs to consider dividend income as a significant part of overall return and also make valid comparisons between different stocks through annualization. Those buying bonds or mutual funds or supplementing a portfolio of stocks by also trading in options face a confusing array of adjustments and considerations required to make return calculations consistent and valid.

The purpose of all calculations of return should always be to ensure that dissimilar holding periods or dollar amounts are evaluated in a consistent manner. It is too easy to overlook the true significance of a trade by failing to recognize the need for adjustment. A $1,000 profit compared to a $500 profit seems like twice the return at first glance. The initial investment amount and the holding period can vary to the degree that you need to look beyond the mere dollar amount, however, and even beyond the percentage. A $1,000 profit on a $4,000 investment represents a 25 percent return. If that return is achieved in two months (a 150 percent annualized return), however, it has far different meaning that if it resulted from a four-year holding period (a 6.25 percent annualized return).

Every investor needs to develop the means for performing comparative analysis that is valid and precise. Thus, comparing any two returns given different circumstances (holding periods, dollar amount of investment, the inclusion of options, reinvested earnings, and so on) is going to mean that the simple analysis of return on investment is not enough. In some instances, it is necessary to reduce the basis for related profits (such as an option premium received for covered call writes). In other cases, overall return has to be adjusted because earnings have been reinvested or because dividends were taken in cash in one instance and not in another.

Many investors place capital in dissimilar areas, including a mix between equity and income mutual funds, direct ownership of stocks in dissimilar industries, and between stocks and other forms of investment. All of these variations require analysis of the overall portfolio. In diversifying risks, you also diversify the potential return. So, it is not realistic to expect to experience the same rate of return from stocks and from directly owned real estate, nor from income funds and equity funds. Because they have different characteristics, both risk and potential return are dissimilar as well.

Because risk and opportunity are inescapably related, the analysis of your own returns has to be comparative between similar types of investments. At the same time, they have to be kept separate in dissimilar investments. Because the risk factors are different, the returns will be different as well. For example, a covered call writer might experience a 15 percent return on a single covered call write while the underlying stock is yielding far below the stock market average. Does the overall return mitigate the problem of low-yielding stock? Does the call profit reduce the basis in the stock? Or, is the stock itself an under-performing investment that should be removed from the portfolio? Is the lost opportunity cost greater than the average return?

These important questions have to be raised and addressed by each investor. The purpose of analysis is to find the truth; and when it comes to the study of comparative returns, the most difficult aspect is going to be ensuring that comparisons are truly valid.

Notes

[1] A classic example of how reports can be distorted is the type of statement made in annual reports of corporations with losses. One example for a company whose losses were higher in the current year than the year before: "The reduction in the rate of acceleration of net losses underscores our move toward profitability."

[2] In the past, dividend earnings were a problem for investors because the dollar amount was too small to justify odd lot purchases. Today, however, many publicly listed corporations offer free *dividend reinvestment plans* (DRIPs). Through these plans, dividends can be converted to additional partial shares instead of being paid out in cash. To find out more, contact the shareholder relations department for the corporation.

[3] As long as your shares are in street name, DRIPs will be run through the brokerage and you might be charged additional fees. As DRIPs become increasingly popular as a way to compound earnings, more and more investors will discover the advantages of registering shares in their own name.

[4] By definition, listed stock option net profits and losses are always short-term with the exception of special long-term options that are not a part of this discussion.

CHAPTER 10

Professional Advice for Investors

The majority of investors consider seeking professional advice at some point, usually when they first begin investing. It is a natural starting point to seek knowledge from more experienced people. It also could be the wrong way to proceed.

In challenging the presumption that it is always best to seek help in investing from someone else, the following points should be kept in mind:

1. *No one else is going to be as concerned with your capital as you.* In fact, one of the chronic problems in the market is an over-dependence on the myth that the right professional is going to take care of our investments for us and will exercise the greatest possible care and concern. The reality, though, is that it is far easier to take risks with someone else's money, and this statement applies to professional advisors just as it does to everyone else. Ultimately, every investor is responsible for his or her investment decisions, even when based on the advice that someone else provides. It is a mistake to trust another person's judgment blindly.

2. *While many professionals are qualified to advise you, many others are not.* It is all too easy to waste time and money in exchange for poor

advice. The financial services industry is regulated only to a degree, and many people are active in the field who are not experts in investing or who do not understand the market any better than the average person. For example, a registered representative who advises clients in the stock market is required to pass a test; however, that test does not really gauge experience, it only ensures that the individual has a thorough knowledge of the rules. Thus, a registered representative might not understand the intricacies of investing to the degree that a client would expect. Holding the license to execute trades also does not ensure that the individual has exceptional qualifications. Many other advisors are licensed to sell insurance but are not qualified to provide advice beyond that area. The problem in this field is inconsistency in qualification, coupled with a self-regulatory environment that is only effective to a point. That self-regulatory effort does not always protect the consumer.

3. *Hiring a professional should be done for the right reasons.* Many people believe, in error, that paying for advice gets them an inside track, and that is never true. This attitude is one of the most common beliefs in the market. Some people think that there are two groups at play. One group has more knowledge than the rest of us, and the other group does not. There is no real "inside track," however, when it comes to providing professional advice. If an individual does possess inside knowledge, he or she is not likely to want to share it with others. In truth, you should hire a professional only when you understand the limitations of the relationship. Trusting someone else to advise you or to make decisions concerning your money should be a decision based on experience, and then only when you know that the person being given that trust is going to act in an ethical and honest manner.

You will need to decide which types of advisors to hire or even to listen to, because there are several different types. Market analysts are thought to be experts in forecasting the future. Some work purely as technicians, concentrating on price trends, while others study the fundamentals and attempt to estimate future earnings levels.

A broker is usually associated with stock trading. A sort of "middle man," the broker traditionally works with clients to place buy and sell orders, conveying those orders to the exchange floor for execution. In recent years, the brokerage business has undergone significant changes. A "full service" broker (meaning that the client would pay a full retail commission to execute trades) was alleged to act not only as the executor of trades, but also as a personal financial advisor, telling clients which stocks were better deals and buying opportunities. As the Internet becomes ever more popular as a medium for trading at relatively low cost, the role of the broker as an advisor is fading. Over the past 40 years, discount brokerage has been taking an ever-growing slice of brokerage business away from the arcane full-cost firms; the Internet will probably speed up the demise of that industry. Few people are going to be willing to pay full price for trades in the future, and this statement is especially true because the history of brokerage advice shows that paying for the service has not produced superior performance. On the contrary, it often has occurred that investors depending on professional advice have suffered financially with lower-than-average performance.

Financial advisors, planners, or consultants offer services for a fee or on commission. They come in a variety of types, some very experienced and others without any particular experience whatsoever. One problem you face in locating a competent financial advisor is that many people use the title; there are few restrictions. So, it is wise to know the professional designations and what they mean and to seek a top professional if and when you determine that you will benefit from hiring a professional.

In the following sections, the various types of professional advisors are discussed in more detail.

Market Analysts

The analyst holds the attention of the market because he or she makes predictions about the future prospects of a corporation. This forecasting function is given far too great a degree of weight and importance among investors. The forecast itself becomes the standard, and actual performance is measured against it. In other words, the forecast becomes more significant than the actual result, which is puzzling when you consider the methods employed to arrive at the analyst's conclusion.

In the corporate world, forecasting is one of the primary occupations and preoccupations. Executives depend upon their expert advisors to anticipate the future. So, internal auditors, accountants, analysts, and most other managers are constantly called upon to estimate the future. Whether expressed in terms of market share, sales, full-blown budgets (company-wide, for a division, or a department), or internal reports, forecasting takes up more time than most other corporate activities. The executive is constantly required to make decisions that place corporate capital at risk, so the dependence on forecasting is all-consuming. The degree to which the corporate employee is able to accurately forecast often defines the difference between career success and failure.

Marketing studies, for example, are compiled with known sales potential, market studies, and interviews in the field. A manager making a recommendation to proceed with a project or to reject it, or to develop a product or abandon it, will base that recommendation on data gathered under proven methods.

Even with the importance of forecasting at the corporate level, everyone knows that the forecast is only an estimate. It is a best guess, given the availability of information and its interpretation. Forecasts are sometimes wrong, and some forecasts fail to anticipate changes in the future that the corporation needs to know about in order to take action today. The entire science of corporate expansion is based on forecasting.

In the stock market, however, forecasting has an entirely different face. An analyst will study a company in considerable depth and review much of the same information: sales and profit history, markets and plans for market expansion, economic prospects, management of the company, and more. The analyst then estimates sales and earnings. While the data are identical in many cases, the analyst is not the same as a corporate manager in a number of ways. First, the analyst probably is not necessarily trained in the same way as a corporate forecaster, who probably has a financial background (and often, experience in accounting and finance). The analyst is more likely to be a market expert. So, the disparity between financial and investment training and education means that emphasis will be dissimilar as well. Second, the analyst is attempting to guess where sales and profit levels are going to end up, given a number of existing factors; the internal forecaster is more likely to attempt to identify market potential and will forecast based on recommendations for specific direction that the company might or might not take. Third, the analyst is advising investors, whereas the financial employee is advising management. It is interesting, with that in mind, to note that the analyst is more likely to make a buy recommendation than to offer investors a sell recommendation.[1]

The philosophy on Wall Street, a sort of unspoken rule, is "never say sell." Fearing that a sell recommendation will drive down the price, it is more likely that an analyst will modify a buy recommendation to hold. The analyst most often is motivated by the fact that his or her firm is working for the corporation whose stock they are recommending. Wall Street firms earn approximately 70 percent of their profits from investment banking; thus, giving clients a sell recommendation is contrary to their motives.[2]

Perhaps the most revealing study on the problem of analysts' recommendations comes from a four-year study done by Investars.com, an online information service. That study revealed that investors lost an average of 53.34 percent when they followed the advice of an analyst whose firm managed the company's IPO. The same study showed that when the firm had no underwriting deal with the company, investors lost only 4.24 percent on average.[3]

The purpose of listening to an analyst is to make money, not to lose it. So, even though the results were dismal in either case, the study makes the point that when the Wall Street firm acts as underwriter, it has not worked for the client. The fact that the average investor lost money when listening to an analyst further supports the contention that this method is not wise for selecting stocks or for timing market decisions.

The analyst's prediction concerning earnings is given a great deal of importance on Wall Street, to the extent that the actual reports are judged in comparison to the prediction, rather than on their own merits. So, the problem is not limited to one of stock selection based on an analyst's interpretation of the fundamentals; it is complicated by the tendency to judge corporate results by comparing them to the forecast. This situation is backward if we return to the premise that a forecast is only a best guess.

When an analyst predicts a 5 percent increase in sales and the corporate results come in at a 3 percent increase, we view this situation as a negative. Because actual results fell short of the forecast, it is likely that the stock price will fall as a consequence, at least in the short term. This situation is true even if the corporation predicted only 2 percent growth and considers the outcome to be excellent. So, the interpretation of fundamentals by the analyst becomes more important than the strength of earnings and the corporate prospects for future growth.

Given the conflicts that analysts have when their firm is acting as investment banker, the *Securities and Exchange Commission* (SEC) is beginning to take steps to correct the problem. The SEC has been urging the stock exchanges to change their rules to do away with the conflict of interest so that investors will not be misled by poor advice. In the meantime, investors need to be aware that a firm is not working in their best interests when it is also working as an investment banker for the company whose stock they recommend.

Analysts augment their recommendations about the fundamentals (sales and earnings) by offering "target price" information to investors. By attempting to identify how high a stock's price will go, analysts attempt to attract buyers. Those prices might be inflated as a means of raising capital, however, with little or no connection to the company's fundamental strength or real value. If the target price were to drive the PE ratio to three-digit high levels, the smart investor should ask, "What is the basis for arriving at that target price?"

A well-known example was the forecast that Amazon.com would climb to $400 per share. The well-known analyst Henry Blodget, who made that prediction, claimed that his target price was based on advanced fundamental analysis. The stock did, in fact, rise to more than $400 per share before it fell drastically. Given the weight of an analyst's prediction, however, it is impossible to know whether Blodget was right or whether the stock rose in response to his predictions. The fact that Amazon.com had never shown a profit belies the claim that the target price was based on good, fundamental information. Without any profits, there are no reliable fundamentals available to make such predictions.

In fact, given the dismal history of analysts' predictions of fundamental outcome, their estimates of future price levels should be given far less weight. Price predicting is elusive at best and should be tied in with a serious analysis of growth trends and future potential. When a Wall Street firm uses target price predictions to sell shares, the buy recommendation should be viewed with caution.

Brokers

Stock market brokers have been around ever since trading began in New York nearly 400 years ago. The origin of brokerage derives from the need to facilitate trading in wheat, tobacco, and other commodities. Dealers in stocks originally met once per day, where trades were executed by auction. The concept of brokerage developed out of the need of commodities and securities dealers to ensure movement of their product. The broker, serving as middleman, originally served the role of matching buyers with sellers. One early function of the broker was to place government bonds in the hands of buyers to finance the Revolutionary War. Secretary of the Treasury Alexander Hamilton encouraged marketing war bonds in 1790, and brokers (as well as bankers, politicians, speculators, and others) traded in the deeply discounted bonds.[4]

In those early days of securities trading, brokers were true insiders. Originally merchants themselves, brokers controlled the market for securities for many years, partly because they created the trading market and partly because communication was inefficient and slow, so the average person could trade in securities only by being at the point of sale. Thus, brokers traded with one another for the most part. In 1792, the brokers of the day used to meet beneath a buttonwood tree at 68 Wall Street. They formed an agreement among themselves that has become known as the Buttonwood Tree Agreement. It read:

> We, the Subscribers, Brokers for the Purchase and Sale of Public Stock, do hereby solemnly promise and pledge ourselves to each other, that we will not buy or sell from this day for any person whatsoever, any kind of Public Stock, at less than one quarter of one per cent Commission on the Specie value and that we will give preference to each other in our Negotiations. In Testimony whereof we have set our hands this 17th day of May at New York, 1792.[5]

This early agreement among brokers became the basis for the organization of stock exchanges. Few issues were active other than government securities for many years, and the relatively small group of brokers dominated the securities market. As corporations began emerging in the early 19th century, brokerage business in New York moved indoors for the first time. Meanwhile, brokers in Philadelphia were far more organized and had set up a formal exchange in 1790. The Philadelphia Stock Exchange, as the first stock exchange in the United States, served as a model for the New York brokers, who modeled their organization after it. In 1817, following a visit to Philadelphia, brokers formed the New York Stock and Exchange Board, housed in a rented room at 40 Wall Street.

This history is significant because it was always viewed as being the exclusive club for the business of brokerage. In other words, brokers organized themselves as members of the exchange and ensured that only fellow members were allowed to trade. The business of brokerage involved speculating in government, railroad, and corporate stocks and then selling shares at marked-up values to banks, speculators, and investors. Changes were sparked by events such as the California gold rush and resulting speculation in the still limited market. During the 1850s, brokers were known to use the capital of their exchange for their own purposes. It was not uncommon for brokers to deposit small amounts and immediately withdraw funds 100 to 200 times greater. The market crashed in 1853, and the abuses of the brokers nearly destroyed the entire system; within two years, however, the panic ended and business was back to normal. By the end of the decade, brokerage membership was seen as a status symbol and exchange members were known for their expensive clothing. Exchange initiation fees were raised to $1,000, excluding most people from considering membership.

The Civil War brought about a surge in the securities market. Four new exchanges opened to meet the growing speculative demand, including an open-air exchange (later called the American Stock Exchange). Wild speculation in gold during the war years dominated exchange business as currency values declined with Confederate victories. Gold values mirrored war news, and attempts by the government to control speculation in gold were not effective. After the Civil War, a period of manipulation and abuse characterized the market. An individual named Jay Gould tried to corner the gold market in 1969 and held contracts to deliver $50 million in gold, although only $20 million worth of gold was on the market. When the government reacted by selling its own gold holdings on the open market, however, the scheme fell apart and many people lost fortunes. The attempt to corner the market failed, but a few brokers made fortunes. Gould convinced the two brokers heavily involved in the transactions to go into bankruptcy, and in exchange he supported them for the rest of their lives.

This corrupt incident was the initiation of a period lasting until about 1900, in which corruption and manipulation were widespread and virtually no regulation over the markets existed. In historical perspective, the brokerage business has been deeply involved in the many scandals of the stock market because, for so many years, they had exclusive control over trading and management of money. Thus, wash sales, corners, collusion, and insider trading are nothing new. Unlike the past, the opportunities to misuse the market today are greater than ever, and they are no longer limited to the exclusive club of traditional brokerage. The Internet has made it possible for even the average investor to attempt to manipulate markets through devices such as the "pump and dump."[6]

The brokerage business was changed not only by the rapid expansion of wealth in the United States, but also by significant changes in communications. As more people gained access to the exchanges, the nature of brokerage changed as well. The expansion of the railroads during the 1870s had a significant impact on exchange business in two ways. First, the railroads issued stocks and bonds that increased investment volume substantially. Second, railroad traffic enabled people to travel great distances in moderate comfort, meaning that lifestyles changed as well. This situation also had an effect on the way that people invested their capital.

The electric stock ticker, introduced in 1867, enabled instantaneous communication of market news. This invention was followed 11 years later by the introduction of the telephone, which linked the trading floor to brokerage offices for the first time. As the United States telegraph expanded during the same period, city-to-city communication became convenient and immediate. The combination of the telephone and telegraph were as significant in the late 19th century as the Internet in the 20th and 21st centuries.

As these improvements in communication were taking place, more and more people were able to take part in the investment world. Brokerage, once limited to a handful of members, evolved to become an industry of representatives for thousands of individual investors. Fewer and fewer brokers limited their activities to trading in their own accounts as the demand for public trading grew from year to year. During this period, the abuses of the system continued. Brokers could deposit relatively small sums and draw larger sums for speculation in their accounts or in the accounts of their customers. Leveraged speculation inevitably led to reversals such as the Panic of 1893. One of every four railroads went bankrupt that year. Another depression hit the United States between 1897 and 1903. While the abuses of the brokerage business did not cause these depressions, they augmented the losses that speculators suffered. The cyclical nature of the economy led to slow-downs in business activity, so a highly leveraged, speculative position in stock meant that losses were matched in severity. The greater the speculation, the worse the financial consequence. The remarkable surge in values in American stocks following World War I brought record numbers of first-time investors into the market. Annual volume of 171 million shares in 1921 grew to 1.1 billion by 1929. At the same time, brokers' loans rose to $8,549 million, and 300 million shares were held in margin accounts.[7]

A severe drop in the market value of stocks signaled the beginning of the Great Depression. The excessive speculation and margin trading resulted in an 89 percent decline in the DJIA, with listed price dollar value losses of $74 billion. The devastation in the market led to an in-depth Senate investigation lasting 17 months between 1933 and 1934, resulting in the disclosure of the widespread abuses among brokers and speculators. Several federal laws were written and enacted as a result. The most significant for the stock market were the Securities Act of 1933 and the Securities Exchange Act of 1934, which led to the creation of the SEC and placed all public exchange business under federal jurisdiction. This situation ushered in the modern era of exchange operations and the regulatory environment under which the public exchanges operate today.

The new laws and regulatory environment caused great unrest in the exchange and brokerage businesses, and by 1937 the conflict led to a call for a complete overhaul. The chairman of the NYSE, William O. Douglas, observed that the evolution of the brokerage industry needed to undergo a drastic change in structure and philosophy. He said:

> Operating as private membership associations, exchanges have always administered their affairs in much the same manner as private clubs. For a business so vested with public interest, this traditional method has become archaic.[8]

The observation was profound. Breaking down a well-guarded and strongly held position dominating the industry was no small task, and those holding the power resisted change. The reforms went into effect in 1938, however, and the past abuses were greatly curtailed.

The desire to bring the markets together and make them available to an ever-growing public interest in long-term stock ownership was encouraged by development of the National Marketing System during the 1970s. Electronic linkage developed by the NYSE in 1978 enabled different markets and exchanges to communicate efficiently so that brokers were able to execute trades on seven major exchanges, with later expansion to include over-the-counter issues as well.

The ongoing improvement in automated trading throughout the second half of the 20th century led to the greater efficiency of intermarket trading; and brokerage was once again changed with the introduction of discount brokerage in the 1970s. In previous times, the brokerage industry had always worked with relatively set commission rates for trades, often on the argument that customers were paying for the expertise of a talented broker. Challenging that assumption, the SEC approved "negotiated" commissions on May 1, 1975, and the control over commissions previously held by retail commission firms began to erode. The old argument that customers were paying for expert advice simply did not hold up with the record, and to this day, an ever-growing number of investors choose to forego the advice of a broker and prefer to save money on their commission costs.

Full-commission brokerage continues to fade as the Internet becomes the medium for stock trades. With growing numbers each month, the transaction of investment business is becoming an online industry. Traditional methods of in-person visits to brokerage offices and even use of the telephone are being viewed increasingly as inefficient in comparison to the nearly instantaneous access found on the Internet. The ease of trading and low cost, coupled with free online stock quotes and charts, has opened the market to millions of investors who previously needed to work through the traditional brokerage relationship.

With the advances on the Internet and its almost universal use of discounted fees for executing trades, brokerage has taken on an entirely new face. No longer the private club referred to by NYSE Chairman Douglas, the brokerage industry has also lost its price controls in the transaction of trades. As the inefficiencies of the old methods become increasingly obvious, the brokerage industry is being forced to evolve into an entirely new business. Today, the broker actually is a streamlined Web site organized to execute trades with great efficiency and at a lower price than its competitors. While some brokers continue to try to offer financial advice in much the same way as the Wall Street analyst, experienced investors recognize the dangers of trusting brokers too much, often to their detriment rather than benefit.

Some brokers continue to try to offer services akin to the analysts by operating in the mixed role of broker and investment banker. By its nature, firms operating as investment bankers attempt to talk its customers into buying shares, but in the electronically efficient world of automation, the traditional methods are becoming less efficient over time. Many brokers have also attempted to hold onto some traditional income by offering financial consultation. Some novice investors might try working with fee-based planners (see the next section), and even some experienced investors will retain a trusted advisor based on past success, notably those with little time to research the market and make their own decisions. For those millions of individuals in the middle, however, the combination of thousands of mutual funds, low-cost online trading, and dividend reinvestment plans offered directly by many listed companies, the need for the old-style broker is becoming increasingly out of date. One idea persists, however. The remaining full-commission brokerage firms still maintain that their customers get greater value when they pay a full retail commission.

Fallacy: Paying full commission gets you better information.

This statement is an appeal to the natural tendency among investors to look for good advice elsewhere. Investing is complex, and few inexperienced investors are willing to go forward without some form of advice or help from a more experienced source. Thus, the myth that paying more gets better advice has its adherents today. Many investors, proceeding with the need for security, begin by trusting a full-commission broker but might be disappointed with the results. The fallacy should be replaced with the realization that brokers are really commission-based salespeople. They are motivated to transact buy and sell orders as a means for earning a living.

With this situation in mind, a natural conflict of interest arises between what translates to a profit for the broker and what might or might not be a profit for the investor. Those who experience less-than-satisfactory results might end up moving their accounts to a discount brokerage firm, where they save significantly on the costs of transacting business.

TIP

For more information about the workings of investment clubs, check the
NAIC Web site at www.better-investing.org/index.html.

As an alternative to trusting an expensive brokerage firm to advise them, beginning investors will probably succeed with a combination of other ideas. For example, putting capital in a no-load mutual fund with a good track record in both up
and down markets is a wise first step to developing a diversified portfolio—and
one that enables them to reinvest earnings automatically. To gain experience and
knowledge, the inexperienced investor should consider starting out by joining an
investment club. The premise behind most clubs is that by dividing up the
research, the membership (usually 10 to 15 people) collectively gains a lot of
information. The experience of investing through a joint effort not only succeeds
because of the in-depth research, but it also helps the inexperienced investor to
move through a learning period without the insecurity of making decisions without the advice of others.

The long history of the brokerage industry is more easily understood if it is
viewed as several different evolutionary changes, rather than as a single industry. Changes in the regulatory environment, communications and technology,
and publicity concerning past abuses have all helped to end one era and begin
another. At the same time, brokerage practices have evolved and changed with
the times and will do so again in the future. As the Internet replaces the previous trading norms with greater efficiency and speed, old-style brokerage will
be replaced as well.

The history of the brokerage industry is marked by well-known abuses and
sudden reversals of fortune. This situation does not mean that the entire industry has been corrupt in the past, but only that the problems of lax regulation,
rapidly changing economic times, and an expanding economy have presented
opportunities for unscrupulous brokers—and those are the events that history
remembers. Whenever large sums of money change hands, it is inevitable that
such events will occur. For the present and the future, the markets benefit from
the mistakes and abuses of the past because those abuses have led to the cre-
ation of protective regulation and the enforcement of laws meant to protect the
public.

Financial Advisors

A field related to brokerage is that of financial advisory services. As with the
case of brokers, the majority of financial planners are ethical and competent

TIP

To review the Investment Advisors Act of 1940 and current amendments, check the SEC's Web site at www.sec.gov/rules/extra/ia1940.htm.

people offering a valuable service; however, over its history, investment advisory services have undergone many problems relating to qualifications of individuals in the field, the proper handling of client funds, and the offering of advice based on knowledge and experience.

A "financial planner" can be many things. An individual using that title might be nothing more than an insurance salesman posing as a more qualified professional. Instead of asking to come into your home to sell you insurance, a "financial planner" might offer you a one-hour free consultation. This sales ploy is smart, but a smart consumer should always check qualifications beforehand and know whether or not the financial planner is qualified to offer investment advice.

Some professional and regulatory designations help separate the true professional from the rest. A registered investment advisor is someone who meets the requirements of federal law as defined in the Investment Advisors Act of 1940.

By definition, an "investment advisor" means:

> any person who, for compensation, engages in the business of advising others, either directly or through publications or writings, as to the value of securities or as to the advisability of investing in, purchasing, or selling securities, or who, for compensation and as part of a regular business, issues or promulgates analyses or reports concerning securities.[9]

Under the law and SEC regulations, the *Registered Investment Advisor* (RIA) is required to make specific disclosures to clients concerning compensation. For many years, the industry has struggled with the problem of compensation. Recommending particular investments generates a commission to the individual who is acting as a salesperson. At the same time, the RIA might operate as a financial advisor and charge an hourly or flat-rate fee. The acceptance of dual compensation is recognized as a conflict of interest; however, it is also improper for the advisor to refund a commission to the client in lieu of collecting a fee (in fact, that practice is specifically prohibited as well).

Some RIA organizations have attempted to deal with the problem in various ways. For example, some have set up a system under which the corporation earns the advisory fee and the individual is paid a sales commission for recommending products. The problem, of course, is that compensation from the two sources goes to the same person, part as an individual and part as a business entity. This solution does not solve the conflict of interest; it only creates the appearance that the individual is not being compensated twice (when in practice, the conflict remains).

It is not always equitable to avoid recommendations that will generate a commission. If an advisor limits his or her recommendations to only no-load mutual funds, for example, then the entire range of directly owned stocks must be excluded. The only way to avoid the conflict altogether is for an individual to act as a fee-based advisor only and to refer clients to someone else for the placement of business. This structure is difficult for the arrangement because clients will invariably prefer to find one person they trust and work with them exclusively. So, the compromise that many RIAs have worked out is to develop a relationship of referrals between themselves and a sales office. The idea is that with enough referrals going back and forth, everyone benefits but no one suffers a conflict of interest.

Another designation to look for is that of *Certified Financial Planner* (CFP). The CFP is an individual who has undergone extensive training and has substantial experience in the field of investing and is qualified to advise clients on a range of alternatives. The CFP Board awards the CFP designation. Qualifications and requirements for obtaining a CFP license include completion of a course of study; passing of a two-day extensive test; no less than three years' experience; and agreement to abide by the CFP Board's code of ethics. The Financial Planning Association, a national professional association for financial planners, encourages its members to study for the CFP designation.

Using a CFP as financial advisor is always a wise step. These individuals are qualified and experienced just by holding the designation; and a non-CFP might be equally qualified but you have no way to verify such a claim.

Whenever investors decide to hire a professional to help with their investment decisions, a good first step is to decide ahead of time what they hope to achieve. Why hire the professional? Some people have unrealistic expectations, and they will be disappointed. For example, if you expect an advisor to give you information that most people do not have access to, then the reasons for hiring an advisor are not well grounded. If you are seeking education about investing, it is an expensive way to proceed. Finally, if you expect the financial advisor to take over responsibility for your investment decisions, it could be an expensive mistake.

The best reason to hire a professional is to make long-term plans and identify the right investment decisions that you need to make today. For example, if you are married and have young children, some of your concerns should

TIP

For more information about the CFP program, check the FPA Web site at www.fpanet.org/cfpmark/index.cfm.

include the following:

Saving for college education

Ensuring that you have adequate insurance of various types to protect your family in the event of loss of life, health, or the ability to earn a living

Identifying investments that will keep pace with inflation to protect purchasing power

Creating a plan for periodic savings and investment

Periodic financial check-ups to update the plan for new information

Financial planning should be focused around the important economic and personal realities that each of us face. For example, major life events—marriage, the birth of a child, college education, career changes, health concerns, divorce, retirement or death, for example—also demand planning and revision to an existing plan. As people grow, their goals change with them. As people gain experience in investing, their risk tolerance changes as well. So, a periodic review of a long-term plan is essential for making sure that the plan itself is up to date. The idea that an advisor can give a client a stock tip would be short-sighted when the more important long-term considerations are kept in mind.

Financial planners offer a range of valuable services related not only to product information, diversification, and risk identification, but also to the methods they employ to help clients identify what they need to do for long-term contingency planning. A competent financial planner not only has the proper professional designations, including CFP license and RIA registration; they also can tap into the resources they need. No one individual can offer expert advice on every possible topic. So, the professional advisor might also use the services of an estate specialist, attorney, accountant, tax professional, real estate expert, insurance broker, and others based on the specific circumstances that each client requires.

Commonly Held Beliefs

Investors constantly hope to find information that will help them beat the averages. If you seek advice, you naturally want to work with someone whose experience is greater than yours and who knows more about how to profit in the market than the average person. Thus, everyone wants to believe that market advisors—specifically, brokers and financial planners—have greater knowledge than the rest of us. That is not necessarily true. Furthermore, it makes little sense. Why would someone with superior knowledge scramble for fees or commissions when they could be making a fortune in the market? The fact is, market professionals are is the sales business and do not necessarily know more than anyone else about how to anticipate price changes, invest to ensure profits, or beat the market averages.

> **Fallacy: Brokers and financial planners know more about investing than most people.**

In fact, most brokers and financial planners are trained in the basics of investing and the regulatory environment. But the important experience, the hands-on knowledge about daily workings of the market, is gained through years of experience. So, as an individual investor, you gain knowledge as you take part in the market with your own money. Brokers and financial planners are not as experienced as you if they have not been involved for as long as you have, so it is a mistake to assume automatically that someone else has more experience and knowledge than you.

Another part of the equation of finding the right professional relates to talent. There is a widespread belief that some people have a flair for investing, a talent for picking winning stocks, and the ability to beat the averages consistently. In fact, outperforming the market is a matter of hard work and analysis and the careful selection of risks. Most investors have this knowledge from mere observation or gut instinct, but many still hope to outperform the market by finding someone else whose superior knowledge can be tapped into for a fee.

Making matters worse, the industry of brokers and financial planners does all it can to further the myth that their membership has superior knowledge. Every brokerage firm charging a commission for its services advertises that its brokers can work to help you beat the market averages; and every financial planning organization and firm attempts to convey the same message.

In fact, you can learn a lot from a competent financial planner as long as you have realistic expectations. A long-ranging plan includes not only well thought-out investment decisions, but also insurance, estate planning, cash reserves, tax planning, and other aspects of the whole financial picture. The scope of matters you need to consider as part of your personal financial plan can be overwhelming, and it is easy to overlook parts of it. One good reason to hire a financial planner is to have someone on the outside look at your total financial picture and advise you about where you need to make changes. Many people are exposed to risks about which they are not aware, and an experienced financial planner can provide a valuable service by pointing out those weak links in your financial plan.

The fallacy that market professionals have more knowledge and experience than most people should be modified. Just because an individual holds a license or a designation does not mean that they are qualified to advise you. The actual experience that person has is the real test of their value, and you can ensure that you are on the right course by hiring an experienced planner to look over your finances and to offer recommendations to avoid different types of risk.

It is a mistake to proceed in the belief that a broker or financial planner will give you specific stock recommendations and that you can simply pass the decision over to someone else. The market professional is not going to serve you well as an educator or decision-maker, even though much of the promotion in the industry implies just that. Ultimately, every investor has to make decisions for themselves, and looking for someone else to take over that responsibility can be an expensive mistake.

Other Professional Help

Once you study the viability of using (or rejecting) the help of a broker or financial planner, you probably also need to consider whether or not to hire other types of professionals. In the arena of personal finance, a variety of different people can be useful in one or more aspects of your personal plan.

Many people prepare their own income tax return, but for exceptionally complicated work, it makes sense to hire a professional. Thus, a qualified accountant or enrolled agent can be of particular value, not only for the annual ritual of filling out forms and calculating how much you owe, but also for the equally important tax planning steps you can take during the year. Decisions such as the timing of a sale of stock can make a difference in your total tax liability. For example, if you sold stock earlier in the year and you have a capital gain to report, you might need to study the rest of your portfolio. If you are holding shares at a loss and you are planning to dump them in the near future, making that decision before year-end can help to reduce the capital gain you will be assessed on your profitable earlier sale.

Using a qualified accountant or other professional for tax planning and preparation is especially important if you have complex tax situations, including the following:

- Schedule C transactions from operating a small business. These involve not only an array of deductions, but also ensure that you are keeping proper records and can document all of the costs and expenses that you claim; depreciation of assets; calculation of beginning and ending inventory; and if applicable, calculation of year-end adjustments such as accruals; selection of the proper accounting method and inventory valuation procedures; and when applicable, payments of the self-employment tax (Social Security for the self-employed).

- Schedule E transactions for real estate and similar matters. This schedule is a summary of income, costs and expenses from real estate, and it is especially complex for those owning more than one property. Also on Schedule E are various other calculations of income from partnerships, trusts, and other specialized entities.

- Complicated capital gains and losses from stocks, real estate, options, investment real estate, and other capital gains. The actual calculation of gains and losses is one of the more complex tax matters, and depending on the nature of the asset, you might need to use more than one Schedule for the calculation. When you have a mixture of long-term and short-term, and a combination of gains and losses, the calculation of what to report may require professional help.

- Depreciation calculations for investment assets such as real estate. Under current rules, depreciation usually is done according to a specific formula under a program of recovery periods and allowances each year. For anyone who is not familiar with these calculations, the required records, forms, and calculations can be quite complex.

- Unusual situations or exceptionally high losses or itemized deductions. Whenever your situation includes unusual items, you might need professional help—not only to report it properly, but also to make sure that you have the right documentation in case your claim of a deduction is questioned.

In rare cases, a tax attorney might be required in addition to a qualified accountant. If you are an officer in a closely-held corporation and decisions have to be made concerning changes from a C Corporation to a S Corporation, for example, you might have several questions about liability exposure. If you own units in a limited partnership, invest overseas, or spent part of the year out of the country, more complex tax questions arise and might need to be addressed from a legal point of view.

Whether the question is legal or just a matter of finding the right form, a tax professional can help to avoid problems later by advising you today. At first glance, it would seem that the most important part of this advice relates to filling out the forms; but for most investors, tax planning is equally important. Under the tax rules, timing is the key to proper planning. This situation refers not only to the decision about when to take profits or recognize losses, but also how to coordinate investment decisions with the rest of your income status.

A qualified tax professional knows, for example, that investing in a passive loss program such as a limited partnership will not help your tax situation whatsoever if you do not have offsetting passive gains. So, before putting money into an investment solely for tax purposes, it would make sense to run the idea past your advisor. Another example is that you might consider buying municipal bonds because they are tax free. Because of the tax benefits, however, the yield will be lower than for other, taxable bond interest. So, the decision to buy municipal bonds should be made only after calculating the after-tax difference between the two types of bonds. Based on your federal and state tax rates, the decision could be profitable or not. It depends on available rates *and* on your tax status. Furthermore, various types of bonds have federal and state exemption, and others are only partially exempt. So, checking first with an experienced tax adviser might help save you from making an ill-advised decision.

A Question of Need

Like every investor, you need to ask yourself how much help you need. Certainly, if your income tax situation is complex enough, you will need to hire a qualified professional to prepare your federal and state returns and to advise you throughout the year about steps you can take to minimize your tax liability. When it comes to direct investment advice, however, the question of whether you need help is more complex; and if you decide that you do, then you need to decide what expectations you have for the results.

If you seek help because you lack knowledge about a specific type of investment or strategy, it is probably a mistake to hire a broker or financial planner. While many of these professionals can help to educate their clients, they are in the sales business; and you will protect your own interests by recognizing that. Perhaps only the most experienced investors should hire a broker, and then only for the execution of trades or management of accounts. The less experienced can certainly gain a degree of guidance from a financial planner, at least to the extent of providing direction to a long-term investment and financial plan.

If you have some experience as an investor, you can probably find the kinds of information that you need through your own research. With books, magazines, subscription services, and online research and news (most of which is free), you can find out a lot about investment information, especially about a company's fundamentals.

You probably seek fundamental information more than anything else— updated financial and earnings reports, sales and earning trend information, and related matters. For in-depth research, consider joining an investment club. Many investors participate both through a club and on their own. The research capabilities of the club membership provide a wide range of in-depth information, which can also be used in your own portfolio.

For keeping track of stock price and volume, go to any of dozens of brokerage or financial news Web sites; they all offer quotes and charts free of charge for every listed company. The Internet is an amazing resource for you, and most of it is free. Avoid investment chat rooms and ignore the advertisement banners, and stay focused on finding precisely what you need. You can make good use of the information found there.

TIP

You can get financial statements and annual reports free online. Check these Web sites:
http://reportgallery.com/
http://annualreportservice.com/

TIP

To get news summaries or find out more about the three major financial newspapers, check their Web sites:
http://public.wsj.com/home.html
www.investors.com/
www.barrons.com/

To augment your contact with the market, consider subscribing to one of the three national financial newspapers. *The Wall Street Journal* and *Investor's Business Daily* are published every weekday, and *Barron's* comes out weekly. Numerous financial magazines can supplement the information in the newspapers, and dozens of online financial news services also provide excellent (and free) news and information.

Because so much financial news, information, and education is free, hiring and paying a professional to become educated about investing simply does not make sense. It also is a misuse of the resource. Financial services should be used to provide expertise that you do not possess, not as a basic educational tool.

Upon hiring a professional, you should also have a clearly defined idea of what you expect to accomplish, and this goal should be discussed with the professional. It makes sense to ensure that both the service provider and the client agree about what services will be provided and for what purpose; otherwise, the relationship will be headed for trouble.

When you consider the complexities of investing and the range of topics that you need to master, you probably will conclude that you already know quite a bit about finance and the workings of the market. Chances are, you know as much about the market as any advisor. For this reason, discount brokerage is becoming more popular than ever. A growing number of investors recognize that they are responsible for their own decisions, and it is not realistic to depend on someone else to tell you how or where to invest your capital. The inexperienced investor might hire a full-commission broker or financial planner out of apprehension about proceeding in the market where they have virtually no experience. As much as this action is a mistake, it is understandable. New territory is difficult to enter into without guidance. History has demonstrated, however, that the guidance provided by some professionals has been expensive for the inexperienced client. The new investor is better off starting with an investment club or by placing funds into a no-load mutual fund than going directly to a broker or planner with the expectation that those resources will educate and guide them.

As long as investors accept the fact that they are responsible for their own investment decisions, one important problem has been put aside. The degree of energy put into educating yourself through the Internet, newspaper and magazine subscriptions, books, and your own direct experience in the market, the more skilled you become at recognizing opportunities when they arise. Investors who resist the temptation of reacting with the crowd mentality defining the market have an opportunity to beat the averages. The market as a whole tends to act and react for many of the wrong reasons, so short-term price changes and trends can be ignored or responded to in a manner contrary to what most people are doing. As a general rule, the majority opinion of the market is wrong more than it is right; in that regard, you are more likely to succeed in your investment endeavors when you think for yourself.

Notes

[1] A "60 Minutes II" study checked analyst stock recommendations before the public. Out of a total of 8,000 recommendations, only 29 were to sell. (Reported on June 27, 2001, "Wall Street Prophets" on CBS's Web site http://cbsnews.com/now/story/0,1597,298260-412,00.shtml.

[2] *ibid.*

[3] Raymond Hennessey and Lynette Khalfani, *"Analysts' Links to IPOs Mean Losses for Investors, Study Finds,"* Dow Jones Newswire, June 13, 2001.

[4] R. I. Warshow, *The Story of Wall Street* (New York; Greenberg, 1929), p. 30.

[5] F. L. Eames, *The New York Stock Exchange* (New York, Thomas G. Hall, 1894), p. 14.

[6] An illegal activity, the pump and dump refers to the process of buying shares of stock and then pumping the company through spreading of rumors, often on investment chat boards. When the price rises in response, the shares are dumped. The SEC actively persecutes those found engaged in this form of stock price manipulation.

[7] R. J. Teweles and E. S. Bradley, *The Stock Market (5th Ed.)* (New York; John Wiley & Sons, 1987), p. 95.

[8] *The New York Times*, November 24, 1937, cited in Teweles, *Op.Cit.*

[9] Investment Advisors Act of 1940, Sec. 202(a)(11).

CHAPTER 11

Developing Your Comprehensive Program

The strategies that you employ and the long-term attitude that you develop depend upon experience and observation. As you learn from your successes and from your mistakes, you also develop a series of opinions about the best ways to invest; the nature and variation of risk; and the timing of your decisions to buy, sell, or hold.

Your comprehensive program has to include a definition of risk tolerance, a thorough understanding of what you expect to achieve as an investor, and how you believe you should go about achieving your goals. This program should remain flexible, because as events take place in your life, your goals and opinions will change as well. So, it makes little sense to define risk tolerance based on your status today when in 5 or 10 years you will have more experience and perhaps an entirely different economic and life status.

Three Market Rules of Thumb

Remain open to the idea that your experiences in the market—good or bad—will shape your philosophy about investing. Also be aware that momentary experiences do not define the market in all circumstances. In times of recession or political turmoil, investor fears and concerns tend to keep prices depressed; but when the economic situation changes, the market's unbridled optimism changes everything. Both outlooks—concerns in slow times and euphoria when matters change—define one of the three rules of thumb about the stock market:

The market thrives on optimism. No matter how much reality one brings to the picture, when investors decide that the good times are here, there is no stopping the trend. For example, when the late '90s dot.com craze was upon us, many investors put all of their capital into companies whose stock price kept rising to record high levels—even though the fundamentals did not support the trend. In fact, many companies had never shown a profit, so the market optimism was senseless. Even so, that optimism was widespread. In such situations, matters change suddenly and without warning, and those who have the most to lose are hurt the worst. If investors borrowed money to invest, bought stocks on margin, and took other risks they could not afford, the turnaround was a disaster.

The most recent events are not the first time this situation has occurred. The puzzling but often-cited "tulipmania" in The Netherlands in the 17th century is a case study in market optimism. Tulip bulbs were inflated in value to the point that individuals invested huge fortunes to own a rare species. Of course, the overvaluation of these commodities was unjustified, and in 1637 the tulip market crashed. In today's stock market, the same thing occurs with shares of stock in varying degrees, perhaps not with the frenzy of the tulip speculator but along the same principle.

In addition to market optimism, a second point to remember is that short-term reactions in the stock market are rarely thought through or rational. The tendency is for overall reactions to big news stories to be unjustified. This rule is the second of three important rules of thumb worth remembering:

The market overreacts to news. This statement is true both for good and bad news. Wise investors know that short-term information is just that. Stock prices will rise to unreasonable levels when the Fed announces a cut in interest rates, only to settle down within a week or two. And upon bad news—economic, political, or financial—the prices of stocks will fall, often significantly, only to return in a short time to more realistic levels.

The astute investor, observing this phenomenon, might actually time short-term decisions according to market overreaction. This action, however, requires the ability to go against the trend. So, the observant investor will buy additional shares when most investors are running in the opposite direction, for example. Following the September 11, 2001 disaster, the stock market closed for the remainder of the week and, upon opening the following Monday, stock prices fell drastically. Within one month, however, the losses (as measured by the various indexes) had for the most part returned to their levels before September 11.

We are not suggesting that investors should take advantage of disasters or tragedies of a massive scale. It does support the contention, however, that the market tends to experience big price changes in the short term for the wrong reasons. The political and social aspects of the September 11 disaster certainly had an impact on many companies listed on the public exchanges. Most stocks fell, however, even though there was no fundamental reason to believe that their values were in fact less. At such times, wise investors know that at the very least, the best reaction is to take no action. Selling after large declines is a panic reaction, just as buying in an unreasonably inflated market might be called a greed reaction. Both decisions are going to lead to losses in the majority of cases.

The third market rule of thumb is that if you wait long enough, a well-researched decision is likely to pay off. Inexperienced investors tend to want results quickly, so they move in and out of positions—accumulating trading fees and missing opportunities. It makes more sense to do your research and then sit back and wait. The third rule of thumb is as follows:

The market rewards patience. Remembering this important point helps you to avoid reacting to short-term information. That is the mistake that so many investors make: deciding to buy or sell shares of stock based on today's news and information and forgetting to wait out the market. The fundamentals tend to disappear from the observer's mind when short-term news is more compelling.

An experienced investor will tend to absorb short-term news and analyze it only to the extent that it might affect the decision to continue with the long-term program. If news has long-term ramifications, then naturally immediate action will be justified. If you remember to always take in news with the fundamentals in mind, however, then you can better manage information as you receive it; and you will also be better able to stay on course when short-term news does not justify some quick action. Patient investors tend to miss fewer opportunities because they do not react along with everyone else. They are content to avoid buying or selling on such news and revert to the hold strategy as a general rule, awaiting changes that are indeed long-term in nature. The day-to-day news and rumor that typifies Wall Street might be observed, but the patient, experienced investor knows not to react.

Theory and Practice

You will experience a more consistent return on your invested capital if you combine patience with an appreciation for reality. In spite of the promises offered by promoters and the get-rich-quick industry, techniques like day trading and other high-risk ventures do not lead to instant wealth. They invariably expose you to far too much risk and ultimate deterioration of your capital.

In reality, making a profit from investing requires one of two approaches. To succeed in relatively short-term strategies, you need to work very hard, performing constant research and trying to identify those short-term and intermediate trends that present momentary opportunities. To succeed as a long-term investor, you need to first identify the most viable stocks (or mutual funds) based on your risk tolerance, then invest capital, then watch and wait. This permanent portfolio should be changed only if and when change is demanded. So, keeping an eye on the fundamentals as well as ever-changing economic conditions enables you to judge your portfolio regularly but without a lot of unnecessary buying and selling activity.

A comprehensive program for long-term investing has to be based, of course, on the desire to earn profits adequate to increase your net worth. In other words, profits have to be high enough to offset losses that you will experience in your portfolio, to beat inflation, and to cover tax liabilities from investing activity. Given the uncertainties of the market, this package of requirements is not an easy accomplishment, but it can be done. It requires reinvestment of earnings, appropriate diversification, a thorough appreciation of risk, and the ability to alter your holdings based on changing economic conditions as well as position and strength of the company.

In addition to watching the fundamentals in terms of earnings reports, you also need to watch the more subtle fundamental features of a company—its management, diversification of products and services, and the ability to change with the times. An example of why this factor is important occurred in the year 2001. Polaroid, a long-established corporation, announced that it was filing for bankruptcy. Those individuals who owned stock had no reason to be surprised, however. In addition to a flattening out of fundamentals over several years, Polaroid had not changed with the times. In its big growth days, it virtually dominated the market with its instant camera products; however, by 2001, the photo business had turned to digital technology. Polaroid did not keep up with its competition by going after a share of that market; so the demise of the company should have been anticipated well in advance of the announcement. Investors might have noticed that Polaroid was not claiming a share of the digital camera marketplace; thus, its long-term growth prospects were limited.

The same critical analysis can be applied to any corporation. Look at the long-term trends in sales and earnings, watching for the inevitable flattening-out effect that invariably occurs when a corporation has reached its growth plateau. Following that trend will be smaller, more aggressive competitors that want to have their growth curve as well. When you see this trend in an industry leader, it might well be time to move capital to the up-and-coming competitor whose growth curve is still attractive.

Another feature to watch for is how well a large corporation is able to diversify its products and services. Once a corporation reaches the maximum growth rate in its primary industry, it might continue to grow only by branching out into other industries. A real test of management is how well it is able to operate in a secondary industry. It is difficult for management to expertly run another company, and the more talented managers know that the only way to succeed in a secondary industry is to keep experienced people around them. So, keeping an eye on how management recruits others, operates its growth through acquisitions, and maintains a growth and profit curve is a sound method for deciding whether to keep stock or to sell it and seek other investments.

Your comprehensive program cannot be limited to a pure study of the financial aspects of a corporation; you also need to study the less-tangible but equally important fundamentals relating to management, product or service, sector diversification, and comparisons to the competition. Given that as a starting point for monitoring your portfolio, your comprehensive program is based on development of four strategic parts:

1. *Immediate decisions and strategies.* What do you need to do today to create a diversified portfolio that conforms to your risk standards, is designed to meet your long-term goals, and provides the potential for long-term growth? Do the companies you select allow reinvestment of dividends in partial share purchase (DRIP plans)? If you need to make changes, what are they, and if they involve moving money, where should that money go? The immediate changes you need to make are comparable to first aid. What are the most critical steps that have to be taken today to fix weak links or problems in your portfolio, to eliminate unacceptable risks, and move capital out of danger?

2. *Long-term goals.* Constantly evaluate and re-evaluate your perceptions of long-term goals. What kind of return do you need to achieve, and why? Do you plan to start your own business, provide for your children's college education, or pay off your mortgage and retire early? Everyone has different goals, and the number of years, risk profile, and financial requirements of your goals should dictate the amount you save to invest, where you put your money, how you diversify, and what types of long-term growth you will want to seek.

3. *Risk analysis and identification.* So often overlooked, the definition of risk has to be at the core of your portfolio selection. Every stock and every sector can be distinguished by its ever-changing risks. Some stocks are cyclical by definition, and others tend to change with economic conditions. A study of a particular sector helps identify the kinds of risk and growth potential, and it is not enough to buy many stocks if, in fact, they all contain similar or identical risk elements. Risk is dealt with by diversification. A simple form of diversification, involving the purchase of many similar stocks, is not adequate. You need to diversify between dissimilar sectors and perhaps outside of the stock market as well. While gold and other precious metals once were recognized as hedges for stock market investment, that has not been true in recent years. Real estate is a more likely offset. Buying your own home provides investment diversification for a strong stock portfolio.

4. *Flexibility to change as needed.* Setting up a well-rounded portfolio and identifying long-term growth potential is only the starting point. Flexibility is important, too, because everything is likely to change. In other words, today's strong growth candidates might lose their lead in the future. You will want to identify the signs as they begin to emerge and take action to move your capital elsewhere. Maintaining your long-term goals could mean having to move capital out of one company's stock and into another. You also need to remain flexible about your goals. As you grow and gain experience, and as your economic status changes, your goals are probably going to change as well. Don't make the mistake of staying with a portfolio designed for yesterday's goals.

In the past, investors depended on brokers and other insiders to provide information and to make recommendations about how and where to invest money. This situation placed investors at a severe disadvantage. Depending on individuals whose income is based on commissions and whose historical record is spotted with examples of abuse is not a reliable method for approaching the market. Today, however, you have a tremendous advantage over investors of the past generation. The Internet provides a wealth of free, easily accessed information. If you perform searches on key words, you are likely to find all that you need as well as easy links directly to free annual reports and detailed financial statements.

Whenever using the Internet, it is important to remain focused on the information that you seek. Don't allow yourself to be distracted by advertising banners or well-worded hype designed to draw you into a Web site. Stay out of investment chat rooms, recognizing that you cannot rely on anything you read there. Remain in control of your research and look for sites that you can use that provide you will easily used information and useful links. If you invest online, seek a company that provides a combination of reasonable cost and access. Remember, the very cheapest transaction service is going to have the greatest number of subscribers; so even though you save on costs for buying or selling, you are also going to find it very difficult to sign on during heavy-volume periods. So, a real bargain is going to be a site that has a competitive price and a fast Web site, but not necessarily the cheapest one.

All of Wall Street is accessible online. This is the great advantage and wonderful resource that will define 21st-century investing. In the past, the world of investing took great leaps with development of the telegraph and the telephone, and in this century we will see even greater accessibility for everyone. As more people go online and discover the convenience of automated investing, they will be faced with new problems and opportunities; greater speed and more information; and the ability to get information they need to make smart, informed, and profitable decisions.

Index

246 INDEX

Certified Financial Planner
(CFP), 231
CFP Board, 231
Chart patterns of stocks, 12, 139
Compound rates of return, 195–199
Confirmation in the Dow Theory, 48
Contingent liability, 127
Cook, Thomas, 44 *n*
Cooking the books, 29
Covered calls, 119, 213
Current price per share, 5–9
Current ratio trends, 120–121
Customer/client service, 32
Customer's Afternoon Letter, 46
Cycles, investment, 75–76

D

Debt ratio analysis, 121–122
Debt service, 174
Devil's Dictionary, The, 22 *n*
Discount brokerage, 227
Diversification
asset allocation, 97
broad forms of, 97–99
defined, 93
fundamental, 99–102
lost opportunity, 95
market, 109–11
market risk, 106–109, 138, 175
misunderstood concept of, 94–97
mutual fund, 102–106, 215–218
product or service, 124–125
risk and, 88–90
simple, 94
Dividend Reinvestment Plans
(DRIPs), 92 *n*, 218 *n*
Dividend trends, 25–26
Douglas, William O., 227, 228
Dow, Charles, 46, 56
Dow Jones Industrial Averages
(DJIA)

accuracy issues, 50, 53
as the market, 54
basis for decision-making, 54–55
companies listed in, 47
defining the market with, 45–46
problems with, 50–53
scorekeeping, 18–19
technical nature of, 20
Dow Theory
applications, 56–63
basics, 47–50
decision timing, 54–56
individual stocks and, 56–63
origins, 46–47
proponents of, 42
solutions, 53–54

E

Eames, F. L., 238 *n*
Earnings volatility, 150–155
EBITDA, 42, 43
Economic conditions, 31–32,
74–77, 94
Effective tax rate, 77, 92 *n*
Efficient market theory, 4, 9, 42
Emergency cash fund, 125–128
Enrolled agent, 234
Equity conversion, 174

F

Federal Reserve System, 18
Financial Accounting Standards
Board (FASB), 27–28
Financial advisors, 229–234
Financial information, 16–22
Financial Planning Association, 231
Full-commission brokerage, 227, 228
Fundamental analysis
attributes, 120–125
banking of earnings, 29